KT-562-332

Creative Recording 1

Effects And Processors
Second edition

Paul White

CONTENTS

INTRODUCTION

As with most music software, this book has gone through a number of incarnations, revisions and updates since its first edition, but my philosophy of making potentially complicated subjects easy to understand remains central to my approach. The first edition of *Creative Recording I: Effects And Processors* dealt with the use of effects and signal processing in the studio environment at a time when many digital effects units were very expensive, had no MIDI facilities and few had multi-effect capabilities. Now, multi-effects units dominate the effects marketplace, with all but the cheapest models featuring real-time MIDI parameter control and most with effects that go way beyond the original reverb and modulated delay treatments. Add to this the fact that virtually all digital instruments and sound cards include their own effects and you can see that effects are inexorably linked to the way in which modern music is made. Effects and signal-processing units have also escaped their hardware confines and emerged as software plug-ins for computer audio sequencers and workstations. Furthermore, the new generation of digital mixing consoles is starting to embrace plug-in hardware and software from third parties, so the user can update an existing system rather than having to replace it.

The plan is to bring the *Creative Recording* concept up to date, but with each revision the book inevitably grows – it is now considerably more comprehensive than the original! This is due in no small part to the introduction of surround recording and the expanding world of software plug-ins. Here you'll find clear and detailed explanations of all the mainstream (and less common) studio effects and signal-processing treatments, plus tips on how to use these them within your own music production. If you're not sure how a compressor compresses, why a reverb unit has a control for early reflections, or how a vocoder works, this book is for you. What's more, once you've seen how these devices work, you'll learn how to use them to make your music sound more exciting.

As with all my other books, the aim is to go into as much detail as possible while keeping the explanations clear and straightforward. It took me many years to learn everything that's in this book, but you can benefit from that experience in virtually no time at all, enabling you to go forward to help create the future of recording without first having to reinvent the wheel.

1 THE MIXING CONSOLE

The mixing console is at the heart of every recording studio, and today these come in a variety of forms: you might choose an analogue mixer, a digital mixer, or even a 'virtual' mixer that exists only in software. Software mixers may have physical hardware control surfaces or they may be controlled via a mouse and keyboard, but it is important to understand that all these different mixing options have their origins in the analogue studio console, and most of the key analogue mixer concepts have been retained in both digital and software mixers. Although this book is essentially about effects and signal processors, a basic knowledge of the studio mixer is vital because the mixer controls the flow of signals to and from effects devices (both real and virtual). In the analogue mixer world, the effects and processors are usually external rack-mount devices connected either directly to the mixer or via a patchbay system. In a digital mixer there is less scope for connectivity to the outside world, though it is usually still possible to connect a limited number of external devices. The majority of the processing, however, is done inside the mixer – a current design generally offers two or more effects processors as well as EQ, compression and/or gating on individual channels.

In the virtual (software) mixing environment, effects and processors are usually added as software 'plug-ins', often with sophisticated on-screen control panels that replicate the look of traditional hardware.

Equipment designed to alter sound (tone controls, echo, reverb and so on) tend to be divided into effects and signal processors, although the exact distinction between these two categories will be made later in the book. Traditionally, effects were devices such as reverb and echo, whereas signal processing is more about equalisation, compression, gating and so on. Bear in mind, however, that the number of different ways in which a signal can be treated is increasing all the time.

Studio effects are designed to enhance recordings rather than to compensate for poor playing or imperfect recording techniques and, properly used, they can add a new dimension to a good recording. Effects can still be bought as standalone boxes but may also be built into MIDI instruments, digital mixers or available as part of all-in-one digital recording workstations. They also exist as software plug-ins for use with computer-based audio workstations and sequencers, but before you can start to use an effect, you need to know where to connect it in the signal path. To do this properly, you must know you way around your mixing console, and the best way to do that is to examine the purpose and structure of a typical analogue mixer.

Even if you're using a digital mixer, or the virtual mixer built into an audio/MIDI sequencing software package, the analogue-mixer model of signal routing is still the best place to start. If you're thoroughly conversant with multitrack mixers, you could probably skip most of this chapter, though it's probably still worth skimming through it at least once. Don't be tempted to skip it altogether, though, as an understanding of the mixer is absolutely central to being able to use a multitrack recording system of any kind.

If you are moving up from an integrated multitrack recording system to something more sophisticated, you might initially find the complexity of a full studio console daunting – whenever an outsider comes into a studio, the first thing they do is look at the mixer and ask you how on earth you know what all the knobs do! Even if you've used a basic 'live' sound console before, the extra routing functions of a recording mixer may still be confusing at first sight. However, it all falls into place quite quickly – as long as you approach things logically and don't expect to master everything at once. You may also hear scary terms such a split and in-line formats, but don't worry if this doesn't mean much to you now as it will all be explained in due course. The first thing to establish is what a mixer does and why we need one to make and mix multitrack music.

The Need For Gain

All analogue electronic circuitry, including that used in mixers, has an optimum operating range that provides the best noise performance and the lowest distortion. If the input signal exceeds this range, distortion will result, while if the signal falls too far below it, the amount of amplification required to bring it back up to a usable level will also make it noisy. All analogue audio circuitry is designed to work within a particular range of signal levels, usually up to around ten volts, so if the original signal is much smaller or much larger than this, it will need to be amplified (made bigger) or attenuated (made smaller) to put it in the right range. Signals at so-called line level are already within this range, such as the outputs from effects units, tape recorders, the analogue outputs of digital recorders and some electronic instruments, but the signal produced by a microphone may measure only a few thousandths of a volt.

To get a microphone's signal voltage up to a more manageable line level, any mixer designed for use with microphones will incorporate a special low-noise microphone amplifier, right at the input. This brings the microphone signal up to the mixer's internal working level, which is generally similar to line level. This microphone preamplifier may also be fitted with phantom power circuitry enabling it to be used with capacitor microphones or DI (direct inject) boxes that require power to operate their on-board electronics.

Phantom Power

Capacitor microphones need an electrical voltage to polarise the capsule, while both capacitor and electret microphones use built-in preamplifiers, which also require electrical power. The majority of capacitor and back-electret mics are designed to work using phantom powering, though some back-electret models can also be run from batteries. Phantom powering gets its name because the supply current is fed along the hot and cold conductors of a balanced microphone cable and returned along the screen conductor. The standard phantom power supply voltage is 48 volts and is generated within the mixing console. It may be switched on globally or per channel depending on the mixer, but only balanced microphones should be plugged into the mixer when the phantom power is active.

Mic Amps

On a typical mid-price desk, the mic inputs will be on balanced XLR sockets and the line and tape inputs on quarter-inch jacks – which may or may not be balanced (though balanced is preferable if your multitrack machine/audio interface has balanced connectors). If you intend to use capacitor mics, phantom powering on the mic inputs should be considered essential, as external phantom power supplies are relatively expensive. Note that tube microphones require their own special power supply due to the very high voltages needed to power the tubes, so they don't need phantom power. In theory, it is quite safe (although pointless) to apply phantom power to a dynamic or tube microphone, but only if it is wired for balanced operation. Where the console has only a global phantom power switch, ensure that you have no unbalanced mics connected. In any event, it is good practice to connect all your mics and DI boxes before switching on the phantom power to avoid the risk of damage to your microphones.

Because not all microphones produce the same level output, and because the output level also depends on how close and how loud the sound being recorded is, microphone amplifiers are equipped with a variable gain control. Line-level signals also vary in amplitude to some extent, so the line input on a typical mixer will also be fitted with a gain control. On some professional mixers, the microphone and line inputs will each have their own gain control, but on most project-studio mixing equipment, a common control is used for both mic and line gain adjustment.

Pad

Yet another button you might come across at the top of the channel strip is the mic pad switch. This is used to reduce the level of microphone signal on those occasions when the mic output is too high to be handled by the input amplifier. This situation rarely arises, but it could be encountered when a sensitive mic is placed near a loud sound source such as a bass drum. The pad button generally cuts the input level down by 20dB (or by a factor of ten, thinking of it in voltage terms) before the signal enters the input amplifier.

Your mixer may also have a phase button, which inverts the phase of the mic (or sometimes both the mic and line) input. Normally a positive increase in air pressure at the microphone will produce a positive increase in voltage, but when phase reverse is switched in, a positive pressure increase causes a negative voltage increase. Phase reversal is useful in multi-mic situations where phase cancellation may be a problem, but will make no audible difference when a single microphone is being used. If you're using two mics directed towards the same sound source and aren't sure whether you have a problem or not, reverse the phase of one of the mics and see if the resulting sound is better or worse at the low-frequency end, where most phase problems manifest themselves. As a rule, the position that gives the strongest level of bass is the one to use.

Mixer Basics

The fundamental job of any audio mixer is to combine two or more audio signals and to allow their levels to be independently adjusted. More refined designs include equalisation (just another term for tone controls), the provision to connect external effects units or signal processors, and the ability to route signals and mixes of signals to different destinations.

A traditional studio mixer is used to route signals both when recording and when mixing.

Why all this should be so will become apparent shortly, but to start with I'll describe a basic, four-channel mixer able to perform the simple task of mixing four signals into one. Because the mixer has only one output, the output signal in this case will be mono. For stereo, we'd need two signal paths: one to carry the left-speaker signal and one to carry the right-speaker signal.

Figure 1.1 shows a simplified schematic of a four-channel mono mixer with simple bass and treble equalisation. Separate mic and line gain controls have been shown to aid clarity, but in practice a single, shared control is more likely. There are separate input sockets for both the microphone and line input signals, though with entry level equipment, such as some budget multitrackers, it is possible that a single socket will be used for both. A switch is commonly used to select between the microphone input and the line input where two separate sockets are provided – it is not normal to be able to use both mic and line inputs at the same time, although some designs do permit this.

Equalisation

Directly after the mic/line switch comes the equalisation section, which can be as simple as the bass/treble (also known as hi/lo) arrangement shown here, but most mixers used in recording also have at least one mid-range control, which is often sweepable so that it can be 'tuned' to different frequencies. Furthermore, all the common types of EQ control offer cut as well as boost so that you can diminish some parts of the audio spectrum as well as accentuate them. Equalisation is a signal processing function, but tends to be taken for granted because most mixers include it. See Chapter 3 for more information about equalisation.

A refinement of the sweep control is found in the parametric equaliser, which not only enables you to tune into different frequencies but also to vary the range of frequencies it affects. This extra parameter is called bandwidth, or Q for short; the higher the Q, the narrower the band of frequencies affected –

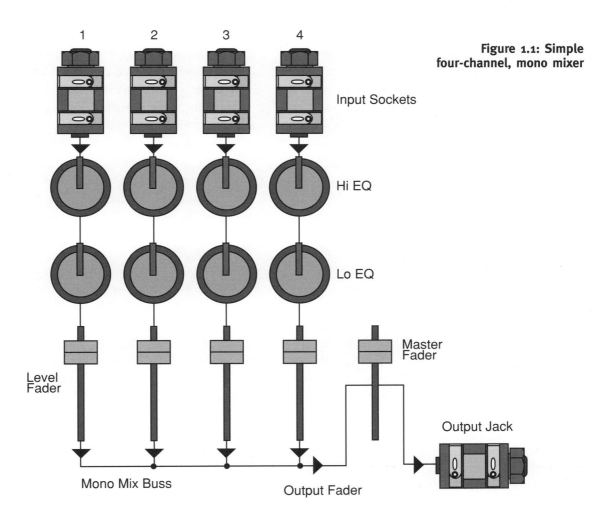

and vice versa. Set to its highest Q, an equaliser might be precise enough to affect a section of the audio spectrum less than a semitone wide, whereas a wide setting will affect several octaves.

Before resorting to EQ, you should endeavour to get the best possible sound at source. It cannot be stressed too highly that if the sound is wrong to begin with, no amount of processing and EQ adjusting will put it right – the old saying about 'fixing it in the mix' is pure myth when it comes to poor quality sounds. The only exception to this is when you are using the EQ to create a special effect rather than to restore tonal balance. What's more, unless used sparingly, the EQ controls in low-cost mixing consoles can easily make your sound muddy or unnatural. Using more sophisticated external equalisers, it may be possible to make greater tonal changes without

the sound becoming unnatural, but it's still good practice to use as little EQ as you can, especially where EQ boost is required.

If you have a very sophisticated desk there may well be other features in the EQ section. The frequencies at which the hi and lo controls come into effect might be switchable between two preset values, and there may also be a sub-bass filter you can switch in to attenuate any frequencies below the normal range of hearing. Sub-bass frequencies might be picked up from a resonant floor via a mic stand, or there may be traffic rumble you need to keep out. Another advantage of using sub-bass cut is that by stopping these unwanted frequencies getting into your recording system you are preventing them from using up valuable 'headroom' that could be better employed recording wanted signals.

At the other end of the scale, there may be a filter to cut out frequencies above the range of hearing. Such supersonic frequencies are often generated by electronic instruments and are best excluded, not only because they too use valuable headroom, but also because they can 'beat' with other high frequencies to cause audible frequencies unrelated to the music. Avoid using high-cut filters on natural sounds such as voice or acoustic instruments whenever possible as the 'openness' of the sound will be degraded. On the other hand, electric guitar and bass can sometimes be treated advantageously as they have very little natural high-frequency content. Most mixers have an additional switch allowing the equalisation section to be bypassed when not in use, and in general this is desirable, as the less unnecessary circuitry you have in any signal path, the cleaner the signal will remain. Disabling (not just bypassing) the EQ in a software mixer often frees up processing power that might be better used elsewhere, so don't leave EQ in circuit unnecessarily.

The Mix Buss

Finally, the signal level is controlled by a fader before it passes through a piece of wire known as the mix buss (on some simpler mixers the fader may be replaced by a conventional rotary control). There may also be a switch to isolate the output of an individual channel from the mix, and this will be labelled On or Mute depending on the manufacturer. Note that all four input channels of our hypothetical mixer are identical, and a larger mixer simply needs more input channels.

Although Figure 1.1 shows the individual channels being connected directly to the mix buss the circuitry involved is actually a little more complex, but it is not necessary to understand the finer points of audio mixer circuit design to be able to use one properly. It is, however, important to appreciate that under normal circumstances it is not possible to mix audio signals simply by connecting the outputs of several different pieces of equipment to a common piece of wire. To achieve mixing we need specialised mixing circuitry, which is one of the reasons we need to use a mixer.

The combined signal on the mix buss passes through a further stage of amplification known as a mix amplifier, where the gain of the mix amplifier is controlled by the master level fader. The master level fader controls the overall output level of the mixer, allowing it to present the correct signal level to the following device, such as the amplifier, recorder or computer audio interface being fed by the mixer. The master fader may also be used to make controlled fades at the end of songs, though this is best achieved using editing software at the mastering stage.

Stereo Mixers

It requires only a few minor changes to turn our simple mono mixer into a stereo one, as shown in Figure 1.2. This is in many ways similar to Figure 1.1, except that the input channels now have an extra control called pan. Pan is short for panorama and is used to adjust the proportion of the signal being sent to each of the two busses. One buss is used to carry the left signal and the other to carry the right, so when the pan control is turned completely anti-clockwise, the channel signal is routed exclusively to the left mix buss. Turning it clockwise routes the signal to the right buss, while setting it dead centre routes equal amounts of signal to the left and right busses. When reproduced over a stereo system, the sound will move from the left to the right speaker as the pan control is turned from one extreme to the other. These two busses (left and right), are often referred to in the singular as a stereo mix buss.

A stereo mixer has two master faders: one for the left signal and one for the right signal, although some mixers use a linked stereo control with a single knob or fader, both to save on cost and space and to make controlled fades easier. Figure 1.2 also shows a stereo level meter that enables the user to monitor the output level of the mixer. This type of meter will be familiar to anyone who has used a stereo cassette recorder, where the actual mechanism could take the form of a moving-coil meter with a physical pointer or it could be a row of LEDs (light emitting diodes) arranged in the form of a ladder. Furthermore, the meter may read the RMS signal level (an average figure that corresponds closely with the perceived loudness of

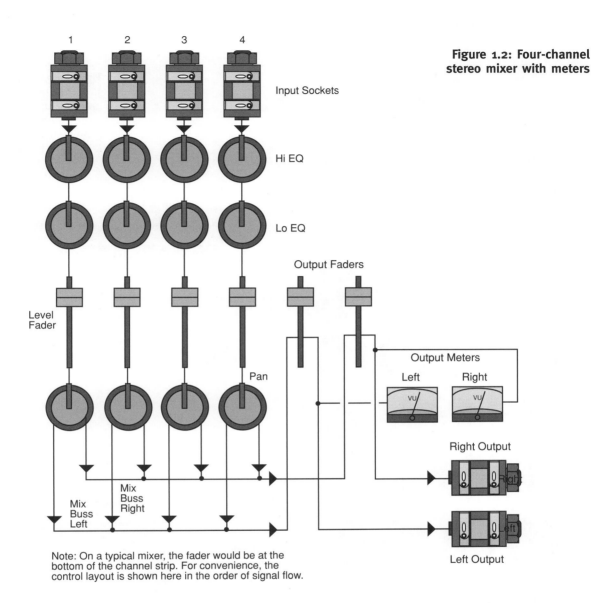

Input Sockets

Hi EQ

Lo EQ

Output Faders

Level Fader

Pan

Output Meters

Left   Right

Right Output

Mix Buss Right

Mix Buss Left

Left Output

Note: On a typical mixer, the fader would be at the bottom of the channel strip. For convenience, the control layout is shown here in the order of signal flow.

the sound), or it may be a peak programme type that follows the signal peaks more closely. As a rule, moving-coil meters give RMS readings while LED, LCD, plasma or VDU meters may be of either type. Computer-based systems have the advantage that they can incorporate any type of metering at no additional cost.

Mixer Format

The simple stereo mixer illustrated so far is commonly found in small PA (public address) systems, and its format is usually described in the form 'something into two'. A 12 into two (12:2) mixer, for example, has 12 input channels and two (left and right) outputs.

The format becomes a little more involved when it comes to dedicated recording mixers as you also have to include the number of output busses and the number of monitor channels. For example, a 32-channel in-line mixer with eight output groups, 32 monitor channels and a stereo output would be classified as a 32:8:32:2. These terms are explained in more detail later in this chapter.

Auxiliaries

All professional recording mixers have some additional facility for connecting one or more external effects and also for producing an alternative cue or monitor mix for

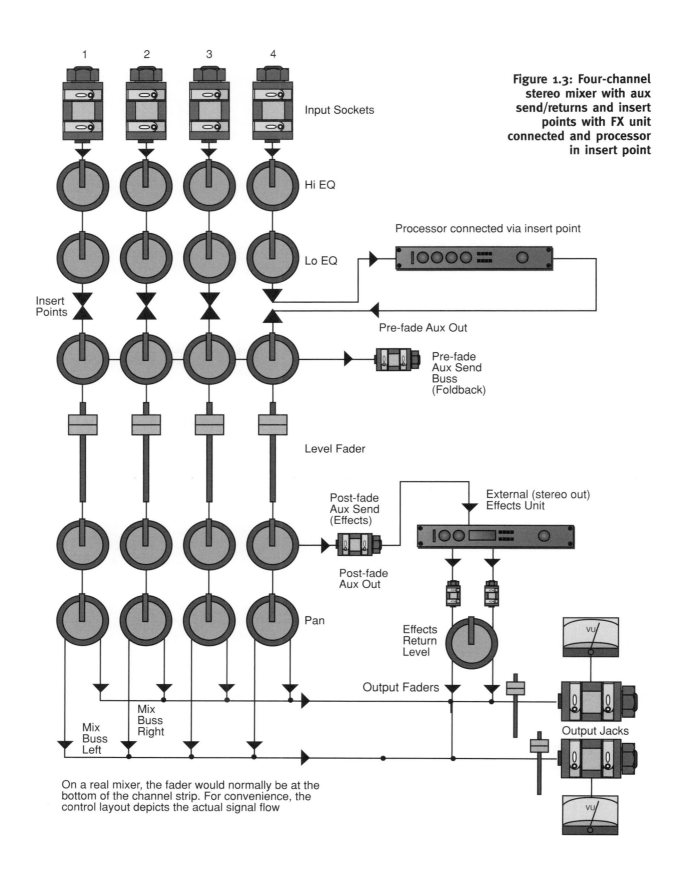

Input Sockets

Figure 1.3: Four-channel stereo mixer with aux send/returns and insert points with FX unit connected and processor in insert point

Hi EQ

Lo EQ

Processor connected via insert point

Insert Points

Pre-fade Aux Out

Pre-fade Aux Send Buss (Foldback)

Level Fader

Post-fade Aux Send (Effects)

External (stereo out) Effects Unit

Post-fade Aux Out

Effects Return Level

Pan

Output Faders

VU

Mix Buss Right

Mix Buss Left

Output Jacks

VU

On a real mixer, the fader would normally be at the bottom of the channel strip. For convenience, the control layout depicts the actual signal flow the performers. In a live situation, the cue mix might be fed to the stage monitors or in-ear monitoring system and may well have a different balance of instruments and voices to the main mix heard by the audience. In the studio, this is more likely to feed the musician's headphone mix so that they can hear what has already been recorded when they are overdubbing new parts. The ability to be able to set up a custom monitor mix is important when, for example, the performance includes complex vocal harmonies and the singers need to hear more of the vocals than the instrumental backing. Adding effects and setting up the performer's cue monitoring can both be handled using what are known as the mixer's auxiliary controls. To understand how these work, it is necessary to look at Figure 1.3: here you can see that two new controls have been added (aux 1 and aux 2, where aux is simply a shortened form of auxiliary).

Pre-Fade Send

Aux 1 is really just another level control feeding a separate mono mix buss that runs across the mixer to the aux 1 master level control and then to the aux 1 output socket. The signal feeding the aux 1 control is taken before the channel fader and, for this reason, is known as a pre-fade send. The significance of a pre-fade send is that once it's set, the level of the aux 1 signal doesn't change if the channel fader setting is adjusted. It follows that a mono mix of all four channels can be set up using the aux 1 controls, and this will appear at the aux 1 master output under overall control of the aux 1 master level control. This mix, being totally independent of the main fader settings, can provide the performers with a monitor mix that is exactly to their liking without compromising the main stereo mix. In the studio, this mix would normally be fed to a headphone-amplifier distribution box so that multiple performers can listen in. On larger studio consoles, multiple pre-fade aux sends are provided so different performers can be sent different headphone mixes.

Post-Fade Send

The other aux control, aux 2, is located after the channel fader (post-fader), and as a consequence its level is affected by changes in the channel fader setting. This is exactly what's needed if aux 2 is being used to feed an effect such as reverb, because when you use an effect connected via the aux send, the unaffected (or 'dry') signal goes via the channel fader onto the stereo mix buss and the effect unit output is added to this later in the signal path.

As the channel fader setting is changed during the course of a mix, we generally want the amount of effect to change by the same amount, thus maintaining the same balance of effect to dry signal regardless of the fader setting. Using a post-fade aux send to drive the effects box achieves this. If we were to feed the effects from a pre-fade send, which is independent of the fader setting, the effect level would remain the same regardless of the fader setting. For example, if you were to add reverb to a guitar this way, use the fader to fade the guitar level to zero; the reverb would remain at a fixed level even when the dry guitar had been faded to silence. Sometimes this can be a cool effect, but not when done unintentionally!

Why do we go to all the trouble of devising an aux send system for connecting effects when you could simply pass the signal being affected directly though an effects unit and into a mixer channel? The answer is that by using different settings of the post-fade aux 2 control on each channel it is possible to send different amounts of each channel's signal to the same effects unit. When the output from this effects unit is added to the main stereo mix, adjusting the aux 2 controls on the individual channels enables different amounts of the same effect to be added to the various channel signals. A typical example might be where one reverb unit is used to provide a rich reverb for the vocals, less reverb for the drums and little or none for the guitars and bass. In other words, the post-fade aux send makes it possible to share effects between mixer channels.

Wet And Dry

It is important to note that an effects unit used in conjunction with a channel aux send should generally be set up so that it produces only the affected sound and none of the original. This is usually accomplished by means of a mix control, which is either in the form of a physical knob or accessed via the effects unit's editing software. The effect-only sound is often known as the 'wet' sound, so the mix should be set to 100 per cent effect, 0 per cent dry.

The output of the effects unit could simply be fed back into the mixer via any spare input channels, but you'll often find dedicated effects return inputs – also known as aux returns – provided for that purpose. Aux returns are electrically similar to regular input channels but usually offer far simpler facilities. For example, they have no mic inputs, little or no EQ and few, if any, aux sends of their own. Normally they feed straight into the main stereo mix, although on more elaborate consoles it may also be possible to feed them to other destinations.

If a spare input channel is used to feed an effect output into the mix (which is a perfectly acceptable way to work), ensure that the corresponding aux send (in this case aux 2), is turned down on the channel used as a return or the effect signal will be fed back on itself, resulting in an unpleasant howl or scream.

Stereo Effects

Since the majority of effects units have stereo outputs, they need to be connected to either two spare input channels or to a stereo aux return input. When using channels, the two mixer channels should be panned hard left and hard right respectively. Figure 1.3 shows an external effects unit connected to the stereo aux return, where the two inputs feed the left and right stereo mix busses. It is sometimes possible to use just one of the effect outputs to feed into a single channel or return where mixer inputs are in short supply, but in this case the effects will be in mono only. Look on the back of the effects unit to see if one of the output sockets is labelled Mono. If it is, connecting to this output only will provide a mix of the left and right effect outputs at the output and not just the right or left output on its own.

Remember that although the controls shown in the figures are arranged in a logical order to illustrate the signal flow through the channel, commercial mixers tend to have the pan and aux controls located above the channel fader as the fader is the control most often requiring adjustment.

Insert Points

There is another standard way to connect an effects unit or signal processor to a mixer, and that is via an insert point. All but the most basic analogue mixers have insert points on the input channels and also on the master stereo outputs. Digital mixers may have more limited insert capabilities, mainly because of the additional cost of the extra input and output converters needed, but most still enable you to configure some of the available I/O (inputs/outputs) as insert sends and returns. However, digital mixers tend also to include internal effects and signal processors that can be assigned to virtual insert points via the software interface. Software mixers generally allow the use of effect/processor plug-ins, and if you have an audio interface with sufficient spare I/O capacity, it's usually possible to route signals to and from an external hardware device using these.

An insert point is simply a means of breaking into a signal path at some point so that the signal can be diverted via a suitable effect or processor device. On most of the analogue mixers you are likely to encounter, the insert points will be in the form of TRS (tip, ring, sleeve) jack sockets, which means you need a specially wired Y-lead or adaptor to be able to use them. The TRS socket is conventionally wired 'tip send/ring return', but if soldering up leads is not your forte (though you'll save a lot of money if you learn), you can buy ready made Y-leads or adaptors that enable you to use off-the-shelf jack leads.

Referring back to Figure 1.3, the insert points are depicted by black arrowheads, which show their position in the signal path – the sockets actually contain sprung contacts that maintain the signal flow when no plug is inserted. Physically, they appear as TRS jacks and are located either along the top edge or rear panel of the mixer. It is important to note that while it is permissible to connect any type of effect or signal processor via an insert point, there are restrictions on what can be used via the aux send/return system. On digital/virtual mixers, there are no physical connections to the internal or plug-in effects as these exist entirely in the software domain. Nevertheless, to make the user interface intuitive, routing displays are frequently used to show an analogue-style signal path, enabling the user to visualise what signal is being sent where.

Effects And Processors

This next section is very important, and understanding its implications will save you a lot of frustration when connecting effects and processors. In fact it's so important that the information will be repeated throughout the book.

While it is fine to connect any type of effect or signal processor via an insert point, there are restrictions on what can be used via the aux send/return system. As a rule of thumb, only delay-based effects such as reverb, echo, chorus, phasing, flanging and pitch shifting should be connected via the aux system, and these are generally referred to as effects. If the box uses delay to do its work, it's an effect, and if there's a dry/effect mix knob or parameter, the box is almost certain to be an effect. The unique thing about an effect is that it is added to the original signal, whereas a process such as EQ doesn't add to the original signal but rather changes the whole of the signal. Processors include compressors, gates and EQ and may normally be connected only via insert points, not via the aux sends and returns. There are workarounds to specific problems that may involve connecting processors to the aux send system, but in normal operation it should be avoided. These exceptions will be described later in the book so as not to cause confusion.

Pre-Fade Listen

Most mixers include PFL (pre-fade listen) buttons that, when depressed, display the channel signal level on one of the desk's meters and isolate the channel in the monitor speakers or headphones. Think of PFL as a kind of solo button, though it is a little different from a traditional solo function. PFL facility provides an easy way of setting up levels independent of channel faders, and it also enables you to check individual signals in isolation. To set the input gain control of a mixer for the best signal-to-noise performance it's simply a matter of going through the mix, one channel at a time, pressing the PFL solo button then adjusting the input gain for a nominal

full-scale reading on the output level meter designated for PFL use. When you release the PFL button, all the other channels will come back on and the meters will revert to displaying the output signal level.

If your mixer doesn't have PFL buttons, the best way to optimise the channel gain is to set the channel fader around three-quarters of the way up, turn the stereo output faders to their odB positions, then adjust the input gain trim control to give a full-scale reading on the main output meters.

Some mixers also include a solo facility – again accessed via a button at the bottom of the channel strip – and its function is similar to PFL in that it isolates the channel signal in the control room monitors, though the signal level and pan position remains the same as before solo was pressed. With PFL, the signal is always monitored in mono at a fixed level regardless of fader position. To solo a channel that has an effect applied, it is generally necessary to solo both the channel in question and the relevant effects returns.

Multitrack Mixers

A studio console doesn't just mix signals, it also acts as a central routing system, sending signals to the different tape/hard disk recording tracks, adding effects from external processors, and mixing the outputs from the tape machine to produce a final stereo mix. At the same time, it has to function as a 'mixer within a mixer' so that a separate control room monitor mix can be set up while the performers are recording or over-dubbing. This makes it a lot more sophisticated than our earlier four-into-two mixer, and perhaps the most difficult areas to come to grips with are the multitrack outputs and the 'from recorder' monitoring.

Tracks Or Channels?

The terminology associated with mixers can be a little confusing, and a common mistake that even experienced users make is to refer to a mixer as having so many 'tracks'. In fact, mixers don't have any tracks, they have channels (inputs) and groups (outputs). It's multitrack recorders and sequencers that have the tracks!

So far we've described a simple input channel with input gain, EQ, aux sends, pan control and a fader, but on a hardware multitrack mixer there are two different kinds of channel. The main input channel generally has the most comprehensive facilities and is used to feed microphones and line-level sources into the mixer – and subsequently to the recorder inputs – while recording. When the recording is complete and you're mixing your recorded tracks, the input channels are freed up to accept the output from the multitrack recorder. The physical location of the monitor channels depends on whether you have a split or in-line mixer.

To hear what's already been recorded while adding new parts we need monitor channels, which are used to set up a guide monitor mix based on the multitrack outputs. This is necessary as without a monitor mix there would be no way of keeping in tune or in time with material that was recorded earlier.

Monitor Channels

Monitor channels are similar to the main input channels, but on analogue consoles often have fewer facilities and may have rotary level controls instead of faders. On an in-line mixer (so called because the main input and monitor controls are located in the same channel strip as the input channel controls), there's often provision to switch all or part of the EQ between the main and monitor signal paths so you can have your EQ where you most need it. The same is often true of the aux sends. On digital consoles it's more common to find both main and monitor channels with the same features. The main job of the monitor channels during the recording phase of a project is to provide a rough mix of the recorded tracks for the performers to play along to.

It's easier to figure out what the monitor channels are doing if you envisage the monitor section as being almost a separate mixer in its own right, fed from the multitrack machine's outputs and routed into the main stereo mix.

Once the recording is complete, there's no longer any need for a monitor mix, which frees up the monitor channels for other purposes. Most often they are used as extra line inputs at the mixing stage, where they can function as effects returns or additional input channels for sequenced MIDI instruments. At mixdown, the monitor channels invariably route into the main stereo mix.

Groups

For multitrack work there must be some facility for sending different signals to different inputs (the track inputs) of the multitrack recorder, which is where groups come into the picture. A stereo mixer has just a left and a right output, but a multitrack mixer needs several additional outputs to feed the individual tracks of the recording machine. Each of these outputs needs its own fader for setting record levels. These separate outputs are known as groups.

If you need to send a different signal or mix of signals to all eight inputs of an eight-track recorder, you need a mixer with eight group outputs in addition to the main stereo output. This is known as an 8-buss console, because the eight groups are fed from eight separate mix busses. However, it isn't limited to eight-track recording – you can work with as many tracks as you like as long as you don't need to record on more than eight tracks at once. This may involve a little repatching, but it's one way of getting a lot of performance from a relatively small mixer. Similarly, a computer-based system equipped with an eight-in-eight-out audio interface may be restricted to recording eight signals at any one time, but there's nothing to stop you adding additional parts after the initial eight. Once all the tracks are recorded, they can be mixed internally using the software mixer and fed to between two and eight outputs at once. Normally you'd mix to two outputs for stereo work, but you would need six outputs for 5.1 surround (surround will be covered towards the end of this book).

Routing Buttons

In our basic mixer, channels could be only on or off, but in a multitrack mixer they can also be routed to any of the groups, usually in odd/even pairs via the channel routing switches. If two or more channels are routed to the same output they are automatically mixed together, so you could mix four drum kit tom mics then route them all to channel 5 if you wanted to. The channel faders still set the relative levels of the various signals being mixed but the master group fader controls the overall level feeding the multitrack recorder. As most hardware multitrack recorders don't have input level controls the mixer group output faders are used to set the record level.

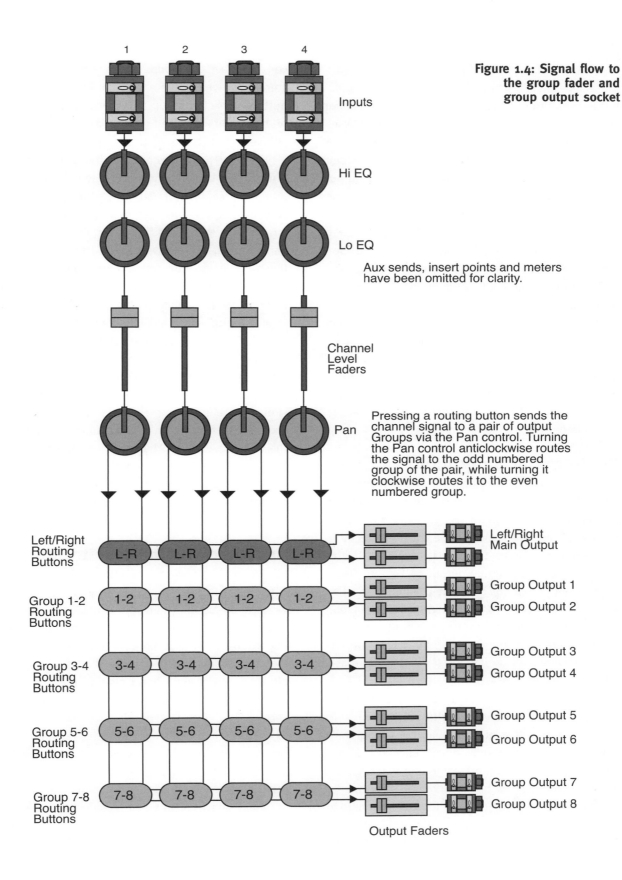

Inputs

Hi EQ

Lo EQ

Figure 1.4: Signal flow to the group fader and group output socket

Aux sends, insert points and meters have been omitted for clarity.

Channel Level Faders

Pan

Pressing a routing button sends the channel signal to a pair of output Groups via the Pan control. Turning the Pan control anticlockwise routes the signal to the odd numbered group of the pair, while turning it clockwise routes it to the even numbered group.

Left/Right Routing Buttons — L-R L-R L-R L-R — Left/Right Main Output

Group 1-2 Routing Buttons — 1-2 1-2 1-2 1-2 — Group Output 1 / Group Output 2

Group 3-4 Routing Buttons — 3-4 3-4 3-4 3-4 — Group Output 3 / Group Output 4

Group 5-6 Routing Buttons — 5-6 5-6 5-6 5-6 — Group Output 5 / Group Output 6

Group 7-8 Routing Buttons — 7-8 7-8 7-8 7-8 — Group Output 7 / Group Output 8

Output Faders

Pan And Routing

In our original basic mixer, the pan control only steered the channel signal between the left and right outputs, but in a multitrack console it also steers the channel signal between the odd and even numbered busses of the buss pair to which that channel is routed. A single routing button handles the routing for a pair of groups. If you want to route a channel to output only group 2, for example, you'd press the routing button marked 1,2 and turn the pan control fully clockwise so that all the signal goes to group 2 and none to group 1. Leaving the pan in its centre position would send equal amounts of signal to groups 1 and 2. To record something in stereo (different tom mics on a drum kit, for example), the relevant channels would be routed to a pair of groups and the pan control used to position the various sounds between them. The outputs from these two groups would then be recorded to two tracks of the multitrack recorder. When mixing, these tracks would be fed into separate mixer channels then panned hard left and right to maintain the original stereo image.

Routing And Subgrouping

On an eight-buss mixer, (the most common analogue mixer format for project-studio use) the routing buttons would be marked 1,2, 3,4, 5,6, 7,8, with a further L,R button for routing the channel directly to the stereo mix. Figure 1.4 shows the signal flow to the group fader and group output socket.

Just as the monitor channels change roles when switching from recording to mixing, so does the group routing system. During recording, the groups are used to route signals to the recorder, but when you mix they can be routed back into the stereo mix. As always, there's a very good reason.

Imagine you have backing vocals recorded over four or five tracks of your multitrack recorder. To change the overall level of the backing vocals you'd have to change the level by moving several faders at once, which is both cumbersome and inaccurate. A more effective approach is to create a 'subgroup' of the backing vocals by routing the vocal channels to a pair of groups rather than directly to the left/right mix. This way, the whole stereo backing vocal mix can

be controlled using just two group faders. Some consoles have the groups permanently routed to the stereo mix while others provide 'groups to stereo' buttons for each group fader, and these generally route all odd numbered group faders to the left and all even numbered ones to the right.

A more versatile system, which is usually missing from budget consoles for cost reasons, is to provide group pan controls. If you have group pan controls, you can create mono subgroups and still pan them anywhere in the stereo mix. If you don't have group pan controls, you always have to use up two group faders for every subgrouping operation (in effect, to create a stereo group) apart from those where the end result will be panned either hard left or hard right.

In a typical mix, you might create subgroups from things like drums, backing vocals and keyboards, which reduces the number of faders that need to be moved during the mix. Note that any effects that are to be added to these subgroups using the aux sends should be returned to the same subgroup (using the channel or effect-return routing buttons), otherwise the effect level won't change when the group fader is moved. Figure 1.5 shows the signal flow at mixdown. In this example, the monitor channels are being used as extra line inputs and the signal flow shows how subgroups actually work.

Split And In-Line Monitoring

Earlier in the chapter I mentioned in-line mixing consoles, and the concept is an important one as virtually all modern hardware consoles – and most software mixers – are based on an adaptation of the in-line format. On a conventional 'split' mixing console, the group faders and the monitor channel controls are situated to the right-hand side of the mixer and separated from the input channels by the master section. The master section includes such functions as the master stereo faders, the group faders, the aux send and return masters, and so on. You may also find a test oscillator, talkback mic, mix/two-track monitor selection, headphone level control and other facilities.

A minimum of eight monitor channels are required to provide a monitor mix from an eight-track recorder, but many split consoles have 16 or more dedicated

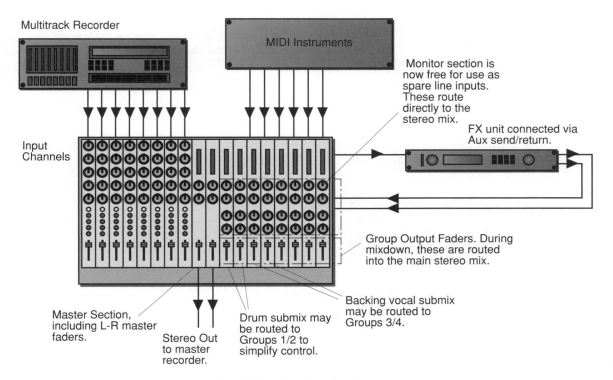

Multitrack Recorder

MIDI Instruments

Monitor section is now free for use as spare line inputs. These route directly to the stereo mix.

FX unit connected via Aux send/return.

Input Channels

Group Output Faders. During mixdown, these are routed into the main stereo mix.

Master Section, including L-R master faders.

Stereo Out to master recorder.

Drum submix may be routed to Groups 1/2 to simplify control.

Backing vocal submix may be routed to Groups 3/4.

This example shows a split console as this makes it easier to visualise the signal flow. However, the majority of project studio consoles follow the in-line format where the Monitor controls are located within the channel strips.

Figure 1.5: Signal flow at mixdown. In this example, the monitor channels are being used as extra line inputs and the signal flow shows how subgroups actually work

monitor channels to accommodate 16-track working. In-line consoles, on the other hand, have as many monitor channels as they have input channels. The basic requirements for a split console monitor channel are level and pan controls, though most also have some form of EQ and aux send controls. Figure 1.6 shows a multitrack split console with the monitor section moved away from the main body of the mixer to clarify signal flow. Figure 1.7 shows an in-line console with similar facilities.

Tape Monitoring

Setting up the monitoring for multitrack work used to be a lot more complicated than it is now, but fortunately the majority of recorders have an auto

monitor mode, which means it's always possible to monitor from the recorder's track outputs and still hear the signal you need to hear. If a track is being recorded, you hear the track input, but if the track is in playback mode, you automatically hear the recorded track. When executing a punch-in, the monitoring automatically changes from track to input as you punch in, then back to track again as you punch out. Usually, when the recorder is stopped, the input signal is monitored.

More On In-Line Consoles

The in-line layout may seem confusing at first because the monitor and input controls reside in the same channel strip, but there are advantages – not

**Figure 1.6: Multitrack 'split' console
with the monitor section moved away
from the main body of the mixer to
clarify signal flow**

Sources to be recorded are fed
via the input channels and
routed via the Groups using the
Pan controls and channel
routing buttons.

**Figure 1.6: Multitrack 'split' console
with the monitor section moved away
from the main body of the mixer to
clarify signal flow**

Monitor section shown
below recorder to
clarify signal flow.

Track recording
levels set via
Group faders.

Split-format recording console

During recording, the Input
channels are routed to the
desired tape tracks using
the channel Pan controls
and routing buttons. The
recording levels are set
using the Group faders. The
control room monitor mix is
normally fed from the
outputs of the multitrack
recorder and mixed using
the monitor section of the
console.

Multitrack Recorder

Track 8

Recorder Inputs   Track 1

Monitor Speakers

Left/Right
Faders

Monitor section of mixer

Monitor Amplifier fed
from Control Room
Monitor output.

Monitor Amplifier

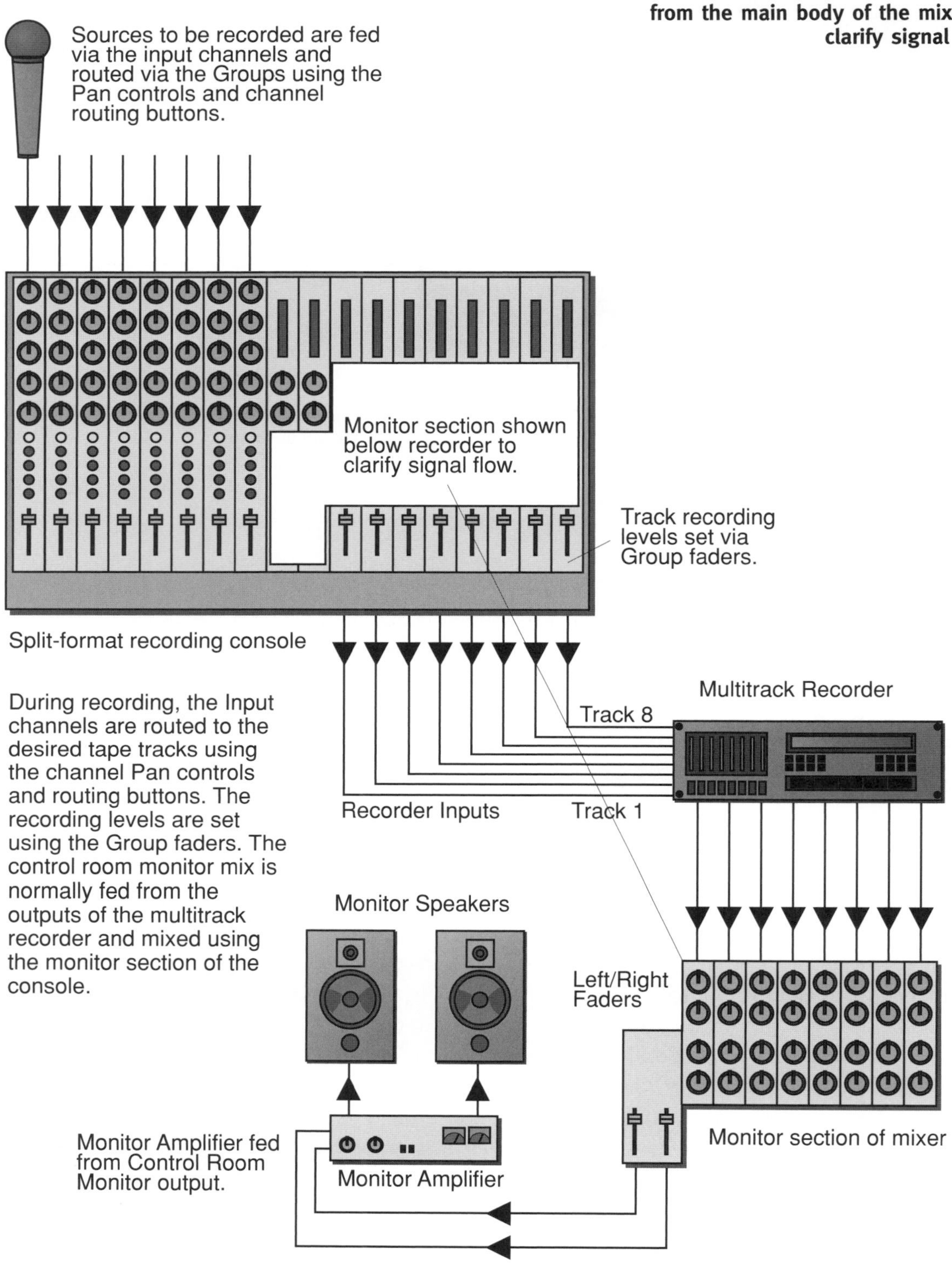

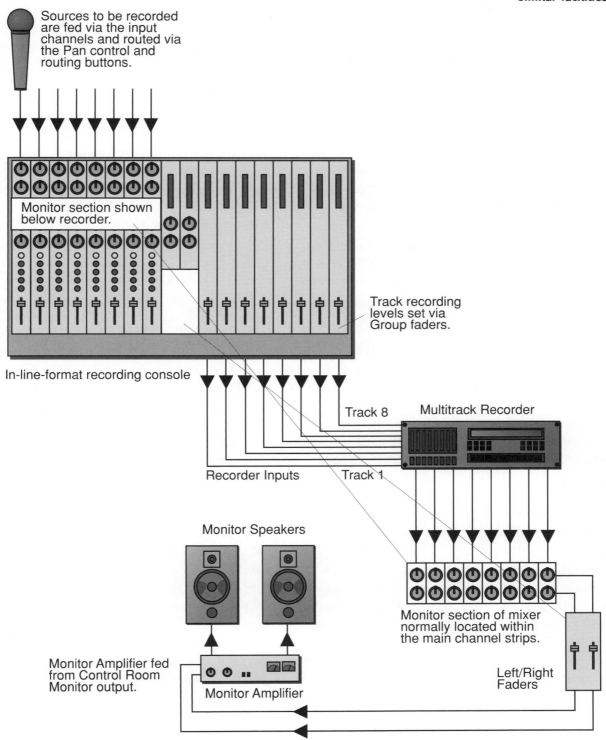

Sources to be recorded are fed via the input channels and routed via the Pan control and routing buttons.

Monitor section shown below recorder.

In-line-format recording console

Track recording levels set via Group faders.

Track 8   Multitrack Recorder

Recorder Inputs   Track 1

Monitor Speakers

Monitor section of mixer normally located within the main channel strips.

Monitor Amplifier fed from Control Room Monitor output.

Monitor Amplifier

Left/Right Faders

least that instead of being limited to just eight or 16 monitor channels, there's one monitor channel for every input channel. This arrangement usually results in a mixer that is deeper front to back than an equivalent split design, but it also it means the mixer can be made less wide for the same number of channels.

Rather than reconfigure the whole mixer after recording, ready for mixing, most in-line consoles have a channel flip switch that routes the track signal through the input channel and connects the unused monitor channel input to the channel input sockets. If channels are flipped as soon as they have been recorded, the input channel fader may be used for balancing the mix, so that by the time the recording is complete, the mix will already be set up on the input channel faders. The spare monitor inputs may be useful at mixdown for adding sequenced MIDI instruments to the mix.

Split EQ And Aux Sends

Split consoles may or may not have EQ on the monitor channels (though they will usually have some aux sends) but in the case of an in-line desk both aux sends and EQ facilities may have to be shared. The majority of split-console monitor sections have at least one dedicated aux send control so that effects may be added to the foldback or cue mix, but there may be little or no room for EQ or further aux send controls.

To get around this limitation, there's usually a switching arrangement that allows the monitor channel to share part of the main input channel's EQ. For example, if the main EQ is a four-band affair with two sweep mids, the monitor channel may be able to make use of the hi and lo EQ leaving the main input channel with two sweeps. In such cases, the sweep range is usually wide enough to allow the two mids to cover the entire audio spectrum.

Another common arrangement is for a couple of the aux sends to be switchable between either the input or monitor channels. This is obviously less than ideal, but providing a full-featured EQ on every monitor and input channel would take up a lot of space and add considerably to the cost of the desk.

Monitors As Line-Ins

When you're mixing down using an in-line console, the channel flip switches are all operated leaving the monitor channels connected to the console line inputs and available to accommodate other line signals that may need to be added to the mix. If you have a large MIDI system synchronised to a multitrack recorder, these additional inputs may well be a necessity unless you have the luxury of a separate keyboard mixer. However, these spare monitor channels may also be used to handle extra effects returns if you run out of conventional effects returns – remember that an effects return is just another kind of line-level input channel.

'All-Input' Mixing

Although this book is mainly concerned with the use of effects and signal processors, this whistle-stop tour of mixing console features is essential if you're to get the best out of your outboard gear – after all, most effects and processors are used with a mixer of some kind. No overview of mixers would be complete without looking at the 'all-input' method of working, which can be applied to both split and in-line consoles. In all-input mode, the monitor channels are never used for monitoring at all. This may sound illogical, but it's actually a very simple way of working and comes close to the way most software mixers work.

If you have an eight-track recorder – and providing that you have enough mixer input channels – you can leave the outputs of your recorder permanently connected to the first eight input channels of the mixer, routing these directly to the stereo L/R mix so that you can monitor them. The remaining input channels may then be used to handle the signals being recorded, routed via the groups. This does away with the need to switch the off-tape signals between the monitor and input channels, so you can leave your MIDI gear permanently connected to the monitor inputs. This way your control room mix becomes your final mix. In fact, I think this is the simplest way to work providing you have at least eight more input channels than you have recorder tracks.

The only limitation of working this way – other than having to ensure you have a mixer with enough input channels – is that the monitor channels can't usually be routed via the groups to create subgroups – they always feed directly into the stereo L/R mix. However, as most MIDI sequencers allow you to automate synth and sampler levels and pans via MIDI, not being able to group MIDI instrument inputs shouldn't be a disadvantage.

Monitor Select

The control room monitor outputs of a console tend to follow the stereo mix present on the master faders, but sometimes you'll want to hear playback from one or more stereo mastering machines, the output from an effects processor, or you may need to check what is being fed out of one of your aux send sockets. A row of buttons in the master section provides a choice of monitoring options, though not all consoles provide the same choices. Pressing a PFL or solo button overrides the stereo mix so that you hear only the solo channel on the control room monitors or headphones, but it doesn't interfere with the stereo output.

The monitor output also has its own master volume control, and often a dim switch, too. Dim is a useful addition as it drops the monitor volume to about 10 per cent so you can make yourself heard in the studio – or perhaps answer phone calls – without having to alter the volume control setting. On most budget desks, the headphone outputs are fed from the same source as the monitor output, though the phones usually have a separate volume control.

Talkback

Talkback is necessary so that the engineer can speak to the musicians in the studio area. Often there is a talkback mic built into the mixer itself, but on some desks there will be an XLR socket on the front panel to accept a gooseneck-style mic. The mic is normally routed into the musicians' foldback system – a headphone amplifier or a small pair of monitor speakers – though it's also common to have the option of routing it to tape so that you can record cues or song titles as you go along. Talkback switches work only when held down to prevent them from being accidentally left on. In the studio, talkback overrides whatever else is being fed to the studio monitor system but doesn't affect the control room monitor system. Effects are not used with talkback.

Automation

Adding automation to analogue consoles is actually a lot more costly and complex than adding it to digital mixers, but there are fader automation systems based on VCAs (voltage controlled amplifiers) or moving faders. Although the most basic form of automation is simple channel muting, which may be controlled from a MIDI sequencer, few modern mixers offer anything this basic. While muting might seem very limited, it can offer possibilities other than simply shutting down channels when not in use (for the purpose of minimising noise). For example, a signal could be split and fed to two channels simultaneously with the mutes being used to select between them. This way, a track shared between, say, lead vocals and a guitar solo could be mixed by pre-setting the appropriate effect and EQ treatments for guitar and vocals on each of the two channels then switching between them automatically at the right moment. Level changes could be performed in the same way – in other words, switching between two channels on which all the settings are identical except level.

All forms of mixer automation need to be synchronised to the time code generated by the recorder so that the mixer knows whereabouts in the song it's supposed to make changes. In the project studio, the sync system will be MTC (MIDI time code) or SMPTE (the video/film time code standard). Automation data is digital and is stored in a computer built into the mixer or in a desktop computer connected to the mixer. Because of the expense of moving controls, affordable analogue mixers tend to be limited to fader and mute automation, whereas a digital mixer can automate just about every parameter the user can adjust. The main modes of an automated mixer will be described later in the book.

Digital Mixers

Digital consoles don't have the same space restrictions as analogue mixers – many of the controls are accessed one at a time by means of a data entry knob, or via a single row of knobs and faders that can be switched to control one type of function at a time. For example, all of the channel levels, all the aux send levels, all the group output levels and so on may be controlled using the same bank of faders. Having four bands of fully parametric EQ on both the monitor and input channels is not uncommon, and you may find the same facilities on the effects returns and busses.

Digital mixers do essentially the same job as their analogue counterparts, the main practical difference being the user interface and reduced flexibility to connect to external analogue devices. There may also be a digital link between the mixer and compatible digital multitrack machines, which preserves signal integrity and simplifies wiring.

Because digital mixers can incorporate more features than analogue consoles, it would be impractical to provide a physical control for each function. Instead, there tends to be a number of physical faders to control blocks of channels, usually motorised, and perhaps one further rotary control to accompany the faders, but there will be only one set of EQ controls – or perhaps even a single data knob on cheaper mixers. The faders may control aux send levels as well as channel, group and send/return levels. A select button by each fader enables the edit control section to become active for that particular channel, and a display screen provides further information as well as a physical representation of some of the virtual controls. If the mixer has 16 physical faders but can control more than 16 channels, a bank switching system is used so that the same faders can access all of the channels. Because the faders are motorised, they will jump to their new positions whenever the fader bank or function is changed.

Most digital consoles include effects, dynamic processing and the ability to automate complete mixes – right down to EQ and aux settings – making it possible to recall an old mix many months later and get it back exactly as it was. As mentioned earlier, however, it's impractical to put analogue insert points on every channel of a digital console, which is one reason that gates and compressors tend to be included. This is a mixed blessing as you're very limited as to how many of your own hardware processors you can connect. Indeed, it may be better in some cases

to feed the digital multitrack back into the mixer via analogue inputs so that effects and processors can be inserted between them when required during mixing. This is most easily achieved if the recorder is connected to the mixer via a patchbay.

Digital Advantages

It's arguable whether digital mixers have any significant sonic advantage over analogue consoles, and they're certainly less straightforward to use, but they do make it possible to access and automate a great number of functions at a relatively low cost and in a very compact form. Furthermore, we've now reached the stage where it is often cheaper for a manufacturer to build a completely automated digital mixer than an equivalent manually operated analogue mixer.

One very real advantage of using a digital mixer with a digital multitrack recorder is that the signal may be kept in the digital domain by using a digital interface such as the ADAT optical protocol, Tascam's TDIF interface, Yamaha's MLAN or Roland's R-Buss. Indeed, if you use a digital master recorder (such as a DAT machine, MD recorder or computer), the signal may never need to leave the digital domain again until it reaches the end user's hi-fi system. As a rule, the most significant signal deterioration occurs whenever analogue signals are converted to digital signals or vice versa, so once a signal is in the digital domain it makes sense to keep it there.

Software Mixers

Software mixers tend to have little involvement at the recording stage as signals are fed straight from either an external mixer or a series of mic preamps directly into the audio interface and from there to the tracks onto which they are to be recorded. Some systems allow plug-in effects to be added while recording while others do not.

Each recorded track feeds its own mixer channel, which provides monitoring when overdubbing and full control over the signal when mixing. Like a hardware mixer, the soft mixer channels can usually be routed via busses for grouping, while plug-in processors and effects can be deployed via virtual insert points and aux send/returns respectively. All channels tend to have full functionality and more channels can be added depending on how many tracks you have recorded – up to the limit of the processing power of your system. The console layout is like an all-input design and is conceptually easy to understand. In a typical audio sequencer everything can be automated – from pans, levels and aux sends to plug-in settings – and because the recorder and mixer reside within the same software package, the user doesn't have to get involved in syncing the mixer to the recording.

Because mixer channels require processing power, it's best to open as few mixer channels as you require and not to assign plug-ins or EQ to a channel unless you need it.

Specifications

The mixer is the centre of your studio and everything you want to record will pass through it. Because of this, it must have the highest possible electrical performance in terms of frequency response, distortion and noise. On budget mixing consoles, the mic input amplifiers are often the weakest links in terms of noise, and you'll find that as you turn up the mic gain control, the background noise increases. This is further compounded by the tendency of budget studios to make extensive use of dynamic or moving-coil microphones due to their versatility and low cost. Unfortunately, the low sensitivity of dynamic microphones means that a lot of gain is needed to record quiet instruments, such as the acoustic guitar, so noise becomes a problem. The only practical way around it is to buy at least one good-quality condenser or back-electret mic as these have a much higher output than dynamic mics.

Signal quality will also be compromised by any equipment connected to the mixer – an audio chain is as weak as its weakest link, so buy effects and processors that have good noise and distortion specifications.

Modern software mixers tend to operate at a choice of 16- or 24-bit resolution and at sample rates of 44.1kHz, 48kHz, 88.2kHz or 96kHz. If you're making audio CDs, then working at 44.1kHz avoids the complication of sample rate conversion later in the proceedings and also reduces the processor load.

However, it may still be worth recording at 24-bit resolution as some resolution is invariably lost during mixing and processing. This will enable you to produce a high-quality 16-bit CD master at the end of the mastering stage.

Although the internal 32-bit, floating point signal path used in most native or host-based systems has a huge amount of headroom, you still need to take care optimising levels at the input and at the output of the mixer. The best way to get a clean signal from such a system is to use a high-quality mic preamp or voice channel, the main difference being that a voice channel incorporates additional processing such as compression, EQ, limiting, de-essing and so forth.

Effects And Processors

When connecting signal processors to mixing consoles it is best to consider the processors as falling into two categories, each of which must be handled differently. There are those processors that treat the whole signal, and those that add a proportion of treated signal to the unprocessed signal to create their effect. Even though both types are processors of some kind, I have coined the term 'processor' to describe those devices that treat the whole signal and 'effect' for those where a mix of processed and unprocessed sound is involved. Fortunately, there is a rule that may be applied to decide which is which: if the device has some kind of time delay or pitch-shift circuit, and if it has a dry/wet mix control, then it is almost certainly an effect. If not, it is probably a processor.

Examples of processors include gates, expanders, compressors, limiters, equalisers, enhancers, amplifier modellers, pitch correctors and distortion devices – all of which are characterised by having no mix control (with the exception of enhancers, where the mix control determines the depth of the effect). Examples of effects include reverb, digital delay, chorus, flangers, ADT units and pitch shifters. All of these usually have a mix facility, enabling the user to blend the processed and unprocessed sound; however, by setting the mix control to output the affected signal only, mixing can be (and generally is), performed within the mixing console.

An effect may be used either in conjunction with the auxiliary send circuit (in which case mixing is performed by the mixer), or via an insert point (in which case the unit's own mix control is used). A processor, on the other hand, is normally used only at the insert point (or otherwise connected in line with the signal path). Any attempt to use it via the aux send system is likely to yield a variety of undesirable results, although some engineers like to use compressors in the aux send path to combine the compressed and uncompressed sound. This is because it produces a different compression characteristic from regular compression, but it is safe to do this only with analogue mixers. In digital mixers – unless the various signal paths are sample accurate in their timing – the combined sound can seem flanged or filtered due to the time delay between the two signal paths. At best, the resulting sound will be diluted by the addition of the untreated portion of the signal, and at worst phase differences within the circuitry may completely spoil the tonality of the signal, so don't try any of this 'risky' stuff until you've mastered the basic rules.

A valid exception to this rule is when you need to treat one channel with a signal processor, such as a compressor, but don't have an insert point available. In this case you can feed the compressor from the pre-fade aux send and turn the channel fader down. The compressor output may then be plugged into a spare channel. Normally, the compression would be added to only a single channel, so all the corresponding pre-fade sends on the other channels should be turned down. However, if you want to compress a mix of similar sounds, such as backing vocals, then you could feed all these to the pre-fade send buss and compress them as a single mixed signal. The reason this trick is reasonably safe is that the dry sound contributed by the individual channels is removed from the mix so you're hearing only the compressor output.

If it is necessary to split a signal to feed two inputs, a simple Y-lead or two-into-one adaptor will usually suffice. However, the same is not true if two outputs are required to feed one input. If two outputs are joined directly it is likely that circuit damage will result, so the only way to combine two signals is via a purpose-made mixer circuit. Under no circumstances should you connect the speaker output of an amp directly to any input of a mixing console or signal processor. If it is necessary to extract a manageable signal from a speaker output, as may be the case when DI'ing a guitar, then a purpose-made DI box (that accepts speaker inputs) must be used to match the signal levels.

Optimum Effects Connection

The usual way of connecting a reverb unit or other effect is to feed it from a post-fade effects send on the console (effectively mono), then feed the two reverb outputs back into the mixer, either through two effects returns panned left and right or through a pair of spare input channels. The effects unit output mix parameter or control is then set for effect only – no dry signal. If you use input channels as returns, ensure that the corresponding aux send is turned completely off on those channels, otherwise some of the reverb gets fed back to its own input, causing feedback or tonal colouration.

To make absolutely sure that your reverb unit or multi-effects processor is working as quietly as possible, set the aux sends on the channels you want to affect to around three-quarters full up. The aux send master should also be set to three-quarters full up – the input level control on the effects unit itself is used to set the signal level going into the unit so that a healthy meter reading is obtained. You should set the output level of the effects unit to be close to maximum and then adjust the effects return level on the mixer to give you the right subjective level of effect. By following this procedure, you have ensured that the gain structure of both your mixer and your effects unit have been properly optimised.

It's also important to turn down any effects sends that aren't being used and to deactivate any mixer channels that aren't being used in the mix. This doesn't just mean turning the fader down – you should also turn the channel off if it has a mute button, and if you are using a console with routing buttons, make sure that unused channels aren't routed to the main stereo mix. It's not often realised that a muted channel with the fader down can still add a little noise (known as mix-buss noise) just by being connected to the stereo mix buss, so always unroute unused channels.

Mix-buss noise also applies to effects send controls, but few consoles enable you to mute these. However, you may have aux send switching, which allows you, for example, to route a channel's aux sends to sends 1 and 2 or 3 and 4. If this is the case and you need to use only two effects units, use sends 1 and 2 for your effects, and on any channels where effects aren't required route the sends to 3 and 4 instead. This has the effect of removing unused sends from the aux mix buss, which can make things considerably quieter.

Finally, if you're adding a specific effect to only one channel, you could take your effects send from the channel's insert send or from the channel's direct output if it has one. This removes the contribution of mix-buss noise altogether. Alternatively, feed the signal to be treated directly into the effects unit and then feed the effects unit's outputs into two adjacent mixer channels panned hard left and right. The effect/mix balance will then have to be set on the effects unit. It should also be realised that a mono-in, stereo-out effects device such as a digital reverb unit will need

to be fed into two mixer channels panned left and right if the stereo effect is to be preserved.

Processors are generally connected via a console's channel or group insert points, although both effects and processors can be connected directly 'in line' between a line-level signal source and a mixer input if preferred. It is, however, important to realise that most outboard equipment works properly only with line-level inputs, not with microphone signals. The only exception to this rule is for equipment that includes a microphone preamplifier, such as dedicated voice channels or vocal processors.

Software mixers simplify some aspects of connecting effects and processors. For example, you don't usually need to worry about the level of the signal passing through the plug-in if the mixer inputs are set correctly, and in cases where this is important, metering will be provided within the plug-in itself, as well as some means of attenuating the signal. Furthermore, a mono-in, stereo-out plug-in inserted into a mono channel will generally reconfigure the channel to produce a stereo output. Figure 1.8 shows a section of a typical software mixer.

Figure 1.8: Section of a software mixer

2 PATCHING AND PATCHBAYS

The previous chapter explained the way in which signals are routed through a typical mixer, and most of the connections in a typical studio are made via the mixer. Even if you plan to use an all-in-one mixer/recorder workstation or a computer-based system, you may still need to add a patchbay to integrate external hardware elements. In any event, many of the concepts of patching are just as relevant to the virtual world as they are to the real one. Incidentally, the term 'patching' came from the original telephone exchanges, where calls were connected using patchbays and patch cables.

With the need to regularly change the signal connections in a studio to accommodate specific situations, it's pretty obvious that plugging and unplugging leads into the rear panels of processors and mixers is going to be both tedious and time consuming. Even in the small home studio, there may be many such connections and the only practical approach when hardware outboard equipment and mixers are being used is to bring all the regularly used inputs and outputs to a patchbay so that they can be conveniently patched together as necessary using short signal leads. Patching is often simpler in a digital studio simply because more processing takes place inside the mixer or inside a software package, but in most real-life situations analogue and digital equipment exist side by side and analogue connections are frequently made between the two. As touched upon in the chapter on mixing, digital mixers tend to have much more limited I/O than analogue mixers, so using the analogue line inputs connected via a patchbay is a useful way of providing insert points for use when mixing down.

Professional analogue patchbays use high-reliability miniature Bantam jack plugs and sockets, often with gold-plated contacts to provide a flexible and durable – but highly expensive – patching system. Budget semi-pro systems are much more realistically priced and tend to be based on readily available, mass-produced plastic sockets, which accept standard quarter inch instrument-style jack plugs. Both unbalanced and balanced versions are available. This is a convenient format for the musician as most musical instruments rely on quarter-inch jack connections.

The physical patchbay format usually consists of a rack-mountable 1U panel, generally with two rows of between 16 and 24 sockets, each socket on the top row being paired with the socket below it. By convention, the top row of sockets is for outputs and the bottom row for inputs. A typical patching system takes the most commonly used inputs and outputs of the mixer, recorders and outboard signal processors to the patchbay, where they can be connected as desired using short jack-to-jack leads. Patchbays are most commonly used to gain access to console line inputs, aux sends and returns, equipment inputs and outputs and insert points, but not all are wired in the same way. Any patchbay socket pair wired to handle an insert point must be 'normalised'.

Figure 2.1 shows how the pairs of sockets in an unbalanced patchbay are wired, although the concept is similar for a balanced patchbay. If your console has balanced ins and outs, it's sensible to make this part of your patchbay balanced too, though the insert points on a typical home analogue console will invariably be unbalanced. The signal ground connections are often permanently linked between the

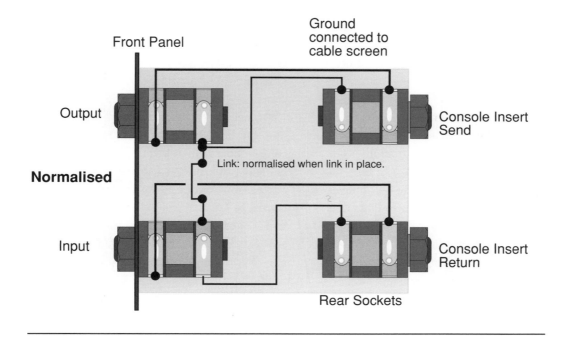

Ground
connected to
cable screen

Front Panel

Output

Console Insert
Send

Normalised

Link: normalised when link in place.

Input

Console Insert
Return

Rear Sockets

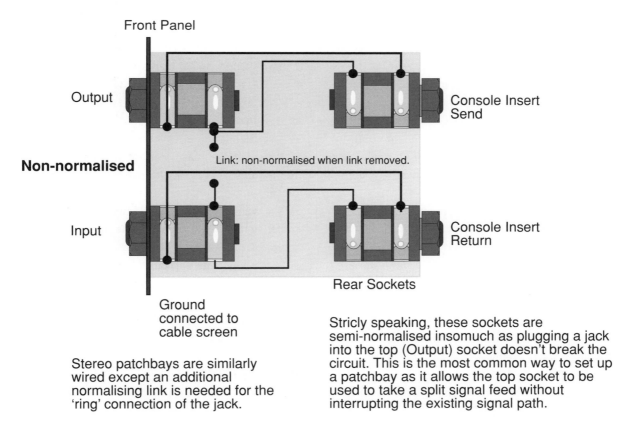

Front Panel

Output

Console Insert
Send

Non-normalised

Link: non-normalised when link removed.

Input

Console Insert
Return

Rear Sockets

Ground
connected to
cable screen

Stereo patchbays are similarly
wired except an additional
normalising link is needed for the
'ring' connection of the jack.

Stricly speaking, these sockets are
semi-normalised insomuch as plugging a jack
into the top (Output) socket doesn't break the
circuit. This is the most common way to set up
a patchbay as it allows the top socket to be
used to take a split signal feed without
interrupting the existing signal path.

Figure 2.1: Patchbay socket pair

socket pairs, and there may be a wire or track link on the printed circuit that 'normalises' the two sockets; all normalisation means is that the top and bottom sockets remain connected even if a plug hasn't been inserted. Without normalisation, the signal path would be broken whenever the sockets were not in use.

The most popular system for normalisation on current jack patchbays is to have each pair of sockets mounted on its own separate PCB with another pair of identically spaced sockets at the back to carry the rear connection. This board can easily be removed and replaced in one of two orientations so that either pair of sockets can be at the front – the circuit board is designed so that one way round the sockets are normalised and the other way round they are not. If you're not sure which way is which, plug an instrument such as a synth into one of the rear sockets and plug the other rear socket into an amplifier. If you get a sound, the sockets are normalised; if you don't, they're not.

Normalisation is necessary at insert points to maintain the signal flow through the console when nothing is plugged into the insert point and, depending on the complexity of your system, you may want to normalise other connections such as the output of your console to the input of a DAT machine. This means your most regularly used signal path is available without inserting patch leads, but you can still get at the mixer output or DAT machine input using patch leads if you need to.

The most commonly used semi-pro patchbays are fitted with jack sockets on the rear so that connection to other parts of the system can be made by means of easily made-up leads. Alternative versions are available that enable cables to be soldered directly to the rear of the patchbay and, in theory, minimising the number of connections produces a cleaner signal path. However, using sockets is more flexible as you may want to make changes to your patching system as your studio expands. From experience, I know that you get a lot of cable around the back of a typical patchbay and if a plug gets accidentally pulled out from the back of one of the units it can be difficult to put the matter right. Keep your cables organised as tidily as possible, and always leave enough slack

so that you can pull the patchbay out of its rack by a few inches to allow access to the rear sockets.

Normalisation

Referring again to Figure 2.1, contacts A carry the signal while contacts C provide the signal ground. The other set of contacts, B, are normally found on only the bottom row of sockets and it is these, in conjunction with the link (shown dotted), which normalise the sockets. Actually, as there is a switched contact only on the lower socket, it would be more correct to say that the patchbay is semi-normalised, and in most systems a semi-normalised patchbay is actually more useful than a fully normalised one. What does this mean in practice?

If there are no plugs inserted, contact B is mechanically switched to contact A, so whatever signal comes in on the back of the top socket is routed via the link directly to the lower socket. This completes the circuit, so that the console's insert send is routed directly back to its insert return.

If a plug is inserted into the lower socket, the contacts open, so no signal flows along the link. If, however, the top socket is patched to the input of an effects device and the bottom socket to the output of the device, contact B opens and all of the signal is diverted via the effects unit before being returned to the mixer. The reason for not fitting switch contacts to the top socket is that it provides a convenient way of splitting a signal on those occasions where you might want to take a feed from a mixer channel's insert send without breaking the normal signal flow. A typical application of this feature would be to split a signal, delay one part of it (with a DDL, for example) and then pan it to one side and pan the unprocessed sound to the other. Without a patchbay of this kind you would need a splitter box – or a split lead, at the very least – to perform this kind of task.

Ergonomics

The other principle of patchbay application is simply to put all of the inputs and outputs of the effects units, console inputs and aux sends and returns conveniently at hand. In fact, any type of audio connection that you might want to access on a regular basis can be brought out to a patchbay. In the case where the patchbay is handling simple inputs and outputs rather than insert points, you should un-normalise the sockets – failure to do this would result in the inputs and outputs of equipment being linked when no plugs are inserted into the patchbay and this might well cause the gear in question to oscillate. Depending on the patchbay type, un-normalising may involve removing a wire link or making sure the reversible circuit board is the right way round.

Side-Chain Inputs

There is one other connection, which is handy to bring out to a patchbay and that is the key – or side chain – input found on the back of some gates and compressors. This, however, is not always as straightforward as it might seem, so before doing anything check the manual relating to the piece of equipment in question to see exactly how the side chain socket is wired. Sometimes they're straightforward inputs selectable via a switch on the front panel, but on other occasions they may be wired in the same way as an insert send/return, in which case you'll have to use a normalised pair of sockets. Most reputable rack-mounted gear is designed to be used in conjunction with a patchbay, so if you haven't got the information you need to bring the key inputs out to your patchbay don't be afraid to phone the manufacturers or distributors and ask for more details.

Patchbay Wiring

Wiring to and from the patchbay should be done using separate screened cables, but for unbalanced insert points where the distance is no more than a few feet you can generally use a twin-core screened cable where one core carries the incoming signal and one the outgoing. The screen connection needs to be connected to only one of the two jacks feeding the patchbay as the two socket grounds are linked in the patchbay itself. Figure 2.2 shows how an insert patch point is wired. Foil-screened cable works well and is easy to strip and solder, though any high-quality co-ax is fine. With budget recording

equipment, console inserts are generally connected via a TRS stereo jack at the mixer end, so this method of wiring is the most convenient.

If you find that your desk behaves oddly and has a tendency to hum once the patchbay is wired up, suspect ground loop problems and check your wiring to ensure you don't have multiple earths connected to any single piece of equipment. (See the section on ground loops for more information on how to tackle this irritating problem.) As a rule, don't join the cable grounds to any metalwork or to the mains earth, and in the case of balanced connections it's usually wise to leave the screen disconnected at one end of the cable. Don't wire speaker signals to your patchbay as you could connect them to signal inputs by mistake, where the high signal level could cause severe damage.

Routing And Patching

The roles of the various signal processors and effects used in audio production are fully described elsewhere in this book, but it's not always obvious where they should be patched into the signal chain to give the best results.

If you're using a cassette multitracker, you have few options and everything is simple, but if you move up to a separate multitrack recorder and mixer you find yourself confronted by aux sends, insert points and mixing consoles with routing systems so advanced that they rival those of professional desks. Even if you've read the rest of this book and know the basic ground rules, there may still sometimes be a better way of doing things if you stop to think about it.

I've already grouped outboard equipment into the categories of effects or processors according to what they do and how they do it. You might think this seems pedantic, especially when most boxes that don't actually produce noise in their own right tend to get referred to as processors, but it does help avoid patching mistakes. As touched upon in the previous chapter, the main reason for separating boxes into these two categories is that there are certain restrictions on how processors can be connected, while effects (or FX as they tend to be called) enjoy a little more flexibility.

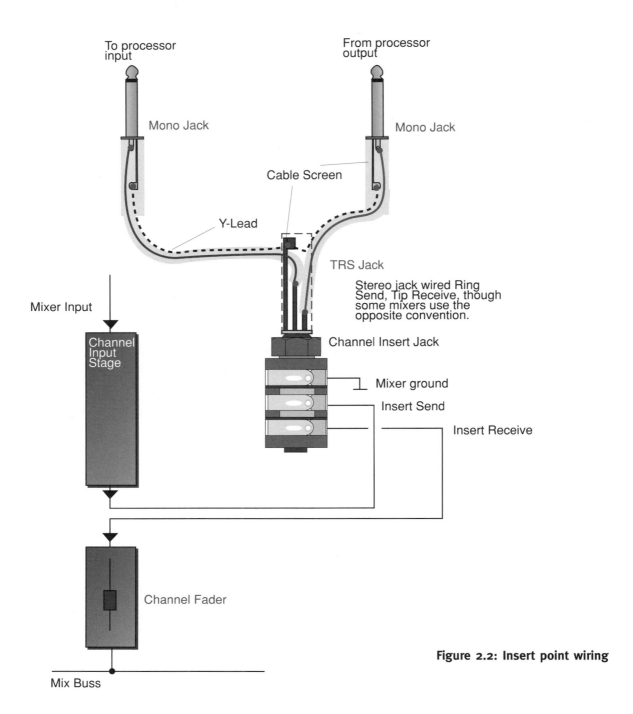

To processor
input

From processor
output

Mono Jack

Mono Jack

Cable Screen

Y-Lead

TRS Jack

Stereo jack wired Ring
Send, Tip Receive, though
some mixers use the
opposite convention.

Mixer Input

Channel
Input
Stage

Channel Insert Jack

Mixer ground

Insert Send

Insert Receive

Channel Fader

Figure 2.2: Insert point wiring

Mix Buss

Multi-Effect Patching

A potential dilemma arises when it comes to multi-effects boxes because most can function as either effects or processors, and a multi-effects patch might comprise both! If you set up a patch where processors feed into effects, then treat the whole patch as an effect. However, if you have a chain of processors with no effects (for example, a compressor followed by an equaliser), then treat the combination as a processor and patch it via an insert point.

Routing Rules

On a modern mixing console, the post-fade aux sends, commonly known as effects sends, allow some of the signal passing through a mixer channel to be sent to an effects unit such as a reverb or delay device. Using a patchbay makes these devices much easier to connect. The output from the FX device is then brought back into the mixer through a spare channel or an effects return (which is really just another channel but without the frills), to be mixed in with the original sound. Again, effects returns and spare line inputs should be made accessible from your patchbay. Stereo effects will, of course, take up two channels or returns (unless your mixer has dedicated stereo aux returns), and to keep the effect in stereo the two returns must be panned hard left and right. Because each channel has its own aux send level controls, the same FX unit can be used by several channels simultaneously; the aux send controls simply work as 'more-or-less-effect' knobs enabling the user to set up different levels of effect for each channel – and when the channel fader is turned down the effects level changes accordingly. This is explained in more detail in the first chapter.

Under normal circumstances, only effects should be patched in via the aux send return system, and I make no apology for repeating this as it's a very important concept. If you were to do the same with a processor, such as an EQ unit, you'd just be adding EQ'd sound to the original sound, which would, in effect, 'dilute' the effect of the EQ. This is bad enough with an analogue desk, but in a digital desk where there is a delay of a few thousandths of a second between signals going into the desk and coming out again, the effects of routing a signal to the same destination via two different routes can lead to very obvious comb filtering, which makes the sound appear phasey.

The other main method of patching external boxes is to use the channel, group and master insert points, all of which may be brought out to normalised patchbay points. Processors should always be connected via insert points or patched between the output of one piece of line-level gear and the input of another. Effects may also be patched into insert points as long as you need the effect only on that particular channel or group of channels. If you plug

an effect into an insert point, you'll need to use its own mix control to set the dry/effect balance. If you plug an effect into an aux send, you generally set it to produce 100 per cent wet sound. To make reference easier, I've condensed some of the main routing information into a series of short points.

- Insert points are invariably presented as stereo jacks wired to carry both the send and return signal, so if you don't have a patchbay you'll need a Y-lead with a stereo jack on one end and two monos on the other.

- Processors must be used 'in-line' with a signal and not in the effects send/return loop.

- Most processors work at line level, so you can't plug a mic directly into them. The correct way to compress a mic signal, for example, is to patch the compressor into the insert point of the mixer channel, which comes after the mic amp stage. This doesn't apply to mic channel processors that combine a mic amp with one or more processors.

- If an effect is used via the aux/send return system, it is normal to set the FX unit's dry/effect balance to 'effect only' so as to allow the console's aux send controls to control the effect balance.

- If an effect is used via an insert point, it is normal to use the FX unit's dry/effect balance to control the effect balance.

- Some effects, such as phasing and flanging, rely on a precise effect/dry balance, which may be better accomplished in the effects unit itself. In this case, either patch the FX unit into an insert point or, if you must use the aux/send system, you can either de-route the channel from the stereo mix to kill the dry signal or feed the effects unit from a pre-fade (foldback), send and turn the channel fader right down.

- To use a mono-in, stereo-out FX unit (such as reverb or stereo delay) via insert points, simply route one output of the unit to the insert return of the channel feeding it and the other to the insert return of a free adjacent channel. Match the levels, pan one track hard left and the other hard right for maximum stereo effect.

- To use a stereo-in, stereo-out FX unit via insert points, use two adjacent mixer channels panned hard left and right.

- To treat a whole mix, say with compression, patch your processor into the master insert points. This places your unit in the signal path just before the master stereo faders, which means that if you're using a compressor it won't try to fight you if you do a fadeout. Similarly, any noise generated by the processor will also be faded as you pull the faders down.

- If you don't have master insert points, you can patch a processor between the mixer's stereo out and the input to your stereo mastering recorder, but if you want to do fades with a compressor patched in, you'll need to do them using the input level control on the mastering machine, not on the desk. You'll also need to monitor the output of the master recorder to hear the effect of the fade.

Advanced Routing

If you want to process a group, then use the group insert points. Stereo groups require a stereo signal processor. A typical application might be to compress a stereo backing vocal mix, or even a drum mix, which means using a stereo compressor patched into a group pair. Don't forget to set the compressor to stereo link mode in this instance so that both channels are treated equally at all times.

If you want to compress or otherwise process a line-level signal, the simplest thing to do is to patch in the processor via the channel insert points. However, on most semi-pro desks the insert points are unbalanced and there may be an advantage in feeding the line-level signal through the processor first, then plugging the output of the processor into the mixer's balanced line input. The main advantage

of using balanced connections is that there is less likelihood of running into ground-loop hum problems.

Similarly, if you have enough spare balanced line inputs, you might find it better to use these for effects returns when working with consoles that have only unbalanced dedicated return sockets.

Lateral Thinking

Catering for every patching possibility means a lot of patchbays, a lot of cable and a lot of plugs. On top of the obvious cost, patchbays invariably compromise the quality of your audio signal to some extent simply because of the additional cabling and plug/socket connections your signal has to pass through. Unless you design your system very carefully you can easily introduce ground-loop hum, and though this may only be at a very low level it soon adds up when you have a number of FX and processors on the go.

Normalised patchbays sockets used to handle inserts invariably attract corrosion and grease over a period of time, which can result in audible signal distortion and, eventually, intermittent connections. This situation can be improved by treating the socket contacts with an advanced contact cleaner such as Deoxit. Don't use cheap cleaning sprays as these tend to leave a greasy film that attracts dust.

While patchbays are invaluable, it pays to plan your system to keep patching to a minimum. By thinking about how your system will actually be used you can usually avoid connecting every single item to a patchbay. For example, many modern mixers have six or even eight aux send busses, so unless you have more than eight effects units you could opt to permanently wire your effects direct to the aux sends and returns of your desk. This saves patching, money and maintains the best possible signal quality. If you have fewer effects units than you have sends, you could usefully wire up the spare sends to a patchbay so that you can plug in 'visiting' effects.

If your studio is for your own use rather than for commercial use, you could permanently plug your favourite vocal compressor into, say, channel one of your console and always use this channel to record your lead vocal. If you also make sure that you record your lead vocal onto tape track one every session, you can bring it back through the same compressor without having to repatch.

The same philosophy can be applied to gates: if you only ever use them after recording, you could connect them between your multitrack and desk rather than via the insert points, which would enable you to use balanced wiring (if your gates and tape machine are balanced). This maximises signal quality, reduces the risk of hum and, again, saves on wiring and patchbays. Of course, you do have to plan your sessions more carefully, so that anything that needs gating is recorded onto the tape tracks that correspond to your gates, but after just a little thought about your own working methods, you'll probably find that you can cut the complexity of your patchbay down to around 25 per cent or less of a full patchbay system.

The same applies to exciters or enhancers: if you always enhance the whole stereo mix without adding any other overall processing to your recording, simply wire your enhancer directly into your console's stereo insert points. If, on the other hand, you prefer to use it on just some parts of a mix and not others, you could wire it instead into a pair of group inserts.

If you're using a mixer that connects via standard jacks and you've made a number of permanent routing decisions as just outlined, you might even be able to do away with the patchbay altogether, because on the rare occasion that you do want to set up something out of the ordinary, you can always change the connections to the mixer. While this is inconvenient if you have to do it every session, it's less of a problem if you need to do it only occasionally.

I must stress that if you want an efficient patchbay system, you have to plan it carefully before you start, and one consideration often overlooked is that it's often unwise to put patchbays above other pieces of equipment in a rack as the cables tend to get in the way when you're trying to adjust controls. Put patchbays near the bottom of the rack or in a rack of their own.

Labels

Different patchbays come with different labelling systems, most of which are less than ideal. I find the easiest and best-looking solution is to use self-adhesive photo-quality inkjet paper and print my own using a simple computer graphics program. Once printed, the labels can be cut into strips using a guillotine or sharp knife and steel straight edge. Bold, condensed typefaces are the easiest to see, and background colours are useful to separate different areas of the patchbay.

Patching Suggestion

The following list suggests some of the connections that you could bring out to a patchbay and whether or not the normalising link should be left in. Those connections that are not insert points, but where normalisation has been recommended provide, in effect, new insert points between the individual pieces of equipment concerned. For example, the mixer group outs and multitrack line ins would normally be connected, but putting a patchbay between them lets you access the mixer outs and the recorder ins independently as well as enabling you to insert processors directly between the mixer outs and the recorder inputs should you wish to.

Signal	Normalised?
Channel insert points	Yes
Group insert points	Yes
Line inputs to desk	No
Line inputs to multitrack	Optional
Line outputs from multitrack	Optional
Line inputs to two-track	Optional
Line outputs from two-track	Optional
Effect sends from desk	No
Effect returns to desk	No
Input to effects	No
Outputs from effects	No
Key inputs	Consult manual

It is good practice to use a separate patchbay for MIDI signals on DIN connectors – and the same applies to gate pulses and control voltages if you have a collection of vintage analogue voltage-controlled synths.

Mic inputs would normally be routed to a wall box and connected using balanced XLR plugs and sockets (if the mixer input is balanced).

Special Cases

So far I've covered all the basic patchbay connections, but there are some less common situations that may have you scratching your head. For example, what happens if you have a gate with a key input that becomes active as soon as you plug in a jack? If you connect this to a patchbay, the key input will be permanently active and there's no easy wiring dodge to get around this. Fortunately, most gates have a switch to activate the key input. If you have a model that doesn't, you'll have to resign yourself to visiting the back of the rack once in a while.

Another hardware problem you may encounter is an effects unit that has stereo inputs but allows you to use it in mono by plugging in only one input. As soon as you connect both its inputs to a patchbay, it thinks you want to send it a stereo signal, so if you send a mono signal to just one of the inputs you may find only one channel works. To get around this you need to create your own cross-normalising system between the two adjacent sockets handling the FX unit inputs, as shown in Figure 2.3. This involves soldering two short wire links as shown in the diagram, so that when either of the inputs is used on its own the signal is also linked to the other input jack via the socket's normalising contacts. If both inputs are used, the unit reverts to normal stereo operation.

Keep It Quiet

Route as few channels to the mix buss as are strictly necessary. This will reduce mix buss noise. Most aux send controls don't have routing buttons, though if your console uses switching to swap an aux send between one of two busses, there is another way. The best way to explain this is by example.

Let's assume that your console has a switch that allows one of the aux sends to be swapped between aux 1 and aux 3; if you connect your effect to aux 1,

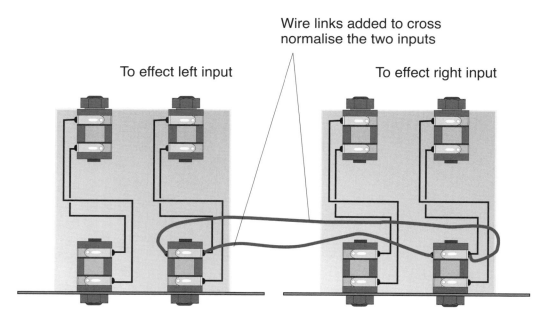

Wire links added to cross normalise the two inputs

To effect left input   To effect right input

Using this arrangement, if only one input of a stereo effects unit is patched, the patchbay will automatically route the same signal to both inputs.

Figure 2.3: Cross normalising stereo inputs

but set any channels where the effect is not needed to aux 3, the mix buss noise contributed by the 'no effects' channels will be shunted to aux 3 (which you're not using) rather than to aux 1, which you are using. On a large console, this can make a considerable difference in background noise.

A similar thing applies to unused mixer channels: if you de-route them by making sure all the routing buttons are up (rather than simply muting the unused channels), they won't add noise to your mix. Contrary to expectations, if you simply mute the channel, some mix buss noise will still be added.

Finally, when wiring your patchbay, keep mains wiring away from your signal wiring. If they definitely have to cross, make sure they do so at right angles, as that will minimise the risk of interference.

Digital and MIDI Patchbays

Most multi-port MIDI interfaces can act as MIDI routing systems, but sometimes you need to arrange things so that you can make manual changes to other parts of your system. In most cases, a straightforward MIDI patchbay is adequate where your regular MIDI cables plug into the back of the patchbay and short MIDI cables are used to make connections at the front. There are no normalising or balancing issues as there are with audio cables.

Digital patchbays are somewhat more complex, simply because of the number of digital formats (both stereo and multitrack) that are in use today. Commercial models are available with integral format converters, though it's often useful to make up a mechanical patchbay to handle S/PDIF (phono and optical) or AES/EBU (XLR) connections so that you can re-route your DAT/ADAT machines, CD player outputs, MD ins and outs, sound card ins and outs and so on without having to go around the back of the rack. Ensure that you use the correct type of cable for these connectors and make up patch leads using the same cable. Most studio supply companies offer specialised digital cable for both S/PDIF (unbalanced) and AES/EBU (balanced), which are of the correct impedance.

TOSLINK optical connections used for ADAT and optical S/PDIF signals can be handled using double-ended optical connectors. By mounting these in your patchbay, optical cables plug into the back and short optical cables are used for patching at the front. Note that optical connectors are slightly lossy, so you shouldn't run a signal through more of them than is necessary. Patch panels are available where multiple types of connector can be fitted to the same panel, enabling you to design your own custom digital patchbay.

3 EQUALISERS

The term *equaliser* was originally used to describe a filter that compensated for, or equalised, imperfections in the microphone signal chain but, in the context of recording, equalisation – or EQ for short – is really just another word for tone control. While early studio equipment and, to a greater extent, the analogue telephone lines for which EQ was first developed, needed a lot of corrective EQ to make them sound natural, modern recording equipment is capable of storing and reproducing sound that is virtually identical to the original. Nevertheless, the original sound isn't always what we want to hear, so EQ has evolved to take on more of a creative role.

Equalisers are based around electronic circuits known as *filters*. Strictly speaking, a filter is a device that removes something, but in the context of active equaliser circuits, filters can be arranged within special circuit configurations so that they boost as well as cut. Early equalisers were very simple affairs, usually no more than a single tone control offering only varying degrees of treble or bass cut. The first 'serious' active equaliser to find popular acceptance was designed by British electronic engineer Peter J Baxandall and comprised separate bass and treble controls – both of which could provide either cut or boost. This meant that the controls had to be set to their centre positions if the signal was to pass through unaffected.

What EQ does

So, how does an equaliser work? If you examine how an ordinary gain or volume control operates, you'll find that it turns the whole signal up or down in level without affecting the tonal balance. All the frequencies present in the input signal are increased or decreased by the same amount, so that what comes out is exactly the same as the signal that went in – other than in level. A circuit that changes nothing but the level of a signal is said to have a flat frequency response. It's technically impossible to make a circuit that has an infinitely wide frequency response, but in the context of audio, a circuit that is flat between the upper and lower limits of human hearing (generally 20Hz to 20kHz) is said to have a flat response.

Unlike the level or gain control, the equaliser is designed specifically to affect the level of some frequencies more than others. A typical treble control, for example, raises or lowers the level of the high frequencies while leaving the low-frequency level virtually unchanged. The reason I say 'virtually' is that if you were to plot out the gain versus frequency characteristics of an equaliser on a graph, you'd find that the graph followed a slope or curve – you don't see a sudden step at the frequency where the equaliser is set to operate. Cutting or boosting frequencies above 5kHz by so many dBs doesn't simply leave frequencies below that point unaffected – the transition is progressive – but the further below 5kHz you go, the less those frequencies are affected. This is much easier to understand if you take a look at Figure 3.1.

Figure 3.1 shows the bass cut curves of a Baxandall-type equaliser in graphic form. Notice that the cut and boost curves eventually flatten out, rather than continuing to rise indefinitely. This particular equaliser characteristic is described as a *shelving response*, because the cut or boost part of the curve eventually forms a flat shelf. It is possible to make an equaliser with a degree of boost that continues to increase with frequency, but this is usually

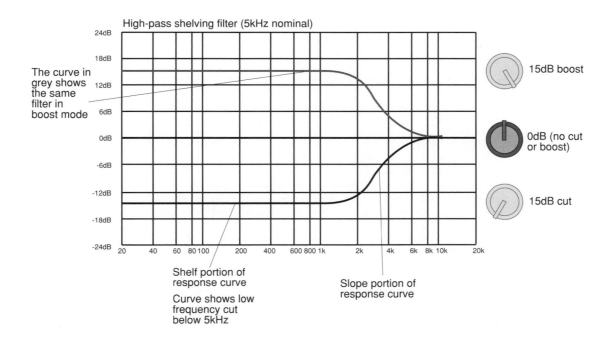

The curve in grey shows the same filter in boost mode

High-pass shelving filter (5kHz nominal)

15dB boost

0dB (no cut or boost)

15dB cut

Shelf portion of response curve

Curve shows low frequency cut below 5kHz

Slope portion of response curve

Figure 3.1: Shelving equaliser

undesirable in cases where the EQ will be used to add boost rather than cut.

In the case of a treble control for example, it would mean that the higher the frequency, the more boost you'd have, and so far more boost than necessary would be applied at very high and even supersonic frequencies – this would lead to an increase in high-frequency noise. Conversely, a bass equaliser with similar characteristics would give more boost and so give rise to rumble and hum problems, which can overload the electronics very easily. This is why most equalisers used in studio work tend to be either shelving or 'bandpass' types.

The slope of an equaliser filter is usually specified in dBs per octave, and for music applications slopes of 6dB/octave and 12dB per octave are common. The greater the number of dBs per octave the sharper the filter slope, and fewer frequencies outside the band are affected. If it is required to filter out subsonic signals using a cut filter, say below 50Hz, or very high frequencies above 20kHz, then sharper slopes of 24dB per octave are used and the filters are non-shelving to allow them to cut as deeply as possible. Such filters

are called high-pass and low-pass, as they allow high and low frequencies respectively to be passed and are often found on more comprehensive mixing consoles, mic preamps and sometimes on standalone equalisers. Figure 3.2 shows typical response curves for such filters.

Bandpass Filters

Shelving filters either cut or boost the level of signals above or below a certain value. However, there's another kind of filter, commonly used in mid-range controls, known as a bandpass – or bell curve – equaliser. These confine their activities to a specific band of frequencies, leaving frequencies above or below their range essentially unaffected. Figure 3.3 shows the characteristics of a typical bandpass filter in both the cut and boost positions. The range of frequencies affected is a function of the EQ circuit design and it's apparent that the wider the band of frequencies affected, the wider the response curve will be. The filter's bandwidth, or range, is defined by the width of the curve at the two points where the level is 3dB below the peak level. This is marked on Figure 3.3.

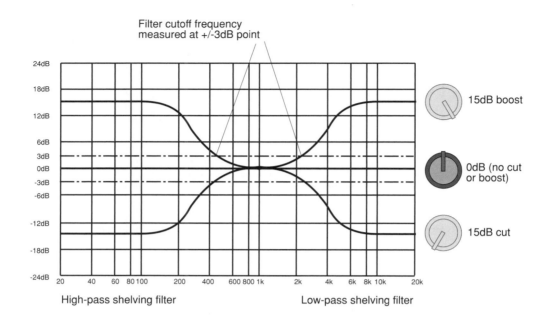

Figure 3.2: Low- and high-pass filters

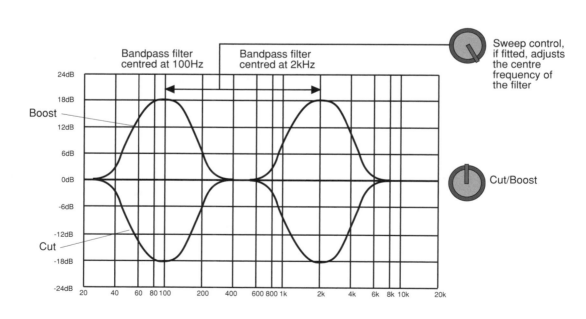

Figure 3.3: Bandpass filter

If you divide the centre frequency of the curve by its bandwidth you get a figure known as the 'Q' of the equaliser. This is useful to know because the larger the Q, the sharper the filter. High Q values are useful for picking out sounds that occupy a very narrow part of the audio spectrum, whereas lower Qs produce a smoother, more musical sound. In fact, it is possible to build high-Q analogue filters that affect a range of frequencies narrower than one semitone. Digital filters can be designed to be much narrower than this.

Because of their ability to affect only a specific band of frequencies, bandpass equalisers are often chosen for use as mid controls, where one or more may be used. In a simple equaliser, the bandwidth and centre frequency would be fixed – all the user would be able to do is to vary the amount of cut or boost. However, most serious recording mixers have what are known as sweep equalisers, where the Q is still fixed, but where the centre frequency of the equaliser can be adjusted.

Some console manufacturers also make the bass and treble (hi/lo) controls switchable from a shelving to a bell or bandpass response, which makes the equaliser yet more flexible. One example of when a bell response might be useful is when trying to add punch to a bass drum sound. Most bass drums have a 'note' around 80 to 90Hz, so using an 80Hz bell equaliser enables the bass drum to be brought up in level without unduly increasing the level of other unwanted low-frequency sounds occurring below this frequency. A shelving equaliser, on the other hand, would increase the level of anything below 80Hz by the same amount. In musical terms, using the bell equaliser might produce a noticeably tighter sound than using a shelving equaliser to boost the whole bass end in an indiscriminate way.

It is usual for the maximum cut or boost of equalisers used in recording to be limited to somewhere around 15dB, although some designs offer as much as 18dB. Adding any more boost than this may increase the level of the signal at the filter's frequency to the point where it exceeds the available headroom (ie the circuit's safety margin), resulting in distortion.

Parametric EQ

If a third control is added to provide a continually variable Q, the sweep equaliser becomes a fully parametric equaliser. Here, all the important parameters are placed under the user's control: the degree of cut or boost, the frequency at which the cut or boost is centred, and the width of the audio spectrum affected. An outboard parametric equaliser usually comprises at least two filter sections – and often four – so as to provide independent control in different parts of the spectrum. Because there are three controls per band, setting up a parametric equaliser takes time and experience, and models that have individual bypass buttons for each of the bands are easier to set up than models that have just a single bypass button for the whole unit. The response of a parametric equaliser is shown in Figure 3.4.

If you set up an equaliser with a very high Q, set the boost to maximum and then sweep the frequency control from low to high, you'll hear a very pronounced resonant peak, not unlike that produced by a wah-wah pedal. Using a filter in this way provides a useful means of identifying problem frequencies, which may then be addressed using a more restrained filter setting.

Graphic Equalisers

It's possible to gain a good degree of control over the entire audio spectrum by putting several narrow, fixed-frequency bell equalisers together in one box, all operating at different frequencies – and this is the basis of the graphic equaliser. Either constant Q or constant bandwidth filters may be used, and there's some argument over which sounds the best. A constant Q filter, as the name suggests, has the same Q value regardless of the degree of cut or boost applied, which means the bandwidth of the filter actually changes. With a constant bandwidth filter, it's the Q value that changes so that a constant bandwidth is achieved.

The individual filters are most often placed at either octave, half-octave or third-octave intervals and are arranged to overlap in such a way that when they are all set to cut or boost by the same amount, the frequency response remains essentially flat. The sliders often have a centre detent so that the centre position

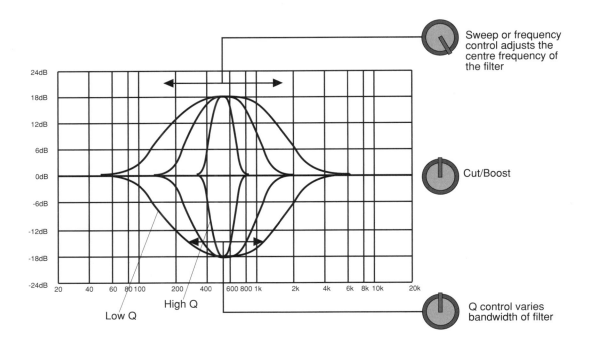

Sweep or frequency control adjusts the centre frequency of the filter

Cut/Boost

Q control varies bandwidth of filter

Low Q

High Q

Figure 3.4: Parametric equaliser

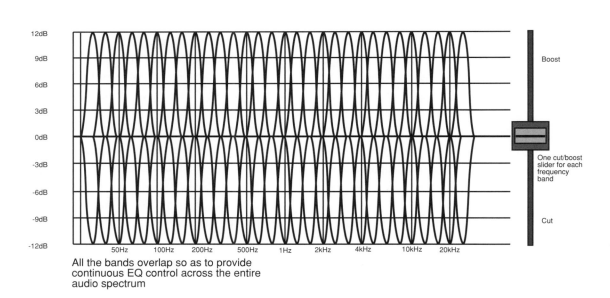

Boost

One cut/boost slider for each frequency band

Cut

All the bands overlap so as to provide continuous EQ control across the entire audio spectrum

Figure 3.5: Graphic equaliser

can be readily identified. It is also common to find that the very highest and lowest frequency sliders control a shelving filter rather than a bell. Figure 3.5 shows the response of the filters in a typical graphic equaliser. Again the filter range is usually limited to a maximum of plus or minus 15dB.

The name graphic equaliser came about because if the equaliser is fitted with slider controls rather than rotary ones, the sliders provide a graphic representation of the frequency response of the equaliser. Graphic equalisers are flexible and easy to set up, but in practice they're better suited to live sound applications than studio work as their fixed-frequency filters make them less precise than a parametric equaliser. Furthermore, less sophisticated designs may adversely affect the sound of the signal being processed, and it's common for adjacent bands to interact in such a way that the actual EQ curve doesn't quite match the curve shown by the sliders.

Paragraphic EQ

The paragraphic equaliser is most often found in digital hardware or software as the sheer number of physical controls would make it very expensive to implement using analogue circuitry. Essentially, the paragraphic is a hybrid of the graphic and parametric EQ where the cut/boost in multiple bands is controlled by sliders (real or virtual) in the usual way, but then each band also has a frequency adjustment and Q control, making it fully parametric. Software offering paragraphic EQ often provides a visual readout of the composite EQ curve in the form of a graphical display, and it's not uncommon to provide a means of adjusting the EQ curve by manipulating the curve display using a mouse. Without the response curve display, paragraphic equalisers can be difficult to set up because the interaction between the various frequency bands can be complex. The display from a paragraphic equaliser software plug-in is shown in Figure 3.6.

Desk EQ

A typical mixing console has shelving high and low controls set at around 100Hz and 10kHz with two sweep mids covering the range in between. There's usually some overlap between the EQ bands, but in the case of an in-line console where it may possible to switch the shelving EQ into one channel path and the two mids into the other, the two mids will generally be given an extended range covering the whole of the audio spectrum.

The fixed bandwidth or Q of sweep mid equalisers is inevitably a compromise: too low a Q will affect too wide a range of frequencies, while too high a Q will sound harsh or peaky if any degree of boost is applied. Unfortunately, different material benefits from different Qs. For example, if you have miked up an electric guitar and find that there is a sharply defined 'honk' caused by cabinet resonance at, say, 500Hz, you could apply some cut at a bandwidth just wide enough to tame the resonance without seriously affecting the sound outside that range. On the other hand, if you just want to add a little boost to the mid range in general, then a lower Q would sound smoother.

Some mid-priced desks get around this by offering a two-position bandwidth switch providing two different characteristics – one moderate and one sharp, which is clearly more useful. But the logical conclusion of this line of thought is to provide an extra variable control in place of the switch so that the equaliser can be made fully parametric. A few mid-price analogue consoles include one or more fully parametric mid sections, but in most cases if you need parametric EQ you'll have to patch in an external parametric equaliser.

Digital Equalisers

As yet there are relatively few digital equalisers available as standalone hardware, although all digital mixers and software audio multitrack systems include digital EQ capability. It is arguable whether digital EQ offers any advantage over analogue designs in terms of tonal quality, though a lot of work has been put into modelling the sound of existing classic equalisers in the digital domain, and some of the emulations are extremely good. It's also true that once a signal is in the digital domain, it makes sense to do as much processing as possible there to avoid the problems of quality loss that occur when signals are subjected to several stages of analogue-to-digital and digital-to-analogue conversion. Furthermore, the potential

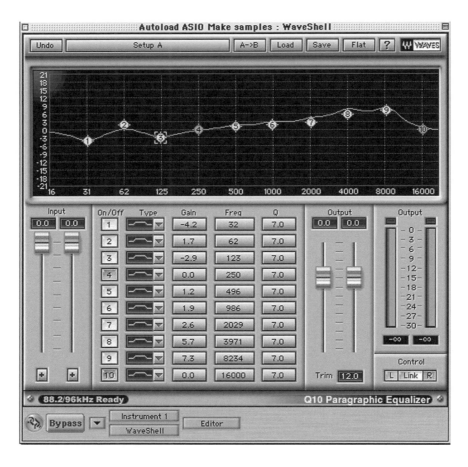

Figure 3.6: Paragraphic EQ plug-in

of digital equalisation far outweighs that of any practical analogue design simply because it is possible to create filter responses by mathematical means that are virtually impossible to reproduce using analogue circuitry. Indeed, the only limits are imposed by the operating software and the processing power available so, in theory at least, it is possible to build a single digital equaliser that can simulate exactly the characteristics of all the most popular equalisers ever built. It is also possible to create extremely sharp filter slopes using digital processing, a factor vital to de-noising and de-humming software.

EQ And Perception

If you check any text book on audio you'll see the limits of human hearing quoted as around 50Hz to 20kHz, though those same books will also point out that very

few individuals, other than young children, can hear pitches anything like as high as 20kHz. A more realistic figure might be around 15kHz for an adult, decreasing further as the years pass. What is puzzling, though – and this area provides scope enough for a book in its own right – is that even if your measured hearing response starts to fall off well below 20kHz, it is still possible to hear the effect of equalisation applied at the top end of the spectrum where you'd not expect to be able to hear any change. The mystery deepens further when reputable studio engineers claim to be able to differentiate between two otherwise identical audio circuits, where one has been modified to handle frequencies up to 50kHz and one handles frequencies up to only 30kHz. In theory, both limits are well above the threshold of human perception, so it seems that what goes on outside the audible spectrum has a way of influencing what we perceive within the range of our own hearing. It's for this reason that most audiophile-quality studio equipment has a frequency response extending to 40kHz or beyond.

EQ In Nature

At heart, no matter how complicated the EQ, it is still really just a frequency selective volume control, but its subjective effect on the sound is often more profound than this simple description might lead you to expect. In less civilised times, human beings relied on hearing for survival, so when it comes to seeing how much of your attention will be grabbed by a particular sound in a mix, it's a good idea to try to analyse what we hear in different natural situations.

Sound at a distance is less bright than sound close to us, partly because air absorbs high frequencies more readily than low ones. This is a natural effect that we perceive every day, so clearly we're used to sound behaving like this as certain sound qualities equate to the impression of distance. Changing the phase of the harmonics within a sound also contributes to a sense of distance, and if we delay the higher harmonics slightly, the sound seems further away again. In recorded sound, however, we're faced with the problem that all recorded sounds travel the same distance – if the hi-fi speakers are 3m (10 feet) from the listener, then that's how far the sound travels. What we need is a way to create the illusion of distance or closeness, and the appropriate use of EQ is one part of solving that particular puzzle.

Level And Phase

We know that EQ acts like a selective volume control, affecting only certain parts of the audio spectrum depending on the frequency characteristics of the filter circuit used. However, it's well known to circuit designers that EQ doesn't only change the level of specific parts of the spectrum, it also changes the phase of the affected frequencies relative to those that aren't being cut or boosted. Because of this phase characteristic, the top cut equaliser creates a similar effect to increasing the distance to the sound source.

This is almost certainly the reason that brightening up a sound makes it seem closer, while winding off some high end makes it seem more distant. In practice, every design of EQ affects the audio spectrum and phase response in a different way and, leaving aside technical criteria such as noise and distortion, this probably explains, at least in part, why some EQs have a more natural, musical sound than others.

Impressions Of Loudness

It's a fact that the human hearing curve isn't flat, but is more sensitive to mid-range sounds than to frequencies at the extreme high and low ends of the spectrum. We don't notice this because we've heard things this way all our lives. Nevertheless, as the level of sound we're listening to increases, the mid boost of the hearing system becomes less, with the result that high- and low-frequency sounds seem proportionally louder. This is yet another of those physiological factors that can be exploited to fool the ear into believing it's perceiving something that isn't entirely true. For example, if we know that extreme high and low frequencies stand out more when we listen to loud music, we can create the impression of loudness at lower listening levels by attenuating the mid range and boosting the HF and LF ends of the spectrum. The loudness button on a stereo system does exactly this, and if you look at the graphic EQs used in a night club or PA system you'll often see them set up showing a smile-shaped curve to promote the illusion of loudness and power. This works just as well in the studio, though it's generally most effective just to treat some of the sounds within a mix so as to maintain a contrast between the different sounds.

To Cut Or Boost?

In general, the less EQ boost you use, the more natural the final sound will be – the human ear is far more tolerant of EQ cut than it is of boost (especially at high Q settings). So, rather than adding lots of top to critical sounds such as vocals to get them to sit at the front of the mix, you could instead try applying high-end cut to other sounds in the mix that are conflicting with the vocal.

Some classical purists might say that you don't need EQ at all, but in the real world of pop recording, where the emphasis is on appropriate rather than accurate sounds, equalisation has become a way of life. The close miking of drums was originally tried in an attempt to cut down on spill from other instruments, but now it's become the normal pop drum sound. EQ plays a very large part in creating the modern drum sound, but because we're not usually trying to emulate the original acoustic drum sound, EQ is used in a creative context rather than a corrective one.

Separating Sounds

EQ can be used in many ways, but one of the most popular applications is to separate two similar sounds within a mix where the degree of overlap is causing the sound to become confused or muddled. If, for example, two sounds are fighting it out in the same part of the spectrum, a peaking equaliser can be used to add a degree of bite to one sound at one frequency while the other sound can be peaked up at a different frequency. Similarly, the top or bottom end of a sound can be 'trimmed' to avoid conflict – a typical example being the acoustic rhythm guitar in a pop mix, where the bottom end can get confused with the vocals, the drums or even the bass guitar. Here you can roll off quite a lot of the bottom end without spoiling the sound of the guitar, though if you listen to it in isolation it will probably sound rather thin. This introduces an important fact about EQ that I'll return to later: it's not what something sounds like in isolation that counts, but how it sounds in the context of the rest of the mix.

When To EQ

As a general rule, equalisation should be employed only after all efforts have been made to obtain the best sound at source. What's more, there's a huge subjective difference in sound between a budget equaliser and a top-quality studio equaliser, so if you have to work with a budget EQ, or the EQ section built into your desk, you'll probably have to use it very sparingly if the overall sound isn't to suffer, especially if you want to make changes in the critical 800Hz to 4kHz region where the human ear is very sensitive. Although the character of a really nice equaliser is difficult to quantify, the best equalisers

enable you to make more drastic changes without the sound appearing unnatural, nasal or harsh.

Most often, a combination of cut and boost is required, but always use the EQ bypass switch to flip back and forth between the equalised and unequalised sounds to make sure you really have improved matters. Equally, if you feel the need to EQ an instrument in isolation, check it against the other recorded tracks to make sure that the settings you're using work in context with the rest of the mix. More often than not you'll have to make further adjustments, but it really is worth striving to get your sounds right at the outset – EQ is an invaluable ally in shaping well-recorded sounds, but even the best equalisers have their limits when faced with difficult material.

What Sounds Are Where

Probably the best way to get to know the audio spectrum is to check out some common musical sounds and see what part of the audible range they occupy. Try feeding a commercial CD through your equaliser and apply a few dBs of boost and sweep through the frequency range to see how different sounds and instruments are picked out. The low-frequency limit of an instrument is usually quite easy to define as an instrument can't produce a pitch below the fundamental frequency of its lowest note, but the high-frequency end is somewhat less well-defined. That's because nearly all sounds include harmonics that extend right to the top end of the audio spectrum and beyond, and even though the level of these harmonics is probably very low, they're still very important in defining the sound and creating the impression of clarity. For the purpose of this section, the most useful thing I can do is pick a ball-park range to show where most of the audio energy from a particular source resides. It's up to you to try EQing above these frequencies to find out exactly how much the sound is affected. For example, a flute produces a relatively pure tone, though the breath-noise harmonics extend to the top of the audio spectrum and will respond to high-frequency EQ. Figure 3.7 shows a few common sounds in chart form so that their frequency ranges can be compared.

If you're using a software recording package, you

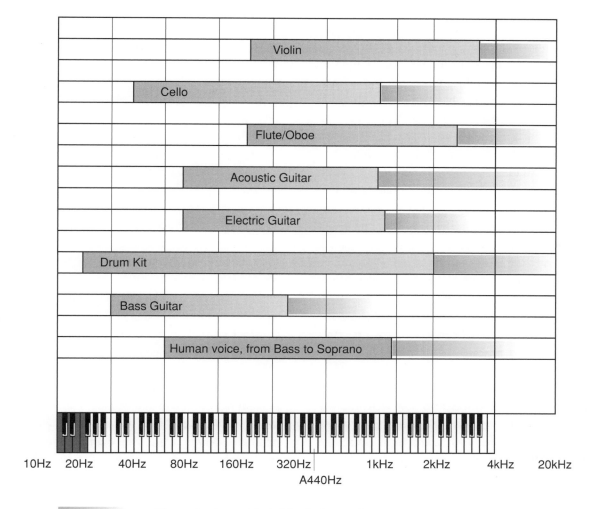

Shows the harmonics of the instrument

Figure 3.7: Common instrument ranges

may be able to buy a plug-in that can analyse the frequency response of any audio signal (a spectrum analyser), which is a good way of seeing how the tonal balance of a commercial track compares with your own mixes. Taking this a step further, there is software available that can automatically adjust the frequency response of your own mix, using multi-band EQ, so that it matches that of a reference recording such as a commercial record. In some instances, this can provide a short cut to getting a tonally well-balanced mix, but I prefer to view such things as educational tools that help you find the best way to do things for yourself.

Using EQ With Instruments: Drums

Drums are a special case when it comes to equalisation because the accepted pop and rock drum sound is not that of a natural kit. What's more, if you include the cymbals, a drum kit covers the entire audio spectrum. The trick is to make the drums sound both bright and solid but not too 'thick'. The following suggestions assume that the kit is being close-miked with one mic per drum plus a pair of stereo overheads to capture the cymbal sound and to add ambience.

The bass drum puts out most of its energy in a narrow band between 50 and 150Hz – depending on how it is tuned – but the attack transients reach right into the upper mid range. This can be confirmed by applying some EQ boost to a bass drum sound at around 4–6kHz; the difference in the attack characteristic is very noticeable. The usual pop music treatment is to add weight by boosting between 70 and 90Hz using a bandpass equaliser.

A close-miked bass drum without EQ will often sound less than ideal, though occasionally you get a great sound straight off. Most often there is a need to add definition to the hit, plus a degree of low-frequency weight. For a punchy sound, a little boost at 80Hz will usually improve matters, but to get a deeper sound without the end result being too boomy try adding 10dB or so of boost with your shelving bass control (most consoles have their bass controls at 50 or 60Hz) and then wind in 10dB or so of cut at around 220Hz using the lower-mid control. The two controls work together to produce a narrow area of low-frequency boost rather than the wide, uncontrollable boost obtained by using the low EQ on its own. The result is a kick sound with a lot of low weight.

To add definition to the beater impact, boost the upper mid range between 3.5 and 6kHz, choosing the final setting by ear. A wooden or hard plastic beater is far better than a felt one for producing a modern rock kick drum sound, and the slap can be further enhanced by taping a piece of thin plastic on the drum head at exactly the spot where the beater impacts. Credit cards work splendidly for this job! For styles other than rock, there are no hard rules because of the diversity of acceptable drum sounds in common usage. Even so, putting the right mic in the right place will always give you more scope for creative EQ.

Toms may be handled in much the same way as bass drums, with boost (using the lower-mid sweep control) in the 80 to 120Hz region, the exact setting depending on the size and type of tom. Careful adjustment of the upper-mid control can help pick out the stick impact, and if the tom rings in sympathy with other drums you can usually afford to roll off quite a lot of bass without the result sounding thin. I often use a gate side chain filter in key listen mode for this because of its sharp response – I know this

isn't what it was intended for, but it does the job perfectly! This kind of corrective EQ is better than applying too much damping to the drum. If you're using a software recording system, use a low cut, 12dB/octave (or higher) filter and adjust the frequency setting so that the right amount of unwanted low end is removed.

Snare drums are unpredictable and you never quite know how they're going to sound until you've put up a mic and listened to the result. The sound can be fattened by boosting the 90–140Hz band, while the bite can usually be located in the 3–7kHz region. It's easiest, when searching for the right area, to apply full boost then tune for the appropriate pitch. Once you've found it, you can back off the degree of boost until you have a sound you can live with. If the drum still doesn't sound crisp enough, consider switching to a capacitor mic or even using an exciter (harmonic enhancer).

When recording to analogue tape (some people still do!), always record cymbals at a low level to prevent tape overload and keep in mind that they cut through more loudly than you expect. Brightness can be added using the shelving high EQ control or you can tune the upper-mid control until you find a sweet spot. In general, cymbals are recorded as part of the overhead mic mix and, in some cases, it can help to roll off the bass end quite significantly to prevent the drum sounds picked up by the overheads from obstructing the drum sounds from the close mics. When recording cymbals into a digital system, there are no high-frequency saturation concerns other than not allowing the signal to clip at any point, so you can use a much higher recording level than you could with analogue tape.

Using EQ With Instruments: Bass Guitar

Whether the bass guitar is recorded using a DI (direct inject) box or with a mic, the equalisation on a typical console can be used to create a wide range of tonal characters. (I'm assuming the use of a console with four-band EQ and two sweep mids, but it is possible to use an external graphic or parametric equaliser to achieve the same result.) The lowest note on the conventionally tuned four-string electric bass guitar is 41Hz, but the higher notes contain significant energy up to 2 or 3kHz.

Boosting at around 80Hz can be used to pull out the low bass, while boosting between 500 and 800Hz adds a nicely aggressive bite. Boosting higher up the spectrum tends to bring out the finger noise and not much else, so if a bright sound is what you're after, get it as close as you can at source.

Playing technique has a lot to do with the tone of a bass guitar and no amount of EQ will compensate for underpowered finger-style playing. A touch of low/mid cut at around 200–250Hz can sometimes be effective in combination with a little low-end boost; this warms up the low bass end without the low/mid area getting boomy. In a crowded mix, on the other hand, applying low mid boost might actually produce a more confident bass sound.

Rather than simply using a DI box and adding compression to record the bass guitar, consider using one of the modelling bass preamplifiers currently available as these are able to get very close to the sound of a miked amp. Alternatively, DI the bass as usual and then process it via a guitar/bass amp software plug-in. Most guitar preamps have settings suitable for bass guitar providing you choose a virtual speaker model with plenty of low end.

Bass synths can be treated in much the same way as bass guitars, though their ability to produce higher harmonics means that EQ at higher frequencies will also be effective. However, be cautious when using very bright bass synth sounds: they can so easily fill up all the space in a mix, leaving the whole thing sounding congested. In this case a high-cut filter can be used to trim out the unwanted high end.

The traditional pipe organ goes an octave lower than the bass guitar, down to 20Hz or so where sounds are felt rather than heard. High organ notes, on the other hand, generate significant energy as far up the spectrum as 8kHz and beyond. Synthesiser sounds can also go this low – or even lower – but there's little point in adding energy at 20Hz when few domestic loudspeaker system extend far below 50Hz.

Using EQ With Instruments: Electric Guitar

The electric guitar has a starting point one octave higher than the bass guitar – at 82Hz – and, because of the restricted range of electric guitar speakers, there's little energy above 4kHz. Even so, it's a mistake to draw too many conclusions from the upper limit of any sound, because EQ applied above this arbitrary limit will almost certainly have some audible effect.

If you need to add warmth to the sound of an electric guitar, concentrate on the area between 125 and 200Hz. There's no point adding boost much below this region as the lowest note's fundamental frequency is 82Hz. Bass boost will only bring up the cabinet boom and make the overall sound muddy – it could also conflict with the bass guitar. Boosting the bass end will also accentuate any mains hum in the signal – most guitar pick-ups, especially single-coil jobs, pick up a surprising amount of hum.

To add attack to the sound, go for the 3–4kHz section of the spectrum, but don't add any really high-end boost unless the guitar is going through a DI box as there's not really all that much coming out of a guitar speaker above the 3 or 4kHz range. All you'll do is bring up the background noise and, if the guitar is being used with an overdrive sound, this will tend to sound buzzy or fizzy.

In a congested mix, two similar-sounding electric guitars can be separated by adding bite at different frequencies, say to one guitar at 3kHz and the other at 4kHz. However, this is rarely as successful as getting a different sound at source. If you can use two different amplifiers or preamp settings while recording the two parts it will help. It also makes sense to use different types of guitar – for example, one with single-coil pick-ups and one with humbuckers. If you're miking the guitar amp try using different mics for the different parts – a dynamic for one take and a capacitor for the other will make a noticeable difference, even if the guitar, amp and player remain the same. As with the bass guitar, digital guitar preamps that use physical modelling can get very close to the sound of a miked amplifier, so if you're using one of these try to use its controls to get close to the sound you want before you consider adding further EQ.

Using EQ With Instruments: Piano

A piano must be recorded using good-quality, properly positioned microphones, otherwise no amount of EQ will restore the natural sound. The bass can be enhanced by boosting at 90–150Hz, while attack detail can be brought out by bringing up the 4–6kHz area. Air can be added by applying wide-band boost at around 15kHz. If the sound is boomy, look for the offending area between 250 and 350Hz and apply enough cut to keep it under control. Because the piano is such a natural instrument, it pays to concentrate on putting suitable mics in the right place from the outset.

Using EQ With Instruments: Vocals

Vocals can range from around 80Hz to 1kHz depending on the style and sex of the singer. Again, there's significant energy above that range, which is why live mic manufacturers often build in a presence peak at 3 or 4kHz, and de-essers have to function at between 5 and 10kHz to remove sibilance. Always use a pop shield when recording vocals as no amount of EQ will fix popping once it's on tape. Try to get as near as possible to the sound you want by selecting the most sympathetic microphone and experimenting with its position. General brightening can be achieved using the shelving high EQ control on the mixer, but keep an ear open for sibilance. Boosting lower down, at 1–2kHz, gives a honky, cheap sound and is not recommended other than as a special effect. Presence can be added by applying a little boost at 3–4kHz using the upper mid sweep equaliser. In a mix of backing vocals, rolling off a touch of bass often helps the sound fit in better with the mix.

Perhaps the most sought-after vocal EQ treatment is what engineers refer to as 'air', where a very broad band EQ is applied at around 12 to 15kHz. The actual amount has to be determined by ear as different models of EQ respond differently. The boosted part of the spectrum is too high to make the vocal seem harsh, yet it still pulls out detail, making the vocal seem more open and interesting. This air trick also works well on mixes and submixes.

Using EQ With Instruments: Brass And Strings

As with vocals, brass and string instruments also tend to occupy the mid range of the spectrum, typically 80Hz to 1kHz (unless you count the tuba, in which case you can add almost an octave to the bottom of that figure). Brass and string instruments work on entirely different principles but they do respond to equalisation in similar ways. At between 1 and 3.5kHz the sound can become nasal or honky, which means a little subtle cutting in this region can sweeten things up. To add high-end sizzle, move up to the 6–10kHz band and try a little boost there, but don't overdo it or the sound will become 'spitty'. For a warm pad sound from string samples, brass samples and synth patches, roll off a little top and add a hint of boost between 300 and 400Hz.

Using EQ With Instruments: Bright Sounds

Few instruments produce much energy at the high end of the spectrum, the piccolo and xylophone coming closest in the 600Hz to 5kHz range. The upper harmonics of cymbals and triangles extend well beyond the limit of human hearing. Where the instrument produces no low frequencies, filtering out the unused lower octaves can help clean up the sound.

Sampled and synthesised sounds haven't been included because they can cover whatever range the electrical circuitry is capable of supporting which, in theory, can be the entire audio spectrum.

Useful EQ Frequencies

Mains hum occurs at 50 or 60Hz (and its multiples) depending on the frequency of the mains supply in the country where you live, so applying cut at 50/60Hz and 100/120Hz using a narrowly tuned parametric can help to remove hum from a recording without significantly changing the overall sound. However, you need a good-quality equaliser to do this as poor equalisers might 'ring' noticeably at the frequency they're tuned to, even in cut mode. A third-octave graphic may also help in this situation, but other types of equaliser are likely to have too wide a range, which means that some of the wanted bass sounds will be seriously affected.

The best anti-hum filters exist as software plug-ins for computer workstations, where some packages are capable of automatically tracking variations in the hum frequency and, at the same time, deploying additional filters to deal with the harmonics. Others may offer manual adjustment of a number of locked frequency bands targeting specific harmonics. There may also be a facility whereby the filter cut becomes less severe when the sound being treated is loud enough to mask the hum, as the less EQ cut you use, the less audible any side effects will be.

- Bass drums and bass guitars: punchiness at around 80Hz, definition at 2.5 to 5kHz.

- Electric guitars: boxy at around 200Hz, harsh or nasal between 1 and 2kHz. Brightness at 3 to 6kHz.

- Acoustic guitars: muddy or boomy between 200 and 500Hz, nasal at 1kHz, zing at 5 to 7kHz. Add a little 'air' EQ to open up the top end.

- Air: to add more top-end 'zing' to a clean guitar or vocal sound, use a shelving high control – or, better still, a parametric with a low Q set to boost at around 12 to 15kHz. This latter setting is useful to add 'air' to virtually any sound that contains high-frequency harmonics. Experiment with applying broadband boost in the 'air' band as this is a very useful production trick both for EQing single sounds and for treating mixes.

- Vocals: boominess at 150Hz, nasal at 1kHz, sibilance at 3 to 6kHz, air at 8 to 15kHz. Avoid excessive use of EQ when aiming for a natural sound.

4 ENHANCERS

Digital recording technology combined with low-cost, high-quality microphones makes it relatively easy to record things very accurately, but somehow it seems that the accurately captured sound of nature is never good or exciting enough for use in commercial music production. Pop music production tends to strive to make everything sound larger and more impressive than it would in real life, but how is this achieved? How do you process a perfectly good mix to make it sound even better – and how do we define 'better'? All kinds of processing can be brought to bear at the mastering stage of a recording, but if there's one box that can be guaranteed to 'hype up' sound in one easy step, it's the enhancer. In this instance, 'better' means making a mix sound brighter, more punchy – enhancing the detail and making it easier to identify individual sounds within the mix. Enhancement devices also tend to make mixes sound louder, even though the peak signal level may not have changed. They're not the solution to all recording problems and shouldn't be considered as a substitute for good recording or mixing practices, but when used carefully they can help your mixes stand out from the crowd.

Psychoacoustics

One important psychoacoustic principle exploited by enhancers is the fact that our perception of the audio spectrum changes as sounds become louder. Those familiar with the text book Fletcher-Munsen curves will already know that at high listening levels, low and high frequencies tend to be perceived as being louder. At lower listening levels, the mid range is more dominant. By using an equaliser to cut the mid range or to boost the high and low extremes, music can be made to sound louder, which is how the 'loudness' button on a hi-fi system works. Some dynamic EQ-type enhancers replicate this effect by cutting the mid range and boosting the highs and lows according to the dynamics of the input signal.

There's also another type of enhancement that works by adding artificially created high-frequency harmonics. This principle is also based in psychoacoustics: whenever an audio signal is subjected to distortion, intentionally or otherwise, high-frequency harmonics are produced. Normally these sound pretty unpleasant but, by using filters to confine the distortion to the upper reaches of the audio spectrum, it is possible to 'fill in' missing or weak HF detail in a way that the human brain will accept as natural. The dynamic element of the process applies the most harmonic enhancement to transient sounds, producing an apparent increase in detail, presence and loudness.

Some of the literature supporting devices working on phase shift claim that in real life, high-frequency sounds travel slightly faster than low-frequency sounds, so the further you are from a sound source the more the high frequencies lag behind. By delaying the bass and mid range to compensate for this effect, sounds can be made to sound nearer and more immediate. Whether this is strictly true or not I have been unable to establish, but manipulating the phase as described certainly makes things appear clearer.

Practical Enhancement

Perhaps the first real enhancer was the equaliser, a device that works by cutting or boosting part of the audio spectrum to alter the overall spectral balance.

EQ can help brighten sounds, change the relative balance of the bass and mid range, or scoop out the mid range to make a mix seem louder, but it can work only with what is already there – if the frequencies you want to hear never existed in the first place then no amount of EQ will bring them out. Another limitation is that when you apply conventional EQ it's there all the time until you switch it off – you can't, for example, decide to add bass boost to only the kick drum beats, or top boost to only the snare hits while leaving the sounds in between untouched. However, this particular effect can be created using dynamic equalisation, a combination of EQ and compression arranged so that the amount of tonal boost varies according to the dynamics and spectral content of the signal being processed.

Properly applied, dynamic equalisation effects can significantly increase tonal contrast within the music, something that fixed EQ can't do unless it's applied only to separate tracks within a mix. Dynamic equalisation is used in several enhancement devices, and one of the most effective systems is to set a bandpass filter to between 6 and 8kHz, compress the output, then add a small amount of the compressed signal back in with the original signal.

Many commercial enhancers combine elements of dynamic EQ with other processes, including harmonic synthesis and phase manipulation. Not all manufacturers use the same combination of techniques so, as you might expect, each type of enhancer has its own signature sound.

Phase Manipulation

Some audio reproduction systems introduce unwanted frequency-dependent phase shifts, and at least one commercial enhancer attempts to reverse this by splitting the audio signal into a number of frequency bands, then applying different delays to each band before re-combining them. Low frequencies are delayed the most (by up to 3ms)

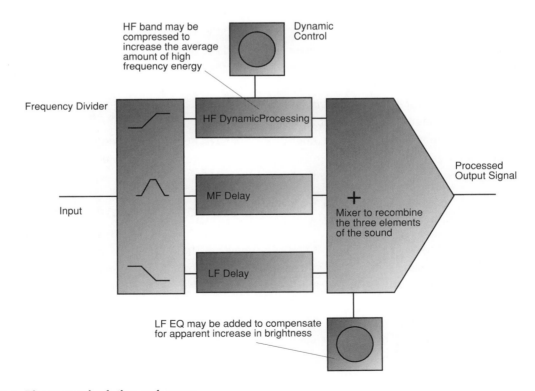

Figure 4.1: Phase manipulation enhancer

with higher frequencies receiving proportionally less delay. Frequencies above 1kHz or thereabouts are not generally delayed at all, but may undergo some form of dynamic processing such as compression or expansion. This can help increase the average level of high-frequency sounds or, if expansion is used, transients will be enhanced at the expense of lower-level signals. A block diagram of this type of enhancer is shown in Figure 4.1. Phase manipulation does not add new harmonics, but rather attempts to realign the relative phase of existing harmonics, as well as using dynamic processing to emphasise transients. Because this process emphasises the high end of the mix it sometimes helps to boost the bass end to compensate, so a typical modern enhancer working on the phase-shift principle will have a low-end EQ control as well as a high-frequency enhancement control. LED metering is used to show the extent of the dynamic processing being applied to the HF band.

Setting up this type of enhancer is fairly straightforward and usually entails adjusting the enhancement control to process the high end to the required extent, then using the low EQ control to make up for any lost bass end. The overall subjective brightness is increased slightly, but without the sound becoming fatiguing or edgy.

Expansion is sometimes included as part of the high-band processing, which may be an advantage when dealing with noisy material. Because of the expander operation, HF boost is applied only when the signal level is high enough to mask any noise that might be brought up by the dynamic control. Low-level sounds receive little or no processing.

Harmonics

A number of commercial enhancers also include some form of harmonic synthesis, a technique first commercially used by American company Aphex, which patented the process. Its system created new high-frequency harmonics that may never have been present in the original recording, but because they are musically related to the existing mid-range harmonics they sound convincing and natural.

It was discovered that by first high-pass filtering

part of the signal then adding a small amount of carefully controlled distortion and compression before adding the treated signal back to the original, the sound actually sounded cleaner and more detailed than it was before processing. This is quite counter-intuitive, as we're always told that distorting signals in any way makes them sound less clear.

The way the process works is that some of the input signal is diverted, via a side chain and a high-pass filter, into a harmonics-generating circuit as shown in Figure 4.2. The high-pass filter, which has a slope of around 12dB/octave, may be adjusted by the user from around 2kHz to over 6kHz (depending on the model in question) – the signal itself being fed into a non-linear circuit where the new harmonics are created. There are also inevitable phase shifts introduced through this process (due to the action of the high-pass filter), and it is believed that these make a significant contribution to the subjective result. Furthermore, a degree of compression is applied to the harmonics-generator output with a carefully set attack time, so that more harmonic enrichment occurs at the leading edges of transient sounds such as drum beats and plucked strings.

Only a very small amount of the processed signal needs to be mixed back in with the original to create the desired effect and, done properly, music appears more detailed, with better separation between individual sounds. However, like the phase manipulation system described earlier, the process doesn't affect the low end of the spectrum, so low-end EQ or other types of low-frequency enhancement may be included to help produce a balanced sound.

Setting Up Harmonic Enhancers

Depending on the design of the enhancer, the user may first have to adjust a drive control to ensure that the correct signal level is being passed to the harmonics-generation circuitry. However, many newer models have been refined to eliminate the need for user drive adjustment, in which case the main controls are the filter and the mix knobs. Careful adjustment of the filter circuit is essential and enables the user to decide whether the new harmonics should just creep in at the top of the

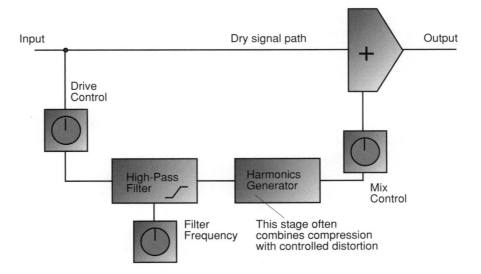

Figure 4.2: Harmonic enhancer

audio spectrum to add a little air, or if they should spread down into the mid range. In the case of a full stereo mix, it may be necessary to add only a little brightness to the top end of the cymbals or to add a little breathiness to a voice. On the other hand, if you are treating a solitary snare drum you may want to affect more of the spectrum to give a completely different sound, so the filter could be set to a lower frequency.

A filter frequency of 3kHz, for example, would cause harmonics to be generated from 6kHz (the second harmonic of 3kHz) upwards. Although the balance of odd and even harmonics tends to be different for different models – or even adjustable – it is generally believed that even harmonics sound the most musical.

Most, if not all, units will have a bypass switch, which enables the processed signal to be directly compared with the untreated sound, and also a mix control, which blends a small proportion of the harmonically enriched signal with the original untreated signal. This has to be done inside the unit rather than by using an effects send loop (as you might with conventional effects) because enhancers

rely on the harmonics being added back to the original signal in the correct phase. Routing the harmonics separately through a mixing console would almost certainly lead to a phase discrepancy between the unprocessed and processed sounds and, when re-combined, the results might not be as anticipated. This is particularly true of digital mixers, which may have a delay of up to three milliseconds between signals going in and signals coming out.

In any event, the mix control will generally not allow the balance to be set to 'effect only' as it might in other effects units. Indeed, the enhancer should not normally be considered as an effect at all, but rather as a processor that should be connected in line with the signal – usually via an insert point.

During setting up, advancing the mix or enhancement control so that the effect becomes obviously excessive will enable you to hear the effect of the filter control on the new harmonics. Once this has been set, the mix control may be backed off so that only the necessary degree of enhancement is added. If a stereo signal is being processed, both channels should be set in an identical fashion – enhancers tend not to have stereo link modes.

Dynamic Filtering

It's not uncommon for enhancers to combine the various processing systems mentioned with new design twists to make the result more distinctive. For example, it's possible to add dynamic low-frequency equalisation in such a way that phase cancellation occurs in the lower mid range, thus preventing the effect of the bass enhancement from spilling over into the mid range. At the high end of the spectrum, a combination of tight filtering and compression can help lift out high-frequency detail.

Even Dolby built its own enhancer based on dynamic filtering, although the exact filter configuration is both complex and secret. The Dolby approach relies upon treating the side chain signal via a bank of dynamic filters, which modify their characteristics according to the nature of the input signal. The filtered signal is subsequently compressed before being added back into the main signal path, so Dolby's system is really a very sophisticated dynamic equaliser.

A number of companies produce general-purpose dynamic equalisers that combine elements of both EQ and multi-band compression, and because all the relevant parameters are accessible to the user they can be very flexible. However, they can sometimes be less intuitive to set up than a dedicated enhancer and require the user to have some knowledge as to what part of the frequency spectrum needs boosting or cutting.

Tube Synthesis

One reason tube circuitry sounds so flattering is that high-level signals are subjected to a musically pleasant type of distortion, so it comes as no surprise that digital engineers have devised algorithms to emulate this process – some with more success than others. Tube emulation is available within both hardware and software products, though for enhancement, the most useful tube emulation system I've come across so far is that pioneered by UK company Drawmer in its 2476 Masterflow mastering processor. Like most mastering processors, this one splits the audio spectrum into multiple bands (in this case three) so that compression and limiting can be applied individually to each

frequency band. However, Drawmer has also added variable tube drive emulation to each band, and by careful adjustment of the amount of drive applied within each band, the signal can be selectively enhanced in quite powerful, yet musically natural-sounding, ways. For example, high-frequency tube drive has the effect of adding a sheen to the high-frequency detail within a mix or track, just as a conventional enhancer does, but applying drive to the low-frequency band has a quite different effect, adding warmth and weight to the bass end without significantly affecting the middle or high end of the spectrum. As a rule, the mid band, where most of the vocal energy resides, should be subjected to the least amount of treatment if a natural-sounding result is to be achieved. By applying most drive to the low and high bands, a Fletcher-Munsen-style 'smile' frequency curve is created, which augments the sense of loudness.

When To Enhance

The first rule must be not to enhance anything unless you think it needs it. The second rule must be to apply no more enhancement than is strictly necessary to achieve the desired result. Although enhancers are often used during mixing to treat individual tracks and submixes, they are also useful in mastering or post-production applications. For example, when treating production master tapes for use in cassette duplication, high-frequency enhancement can help to compensate for the loss of clarity inherent in mass cassette duplication. To a lesser extent, the process can be helpful in adding life to a master tape that has been mixed on inaccurate monitors or to an analogue master tape that has suffered high-end loss because of repeated playing, ageing or minor head-alignment errors during recording.

When mixing, the careful use of enhancement helps make specific sounds stand out in a mix. While it is possible to enhance a complete mix, this is a valuable opportunity to create contrast by enhancing only those elements of the mix that you want to stand out. Enhancement has the effect of making voices and instruments sound more forward in the mix, but if you put everything up front, there's nothing left at the back of the mix to create the illusion of depth and perspective that a good mix needs.

Harmonic enhancement has been used on many occasions to make a lead vocal more intimate, but it is necessary to take care to avoid sibilance as any form of high-frequency enhancement, including conventional EQ, tends to exacerbate sibilance problems. Harmonic enhancers also work well on poorly defined drum sounds, electric pianos and acoustic guitars but, as stated earlier, it's better to use them to augment an already good recording than to rely on them to fix up poor recordings.

Which Enhancer?

Which type of enhancer you use is largely a matter of personal preference, but it's fair to say that different types are better equipped for certain tasks than others. Harmonic enhancers are best at replacing missing high-end detail, which conventional EQ would be unable to recover. For example, an acoustic-guitar recording may be dull because the guitar was fitted with old strings, or perhaps an inappropriate choice of microphone was made for the recording, but a harmonic enhancer can synthesise new harmonics to replace the missing originals. Similarly, dull electric pianos can be given more sparkle, as can old analogue recordings that have been stored under poor conditions.

Because harmonic enhancers process the high end of the spectrum, and because some degree of level compression is used in the side chain, any noise present in the original signal will also be emphasised. For this reason, it is sensible to use as little enhancement as can be applied to get the job done, and always work from the quietest source material possible. Also, make frequent checks between the bypassed and enhanced sound, as it's easy to get used to over-enhancement and apply too much. You could easily discover you've gone too far and made the mix fatiguingly bright.

Phase manipulation or dynamic equaliser-based enhancers tend to be a little less effective at rescuing desperately dull mixes as they can emphasise only harmonics that are present, but it may be possible to apply a greater amount of processing without the sound becoming harsh. Tube emulation can also be used to add brightness to a dull mix, but probably not to the same extent as a harmonic enhancer. Regardless of which type you use, if it has been well designed the sense of detail and separation should be noticeably improved. Multi-band tube emulation is particularly useful at the mastering stage as it allows different parts of the spectrum to be handled differently.

Where possible, use the process to create contrast within a mix, and make sure that your processed mix isn't fatiguing to listen to. The idea is to introduce air and space into your music, but to keep it sounding natural. You'll find that even recordings made with relatively modest microphones can be given an impressive amount of definition by adding a touch of enhancement, making your vocal tracks sound more intimate and up front.

You can also use enhancers to give bite and clarity to synthesisers or samplers that don't have a particularly good bandwidth, and you'll find that bland string sounds take on new depth once treated. If you ever work with Fender Rhodes pianos, you'll find the enhancer gives them all the attack you'd always wished they had! Synthesised or real brass can also be given the kind of attack that normally comes only from a live brass section. As with all signal processors and effects, the key is to experiment as much as you can.

Bass drums or snare drums that lack the required degree of snap can be tightened up considerably through enhancement, and this is one instance where you might find using a harmonic enhancer with a lower filter control setting to be more effective. This can be particularly successful in bringing out the sound of the snares where the original sound is somewhat dull.

Apart from making good recordings sound just that bit better, enhancers are often used to treat old master tapes that have lost brightness due to age or were simply poorly recorded in the first place. Indeed, a popular combination of processors to improve noisy recordings is a dynamic noise filter (to reduce the audible amount of high-end hiss) followed by an enhancer to restore any loss of top that the filter or ageing of the tape might have caused.

Both mono and stereo versions of harmonic enhancers exist and they tend to be similar in respect of the controls available to the user. The signal level

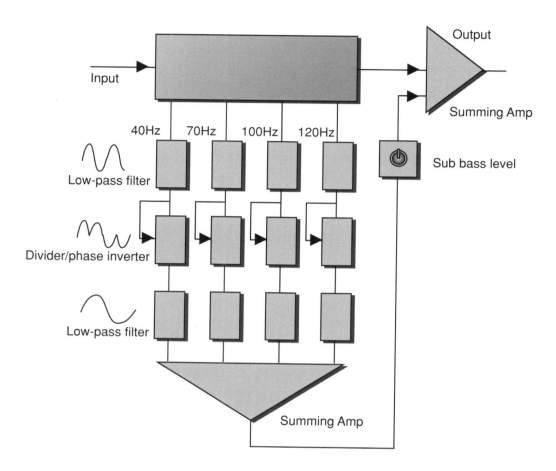

Figure 4.3: Bass enhancer (boom box)

passing from the filter to the harmonics generator is sometimes fairly critical, so most devices have an enhancement control with an associated LED display, which can easily to optimised for a given piece of music.

Bass Enhancement

High-frequency enhancement makes mixes sound more transparent and detailed, but there's often a need to increase low-frequency punch, especially in rock and dance music. The traditional way to do this is to use EQ, but a conventional equaliser with a fixed setting may affect sounds that you'd prefer to leave alone. One answer is again to use dynamic equalisation so that, for example, bass boost is produced only when loud sounds, such as drum beats, are present.

Sub-harmonic Synthesis

Another technique is to synthesise subharmonics one octave below the existing bottom end of the signal, and one way to achieve this is to use a number of bandpass filters between, say 60 and 120Hz, then feed the output of each band into an analogue circuit known as a 'flip-flop' to halve the frequency. The output from the flip-flop is a square wave of fixed amplitude, but if this is used to switch the phase of the original bandpass-filtered signal every cycle, the result is a waveform that's closely related to the original in both harmonic content and amplitude, but half the frequency. By applying more high-cut filtering to these subharmonics to smooth them, then combining them with the original signal, it's possible to create the impression of very deep bass. Figure

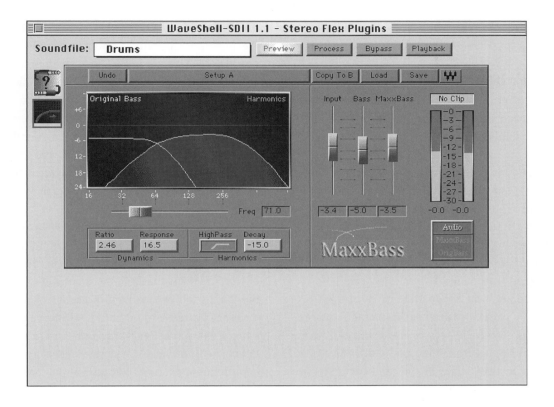

Figure 4.4: Bass harmonics generator

4.3 shows a subharmonic generator with three frequency bands. The advantage of the subharmonic generator is that it's relatively easy to build using analogue circuitry, but unless used sparingly it can easily overtax the end user's loudspeaker system.

Psychoacoustic Bass

Most home hi-fi equipment can't produce the lowest fundamental frequencies of bass guitars, organ pedal notes or some electronic bass sounds, but they still sound punchy because the higher harmonics of the bass sound are reproduced reasonably accurately and the human brain has a tendency to compensate for the missing fundamental. In other words, if the brain can hear the harmonics, it mentally adds the missing fundamental that should also be there.

A relatively new digital process has been developed to enhance the apparent bass energy of sounds destined to be played back through smaller speaker systems, and this is achieved by extracting the harmonics from the bottom octave or so of the original sound, then doubling their frequency. The same system also allows the very low end of the original system to be adjusted by reducing its level to reduce the stress on small speakers. By reducing the level of the real low bass and increasing the level of the newly generated bass harmonics, the sound can actually be made to sound as though it has more bass energy when played back over small speakers, even though the actual low-frequency energy may have decreased. Figure 4.4 shows this process in graphical form. Other techniques such as compressing the level of the newly added harmonics, or the original bottom octave, may also be used. This technique is mainly used in software plug-ins and in bass amplifiers for live use. It is particularly successful in processing the soundtracks from computer games so that they still sound big and exciting when played back over small desktop speakers, but is less applicable to conventional music recording.

Stereo Enhancers

So far I've talked about enhancers that work on the frequency spectrum of the sound being processed to make it sound brighter, punchier, more detailed, more transparent or whatever, but there's another type of enhancer designed to increase the subjective stereo width within a mix. Most stereo mixes use pan controls to position sounds between the two loudspeakers of the end user's stereo system, but by using a little clever processing it's sometimes possible to create the illusion that some sounds in the mix come from points beyond the speakers.

The simplest way to do this is to use a trick employed in ghetto blaster-type portable stereo systems and stereo TV sets to make the speakers sound further apart than they really are. All that's necessary is to take some of the right-hand signal, invert its phase and feed it into the left-hand channel. Similarly, some of the left-hand signal is phase-inverted and fed into the right-hand channel. The result is a subjective widening of the speakers, although if you go too far the mix develops a hole in the middle as centre-panned sounds cancel each other out. Adding even more of the phase-inverted effects causes the left and right images to change sides, but used with caution this trick works quite well and it's also perfectly mono-compatible as all the phase-inverted sounds cancel out and disappear when the sound is switched to mono. However, there are far more sophisticated ways of increasing the stereo width, and in some cases it's even possible to fool the listener into thinking a sound has been panned around behind their head.

The best-known commercial 3D enhancement systems are probably Q Sound, Roland's RSS system and Spatializer, all of which work in similar ways but which were developed using quite different methods. Roland's system was based upon mathematical calculations, while I'm led to understand that the other systems used a more empirical approach. To really understand how these systems manage to achieve what seems to be the impossible, it's necessary to learn a little about the human hearing system.

Two Ears, Three Dimensions

We hear and identify sounds as coming from all directions, including up and down, with only two ears. The reason we have two ears is so that the human brain can measure the slight time delay between sounds arriving at one ear and then the other to help estimate the direction from which the sound came. If a sound is directly in front, behind, above or below, the arrival times will be the same, but if the sound source is directly to the left or right, the arrival time difference will be greatest.

Taken on its own, the arrival time difference between the sounds entering the two ears is not quite enough to determine the exact point of origin, but there are two other effects that give the brain vital clues. Firstly, the head itself casts a kind of acoustic shadow, so if a sound is directly to our left, it will arrive at the right ear not only a fraction of a second later (less than 1ms later in fact), it will also be lower in level and have less high-frequency content because of the masking effect of the head. This is shown in Figure 4.5.

Thirdly, we have the shape of the outer ear to thank, because this acts as mechanical equaliser that has a different response depending on the angle that the sound approaches the ear. Sounds directly to one side are perceived to have a greater high-frequency content than those off-axis, and the shape of the EQ curve is different depending on whether the source is to the front of the head or towards the back. Similarly, the EQ of the outer ear changes as the sound source moves from below to above the head.

Using this knowledge, it doesn't seem beyond the bounds of possibility that building some kind of 3D joystick that varies the inter-ear delay electronically and simulates the EQ effects of both head masking and the outer-ears' polar response could emulate a natural sound arriving from any direction using just two loudspeaker sources. Unfortunately, it's a little more complicated than that, because when we hear a sound over conventional stereo speakers, the right ear hears some sound from the left speaker and vice versa. To make the illusion of the 3D sound work, we need to get rid of this crosstalk.

By calculating the level and spectral shape of this crosstalk it's possible to create a signal that cancels it

Sound from the front reaches both ears at the same time with no masking

Direct path to left ear

Sound reaching the right ear travels further and is shadowed by the head

out, and this is the way Roland approached the problem. Even so, this technique can never be entirely successful because not everyone has the same domestic listening conditions, and not everybody's outer ear has the same polar frequency response. In practical terms, then, these systems can position some sounds outside the speakers very convincingly, but they work better on some sound systems than others, and they also work better on some types of sound than others. What's more, it seems impossible to place a sound behind the listener convincingly, possibly because we use small subconscious head movements to verify the position of sounds coming from behind, and as soon as we do this the illusion is revealed as a fraud. Nevertheless, some sounds can be panned around the listener's head, and providing that they are kept moving the illusion of the source existing in three-dimensional space can be quite convincing. As a rule, harmonically complex sounds work best for this kind of processing.

Such 3D effects are used very effectively on a number of records, but generally only to treat specific elements within the mix. This is because the spectral changes and inter-channel delays needed to create

the effect compromise the mono compatibility of the mix, and even in stereo the tonal changes that take place can be distracting. By confining the processing to effect sounds, incidental percussion, synth stings and suchlike, the mix remains essentially mono-compatible but still gains the added excitement of three-dimensional sound.

Currently, a number of hardware processors are available for stereo width enhancement ranging in price from extreme budget to incredibly expensive. The effect is even available in some stereo multi-effects units, either in the form of a 360 degree panner, or to widen effects such as delay, reverb and chorus. A number of 3D stereo width enhancers are also available as downloadable software plug-ins for digital audio workstations, and in many cases these provide the most flexible control systems and produce the most convincing results.

Summary

Used with care, enhancers of all types can produce a professional-sounding edge to both home and commercial recordings – but it is very easy to overdo the effect. The human ear soon gets accustomed to an increase in brightness, so you may find that what sounds fine at the end of one day's work will sound dreadfully bright or harsh the next. Generally, it is worth switching the unit in and out of circuit at regular intervals to maintain a sense of perspective. Better still, don't use any enhancement until you're ready to set up the final mix. Note that several software plug-in enhancers are now available and some of these sound surprisingly good, especially when you consider that they may be included at no extra charge with your host software, as is the case with the Logic Audio enhancer shown in Figure 4.6.

Another point to watch is background noise. A typical enhancer will not only add definition to your music, it will also do the same to any noise that's present, so ensure that your source signal is as noise-free as possible. Take care also when setting the frequency control (where one is fitted), that it is not too low for the signal being processed because it can add harshness to sounds that are already fairly strong. Be particularly careful if there are distorted guitars in the mix as these can easily become harsh if over-enhanced.

When using stereo enhancement, check that your mix still sounds okay in mono and listen to it on as many different systems as possible before pronouncing it finished. Also be aware that while 3D processing can be effective, it never works as well as a true multi-speaker surround system. Given that home 3D systems are one of the fastest-growing success stories in consumer electronics history, it may be that the need to generate pseudo 3D sound from stereo speakers will soon disappear.

Figure 4.6: Enhancer plug-in

5 COMPRESSORS AND LIMITERS

Pop music production involves strictly controlling the dynamics of both instruments and vocals. 'Dynamics' means the range in volume between the loudest and the quietest parts of a recording of an instrument, voice or complete mix. Some degree of control is desirable on a practical level – for example, to keep the vocal levels relatively constant within a song – but dynamic control is also applied for artistic reasons.

Much of today's music is rhythm based, but if you listen to the drum sounds on virtually any pop, rock or dance record, you'll find that the level is very even: there's little or no use of 'light and shade'. This sometimes makes it difficult to distinguish between a recording of a drum machine and the real thing, or a sampled bass sound and a bass guitar. And this, in turn, sets the pattern for the rest of the instrumentation. If light and shade is required, it is often created by dropping instruments in and out of the mix rather than by changing the balance of the instrumentation to any significant degree. Similarly, the vocal level invariably needs to be kept very even to ensure that the vocals always sit comfortably with the backing music.

Moving slightly away from mainstream pop, you occasionally hear more natural-sounding recordings from those artists who have realised the potential of compact discs for expressing wide signal dynamics. But even here – unless you are listening to a purist recording of an orchestra or other classical work – you are unlikely to be hearing the original dynamics of the performance.

Compressors

Artistic considerations aside, 16-bit CDs are incapable of reproducing the full dynamic range encompassed by the human ear, so for both practical and aesthetic reasons it's often desirable to have some controllable means of reducing the dynamic range of a signal or recording. This is generally achieved using a device called a compressor, and the effect of dynamic range reduction brought about by the use of one of these devices is known as compression.

Compression can be used on just about any sound source or mix of sound sources, but it is almost invariably used on pop vocals – an untrained singer's voice is likely to fluctuate in level considerably, with the result that some words may be obscured by the music while others are too loud. Drum machines and synthesisers tend to have fairly well-controlled dynamics, so further compression is seldom necessary in the context of controlling levels but, as explained later, compression may also be used as a special effect on these and other sounds.

The ability to compress the natural dynamics of a sound in a controlled manner is very important in contemporary music production, and it's probably fair to say that after a reverb unit, a compressor is the most important signal-processing tool in the studio.

Gain Control

To understand how a compressor works, it's useful to examine the way dynamic range control can be achieved manually. Before the compressor was widely available, manual 'gain riding' was the commonly employed technique used to keep signal levels under control. Gain riding involves the engineer sitting, hand on fader, anticipating excessively low or high signal levels so that he can make a quick adjustments to keep the subjective signal level constant. Figure 5.1 shows a diagram of this manual system and illustrates

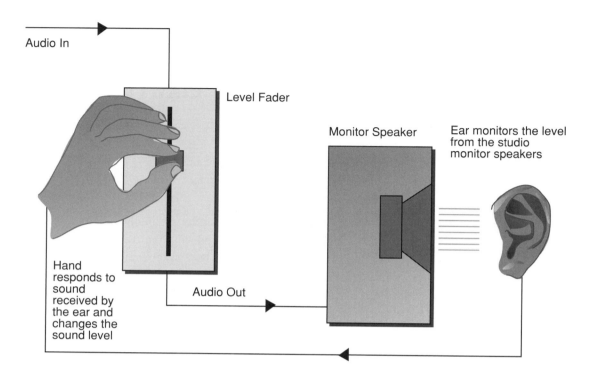

Audio In

Level Fader

Monitor Speaker

Ear monitors the level from the studio monitor speakers

Hand responds to sound received by the ear and changes the sound level

Audio Out

Figure 5.1: Manual gain riding

how the ear follows the signal level from the loudspeaker, enabling the brain to direct the hand, which moves the fader until the level is corrected.

At first sight, putting this process into diagrammatic form may seem a little unnecessary, but the concept it embraces is important because it helps us understand how a machine goes about tackling the same job.

If the session is being conducted by an experienced engineer who is thoroughly familiar with the dynamics of the music being recorded, then gain riding can be reasonably effective in levelling out untoward peaks and troughs in the dynamics of the music, but there are obvious limitations to this approach. Gain riding requires the undivided attention of the engineer and this means that other aspects of the mix may be neglected. In many situations, the only way around this is to enlist the help of other people, particularly when there are several different voices and instruments that have to be controlled separately.

There's also the human response time to consider: it simply isn't possible for an engineer to react quickly enough to the kind of momentary peaks in volume that characterise a vocal or instrumental performance unless he is already thoroughly familiar with the recording – most of the time, adjustments are made a fraction of a second too late.

Electronic Gain Control

Fortunately, the development of early recording systems were closely followed by the invention of a practical electronic compressor design. A compressor works in much the same way as our gain-riding engineer in that it constantly monitors the signal level then makes the necessary adjustments – but it does so much faster and far more precisely. Figure 5.2 shows the block diagram of a simple compressor and, as can be seen, it closely resembles the manual method except that the output signal is monitored before it reaches the loudspeaker – the electronic circuitry relieving the brain of the task of deciding how much gain reduction to apply. The listening part of the circuit generates a control voltage that continually adjusts the gain of a variable-gain amplifier and of the signal being compressed. In practice, an electronic compressor can be designed to work by monitoring its own output, its own input or a mixture of both, but to keep this example simple I've settled on a compressor that monitors its own output as this is the closest model to the human engineer practising gain riding.

Obviously it isn't practical to have a robot arm moving a fader, and even a motorised fader may not be fast enough, so an electronic gain-control circuit is employed in its place. In the analogue world, these may be based on VCAs (voltage-controlled amplifiers), tubes, or LEDs and photocells, though it is also possible to execute compression entirely in the digital domain as evidenced by the proliferation of compressor plug-ins. The optical gain-control circuit

using a photocell is interesting as instead of a VCA, the side chain controls the brightness of an LED, which shines on a photo-resistor. The resistor is placed in a gain-control circuit so, as the LED changes brightness, the signal changes level. Photocells don't always behave linearly and they tend to have a fairly slow response time (though some newer implementations can be made to work much faster), which is part of the reason that this type of compressor has a characteristic sound. A number of optical compressors were designed in the '60s, but renewed interest in vintage recording techniques has led to their rediscovery and some digital compressor plug-ins are also able to emulate their characteristics.

What A Compressor Does

All a compressor does is reduce the level of signals that exceed a pre-determined threshold so as to reduce the overall signal dynamics. In other words,

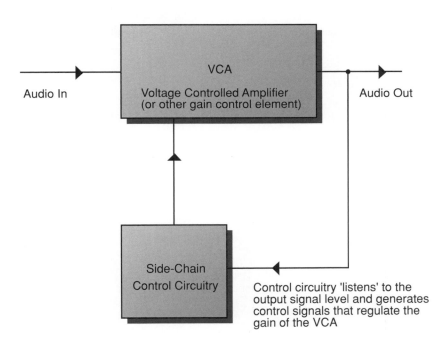

Note that in some compressor designs, the side-chain monitors the input signal level, but in this version, the block diagram more accurately reflects the gain riding model of Figure 5.1

Figure 5.2: Block diagram of a simple compressor

if the signal gets too loud, a compressor turns it down. Most compressors operate on a threshold system: signals lower than a threshold level set by the user remain unaffected, while those exceeding the threshold are reduced in level. The threshold is generally adjusted by means of a front-panel control, and there is often some kind of display to indicate how much gain reduction is taking place. The amount of gain reduction that takes place when the signal level exceeds the threshold depends on something called compression ratio.

Compression Ratio

Ratio is simply the change in output level that results from a given change in input level. For example, a compression ratio of 2:1 means that a 2dB change in input level will result in only a 1dB change in output level. In practice, a 2:1 ratio is adequate for a wide variety of applications but much higher ratios may be chosen to suit specific situations. Ratio is very often user-adjustable by means of a ratio control knob. If the ratio is made very high – say 10:1 or greater – then we have a situation known as limiting, where

an input exceeding the threshold level is subjected to such a high level of gain reduction that the output is effectively prevented from rising above the threshold level by any significant degree. This assumes that the compressor/limiter can respond quickly enough to catch sudden signal peaks.

Compression Or Limiting?

Most compressors have a wide enough ratio range that they can double as either compressors or limiters – hence the title compressor/limiter. Absolute limiting (where the output never exceeds the threshold value at all), requires a ratio of infinity:1, but, in practice, ratios greater than around 10:1 have much the same effect. Figure 5.3 shows how the input and output levels of a compressor are affected by the threshold action and by the compression ratio.

The reasons for employing limiting are rather different from those for compression, and intensive limiting almost always has an audible effect on the sound being treated unless the limiter is very carefully designed. More often than not, a limiter will be set so that it operates only on high signal peaks – most

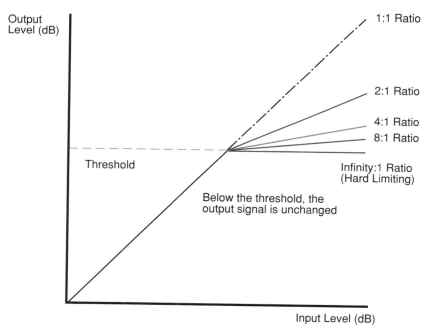

Figure 5.3: Threshold and compression ratio

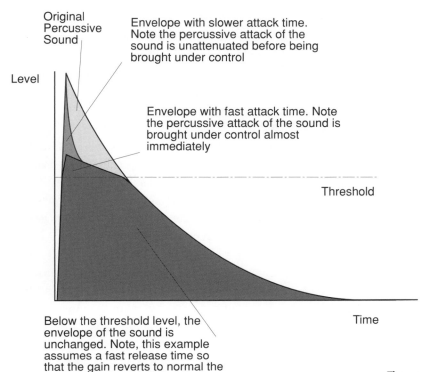

Original Percussive Sound

Envelope with slower attack time. Note the percussive attack of the sound is unattenuated before being brought under control

Level

Envelope with fast attack time. Note the percussive attack of the sound is brought under control almost immediately

Threshold

Time

Below the threshold level, the envelope of the sound is unchanged. Note, this example assumes a fast release time so that the gain reverts to normal the instant the signal falls below the threshold

Figure 5.4: Effect of attack time setting

of the time it will do nothing. In cases where a signal must not be allowed under any circumstances to exceed a certain level, some form of limiting is essential. Typical examples would be in the case of the radio transmitter, where overmodulation is not permitted, or the digital recorder, where there is absolutely no headroom above odBFS (odB full scale). In live sound work (and in some active studio monitor systems), limiters are employed to make sure that power amps are not driven into clipping because the harmonics thus created can easily destroy expensive tweeters. Limiters are also used at the mastering stage of recording to pull down the level of very short signal peaks, thus enabling the overall mix level to be increased by a few dBs to achieve maximum loudness.

Attack Time

Just as our studio engineer takes a finite time to respond to peaks in the programme material, so does the compressor – but it's still much faster than any human. Indeed, modern circuitry is so fast that the gain can be turned down before the input waveform has had a chance to overshoot far enough to cause problems. However, depending on the application, this degree of speed is not always necessary – or even desirable.

The time taken for a compressor to respond to a signal that has exceeded the threshold is called the attack time, and, for reasons that we will investigate shortly this is often under user control, although some compressors also include an auto mode. Likewise, the release time – the time that the compressor takes to return to its normal gain – is again commonly linked to a front-panel control. Release may also be handled automatically by an auto mode on some models and auto modes are described towards the end of this chapter.

The reason for attack and decay times being variable is because their optimum setting depends on the type of material being processed. For example, a powerful bass drum beat in a mix will cause the compressor to reduce the gain of everything in the mix, not just the bass drum. As a result, any high-frequency or low-level detail – such as a hi-hat occurring at the same time – will also be turned down, leading to a dulling of the overall sound. One way around this – apart from using as little compression as is practical – is to increase the attack time so that the compressor doesn't respond instantly. In this case, the leading edge of the beat, including the attack of the hi-hat, is allowed through at full level before the gain is pulled down, producing a more punchy sound. Figure 5.4 shows the effect of different attack times on a percussive sound. Some designs also use a high-pass filter to route a little of the high-frequency end of the input material past the compressor without it undergoing gain reduction. This simple expedient (which is invariably outside the user's control) can greatly reduce the dulling effect of heavy compression on a mix dominated by low-frequency percussive sounds.

The trick of setting a longer attack time is also extensively used when recording bass drums or bass guitars so as to allow the initial click or slap of the strings to come through strongly. Of course, this does mean that the signal may briefly exceed what you consider to be a safe operating level, but any distortion caused by analogue tape overload is unlikely to be audible on such short-duration sounds. In the case of digital recording, it is common practice

to insert a separate limiter into the signal path to catch any brief excesses that might otherwise get past the compressor, and a number of commercial compressors also include a separate, fast-acting limiter. When using plug-ins, a compressor plug-in may be followed by a separate limiter plug-in.

Release

The release time setting is also important to consider because if it is too short, the compressor gain recovers too quickly, with the result that there is an audible 'pumping' or 'breathing' as the gain rapidly changes (have a listen to some of the early '60s singles, paying particular attention to the cymbals, for an example of this). Conversely, if the release time is a bit too long, then the gain may not have recovered sufficiently by the time the next quiet sound comes along, so this may be suppressed more than is necessary.

Another problem that can arise if the attack and release times are set to be very short is that low-frequency sounds from bass instruments may suffer distortion as the gain of the compressor tries to change during each cycle of the signal rather than following its overall envelope. To combat this, some designs incorporate an adjustable hold time, which prevents the compressor from entering its release phase until the hold time has expired. Other models may incorporate a built-in hold time of around 20ms that is invisible to the user. A hold time of 20ms is usually enough to prevent distortion on the lowest

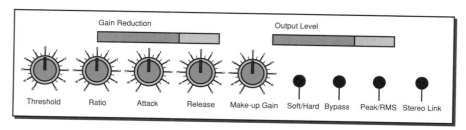

Note: The Stereo link switch would only be fitted either if the unit had two linkable channels or if there was provision to link two mono units. Only one channel is shown in this figure.

Figure 5.5: Typical compressor control layout

audible sounds (50Hz), but a wider range is sometimes available, allowing the user to experiment.

Make-up Gain

Because a compressor reduces the level of any signals that exceed the threshold, the output level will tend to be lower that the input, so an extra stage of 'make-up' gain is commonly used in order that the output level can be matched to any subsequent pieces of equipment. There is invariably some form of meter to show how much gain reduction is taking place at any given time and further meters might well monitor both the input and output signal levels too. Figure 5.5 shows a typical control layout.

Side-Chain Characteristics

The way a compressor performs is in part due to that part of the circuitry that monitors the level of the signal being processed (the side chain), and in part due to the control law of the gain-control device. There are subjective differences depending on whether the side chain circuitry responds linearly or logarithmically to changes in input level and whether or not any filtering is employed to make it respond more to some frequencies than others. This latter measure is sometimes utilised to compensate for the fact that the human ear perceives different pitches as being of different loudness. If the side chain is not frequency conscious to compensate for this effect, then the compressor may appear to be responding more to some frequencies than to others. It also makes an audible difference whether the side chain measures the signal peaks or uses some form of averaging.

An RMS – or averaging – side chain responds to sounds in much the same way as a human engineer would: the human hearing system tends to average out peaks in levels so that short duration sounds appear to be less loud-sounding than longer-duration sounds of the same level. From this description, you may rightly assume that very short, high-level peaks might slip by an RMS compressor unchecked, even if a very fast attack time is set.

Peak-sensing side chain circuitry is far more sensitive to brief transients and responds to even the shortest signal peaks, which means that the compressor is much less likely to overshoot on drums or other percussive sounds when a fast attack time is set. A number of modern compressors have switchable RMS or peak sensing and, as a very general rule, peak works better on percussive sounds while RMS is most effective on non-percussive sounds such as vocals.

Compressor Inserts

The side chain normally 'listens' directly to the signal being compressed, though an insert point or key input is often fitted to enable other processors to be connected into the side chain signal path, or to allow the side chain to be fed from a different source altogether. You might reasonably ask why this is a good thing. Consider, though, what would happen if you were to connect an equaliser into the side chain.

By boosting signals in the 5 to 8kHz range using the external equaliser, the compressor can be made to respond mainly to loud, bright sounds in the 5 to 8kHz range – a technique often used for 'de-essing' sibilant vocal tracks. Sibilance is the harsh, spitting effect sometimes heard on 't' and 's' sounds. Figure 5.6 shows how this type of arrangement could be patched together. In this instance, the equaliser would be adjusted to boost the sibilant portion of the sound by first monitoring the output of the filter and tuning into the offending part of the spectrum by ear. If 10dB of boost is applied in this range, then the compressor will be 10dB more sensitive to sibilant frequencies than to the rest of the audio spectrum. To make setting up easy, some compressors (and gates) have a 'side chain listen' switch, which, when activated, replaces the normal output with the side chain control signal so that it can be monitored over the control room speakers during setting up.

In practice, a dedicated de-esser gives better results than a compressor hooked up to an equaliser, but if you need to de-ess something in a hurry and don't have access to a dedicated unit, this arrangement will work providing you don't process too heavily, otherwise the vocals will become 'lispy' sounding. This happens because we only really want to reduce the level of the frequency band in which sibilant sounds occur, but with the simple arrangement as described, whenever

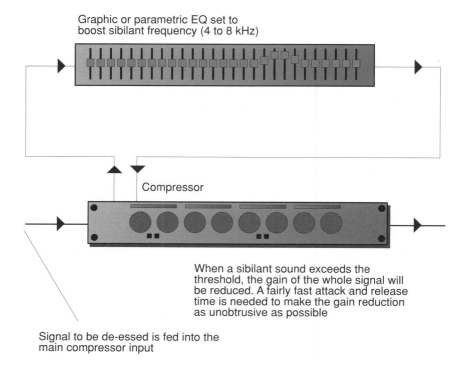

Graphic or parametric EQ set to
boost sibilant frequency (4 to 8 kHz)

Compressor

When a sibilant sound exceeds the
threshold, the gain of the whole signal will
be reduced. A fairly fast attack and release
time is needed to make the gain reduction
as unobtrusive as possible

Signal to be de-essed is fed into the
main compressor input

Figure 5.6: Patch for full-band de-essing

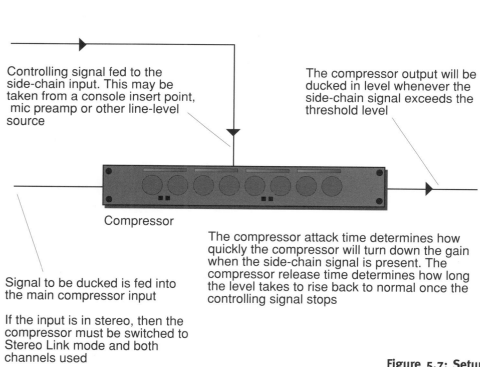

Controlling signal fed to the
side-chain input. This may be
taken from a console insert point,
mic preamp or other line-level
source

The compressor output will be
ducked in level whenever the
side-chain signal exceeds the
threshold level

Compressor

The compressor attack time determines how
quickly the compressor will turn down the gain
when the side-chain signal is present. The
compressor release time determines how long
the level takes to rise back to normal once the
controlling signal stops

Signal to be ducked is fed into
the main compressor input

If the input is in stereo, then the
compressor must be switched to
Stereo Link mode and both
channels used

Figure 5.7: Setup for ducking

a sibilant sound is detected, the level of the whole signal is reduced. A commercial de-esser is more likely to be designed only to attenuate the troublesome frequencies, so it has fewer audible side effects.

Ducking

Another reason for needing access to the side chain is to enable the level of one signal to control another. By feeding music through the compressor and connecting a voice input to the side chain, the music can be reduced in volume to make way for the voice-over. When the voice stops, the music returns to its previous level at a rate determined by the release control. This technique, often used by DJs, is called 'ducking'. To achieve the effect, you will need some kind of mixer that has a mic channel with a direct output or insert send to feed the compressor's side chain. The reason for this is that the side chain input on most compressors will accept only line-level signals and so the mic signal needs to be amplified before it can be used. Figure 5.7 shows a suitable arrangement for ducking.

A more subtle form of ducking can be used in music mixing – for example, to pull down the level of a backing track slightly whenever the vocals are present. A similar technique may also be used on rock music to reduce the level of backing guitar parts when the guitar solo is playing.

Soft And Hard Knee

While most conventional compressors work on the threshold or hard knee principle, there is another popular type that takes the so-called 'soft knee' approach. In some soft knee designs, a degree of compression may be applied to all signals, regardless of level, but the compression ratio is extremely low for small signals and automatically increases as the signal level increases. This makes for an easy compressor to set up as there's no threshold or ratio control, just a compression-amount knob. However, not all soft knee compressors are this simple. More commonly there will be a threshold in the same way as for a conventional hard knee compressor, but rather

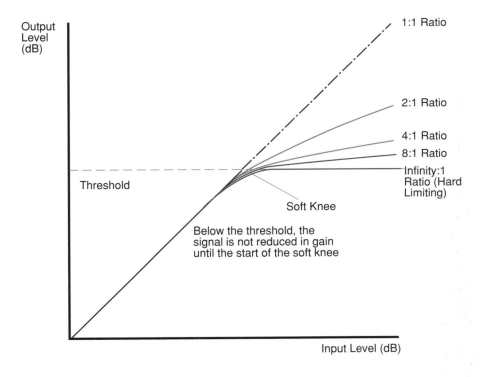

Figure 5.8: Soft and hard knee compression

than everything happening at once when the input signal reaches the threshold, the compression ratio increases progressively as the signal approaches the threshold. By the time the signal actually reaches the threshold, the full compression ratio set by the user is in force. In either case, the idea is to obtain a gentler transition between signals that are not compressed and higher-level signals that are compressed.

Soft knee compressors usually sound less obtrusive than hard knee compressors, but may not exercise such firm gain control. Ideally, you need a model that's switchable between hard and soft knee so that you can match the type of compression to the sound you're processing. Figure 5.8 shows both soft and hard knee compressor characteristics.

Auto Time Constants

While this section has discussed the need for various compressor controls, some of the best compressors I've heard have very few controls, and that's because their attack and release times are automatically adjusted by circuitry that analyses the dynamic nature of the input signal. Naturally such circuitry makes assumptions about what settings sound most transparent for the material being processed, which means you can't experiment with different attack and release times to get deliberately unnatural-sounding effects. Nevertheless, if you're processing something like a vocal line and you want to control the gain without the sound seeming to be processed, an automatic mode can work extremely well. Automatic modes also work well on material that has a changing dynamic character, such as a bass guitar that's being played using a slap technique, or a complex mix.

Built-in Gates

Because a compressor can't differentiate between a small wanted signal and low-level unwanted noise, it tends to emphasise such noise by setting itself to maximum gain during quiet passages, such as gaps between words or phrases in a vocal track, for example. As a result, there is now a tendency for some manufacturers to incorporate simple gates or expanders into their compressors in order to mute the signal at such times. This gate/expander would typically have

only a threshold control and an LED to show when it's closed. The attack and release times are often preset or electronically linked to those of the compressor to keep the number of controls to a minimum.

For a complete description of gates and their applications, refer to the relevant chapter in this book. Suffice it to say here, that the gate should be set with as low a threshold as is practical to deal with the noise, otherwise quieter sections of wanted sounds could be muted. This kind of gating is generally of value only when working on separate tracks within a mix as complete mixes tend to have few, if any, periods of complete silence in which the gate could operate without making its presence known.

Noise is a particular problem when compressing signals that originate from noisy sources, such as analogue tape, guitar amplifiers or some older synthesisers, as the noise will be increased in level by the compressor during quieter sections or pauses. For this reason, it is usual to apply some degree of compression to vocal tracks during recording to analogue tape to ensure a healthy record level at all times. Though digital recording systems tend to be quieter, there's often a low level of hum, mic-amp hiss and background ambience recorded along with the original signal, so gating may still be desirable.

At the mixing stage, further compression may be applied, as needed, paying due regard to the effect of compression on any background noise present. As a general rule, every dB of compression is a dB of deterioration in the signal-to-noise ratio of the signal passing through it. In other words, if you compress a signal to produce 10dB of gain reduction, the noise during quieter sections will be increased by 10dB.

Stereo Linking

Two-channel compressors include a stereo link switch for applications that involve the compressing of a stereo signal. Using two independent compressors in this role can cause image shifts, especially if there are loud peaks on one side of the mix that aren't on the other. What's needed is for both channels to undergo exactly the same amount of gain reduction at all times, regardless of whether the biggest peaks are in the left or right channel, and that's why the stereo link switch is needed. Linking combines the side chain signals in such a way that the compressor responds to an average of the two channel levels, and often you'll find that the compressor can be adjusted using only the controls of the first channel. Other designs may average the control settings of the two channels.

It's interesting to note that for proper stereo operation, each channel still needs a separate envelope follower as part of the side chain. If you were simply to combine the left and right side chain signals (as some cheaper models do), then extract the combined envelope, you could get quite different results caused by phase cancellations between the left and right channels. This could lead to inadequate amounts of gain reduction being applied to some sounds.

Variations On A Theme

Not all compressors work in exactly the same way or have the same control layout. One alternative to the variable threshold system is to have a fixed threshold preceded by a variable gain input stage. This has the same effect as varying the threshold while having a fixed input level – although an output gain control is still desirable to balance up the overall gain through the compressor.

Compressors with gain-control elements based on LEDs and photocells have smooth, vintage sound characterised by a relatively slow attack and fast release time. They are currently very popular, because even though the processed sound is quite obviously being compressed, the side effects are quite flattering to vocals and instruments such as acoustic guitar.

A number of compressors are also built with tubes in the gain-control stage, and these again tend to produce a characteristic sound, which some describe as warm and musical. The precise sound depends on how the circuitry is designed, and whether the tube runs off a full high-voltage supply or a reduced DC voltage. See the section on tube equipment for more details.

Compressor designs are also available that use a complex side chain design to maintain a long-term average signal level as well as compressing peaks in the signal in the normal way. They may also include a facility that detects periods of silence between sounds and prevents the compressor gain from rising. Done

properly, this brings about a significant improvement in signal to noise ratio without recourse to gates. A multi-band limiter might well be used in line with a radio transmitter to ensure that the average signal level is always constant, but there are also applications in mastering for a digital medium where any level overshoots, however brief, cannot be tolerated.

Split-Band Compression

It was explained earlier why compressors usually cause some dulling of the processed sound due to low-frequency peaks such as loud bass drum beats causing attenuation of the whole signal including low-level, high-frequency sounds. One way round this is to use a compressor or limiter that splits the input into two or more frequency bands then compresses each independently before recombining them. This ensures that a loud peak occurring in one part of the audio spectrum won't affect the level of frequencies in other bands but, as you might imagine, this is complicated and expensive due to the fact that each band needs its own compressor circuit as well as the filters necessary to split the bands. Also, some method has to be arranged to make the attack and release times of each band complement each other.

Low-cost, two-band compressors are available, but in more discerning applications special circuitry has to be used to combine the bands intelligently, otherwise unwanted phase changes and other anomalies can be introduced. Typically, a sophisticated multi-band compressor or limiter might cost four or five times as much as a conventional one. The good news is that very sophisticated multi-band compressors are available in both digital hardware boxes and processing plug-ins at an affordable price. Three-band compressors and limiters are often used for mastering complete mixes because of their more transparent sound when compared to that of a full-band compressor, though they may also be used to process individual tracks or submixes.

It's worth remembering that a two-band compressor can make quite an effective de-esser, especially if you can adjust the frequency split-point between the bands. By setting the split at 4 or 5kHz, loud sibilant sounds will cause compression of

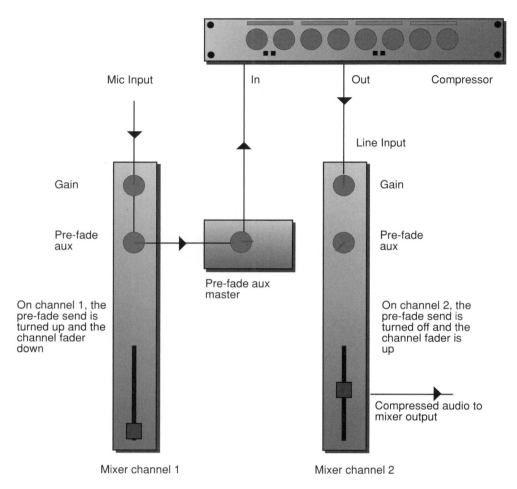

Mic Input

In

Out

Compressor

Line Input

Gain

Gain

Pre-fade
aux

Pre-fade
aux

Pre-fade aux
master

On channel 1, the
pre-fade send is
turned up and the
channel fader
down

On channel 2, the
pre-fade send is
turned off and the
channel fader is
up

Compressed audio to
mixer output

Mixer channel 1

Mixer channel 2

Note: the mixer channels are shown
separated to make the signal flow clear

Figure 5.9: Workaround using pre-fade send

frequencies only above 5kHz, leaving the lower band unaffected. This still isn't as transparent-sounding as using a de-esser that notches out only the offending frequency band, but it's a lot better than using a full-band compressor in this role. I'll be talking more about split-band compression at the end of this chapter as it is a very important tool in mastering.

Compressor Connections

In normal use, compressors are connected in line with a signal, often via the desk's insert points. To compress individual signals, the channel insert points should be used, whereas for compressing submixes,

such as drum kits or backing vocals, it may be best to route the channel to a pair of subgroups and place two channels of compression in the subgroup insert points. The compressor should be set to stereo link mode to prevent stereo image shifts caused by uneven left/right compression.

To compress an entire mix, the compressor should be patched in the console's master stereo insert points, but if there aren't any fitted, you can connect the compressor directly between the mixer outputs and the master stereo recorder's inputs. To hear the effect of the compressor you'll need to monitor the master recorder, not the mixer output, and if you want to do fades you'll have to do these with the record level controls on the master recorder, not the master faders on the desk.

Compressors are not normally connected via the auxiliary send system, though some engineers like to do exactly this when working with analogue mixers, as adding the compressed sound to the uncompressed sound can give a musically useful result. As a general rule, though, you should remember that the compressor is a processor, not an effect, and attempting this trick with a digital mixer or software-based system will probably produce a nasty, phasey sound due to the slight time delays between the two signal paths. Auxiliary sends are normally used only where the 'dry' signal is to be mixed with the affected signal; with a compressor, all the signal is treated and no dry signal is normally added.

Another slightly unorthodox workaround using the aux sends (this time the pre-fade send) is available to those using a console that has no insert points. Lack of inserts is a more common problem with all-in-one digital recorder/mixers and this workaround may be used when you wish to add compression to

one of the channels using an external hardware compressor. The method is shown in Figure 5.9, but it is important that the channel being processed isn't routed anywhere other than to the pre-fade send and that nothing else should be sent to that send. The channel fader must also be turned down and the routing buttons set to off. The output from the effects unit may then be fed back to a spare channel. In effect, you've set up a signal path using the pre-fade send that achieves exactly the same thing as using an insert point.

Digital Compressors

At the time of writing there are still relatively few standalone digital hardware compressors, possibly because so many good digital compressors are already available built into digital mixers and combined recorder/mixers or as software plug-ins for computer audio software. In theory, a digital compressor can do everything an analogue compressor can do, though it has the additional advantage of being able to delay the signal slightly so as to allow the side chain signal to 'see' what's coming a fraction of a second before

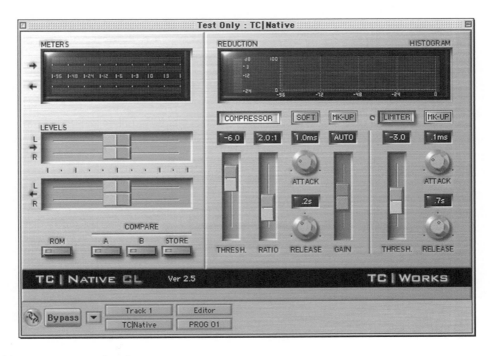

Figure 5.10 (a): Compressor plug-in

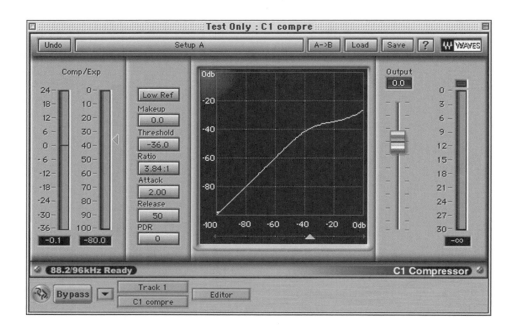

Figure 5.10 (b): Compressor plug-in

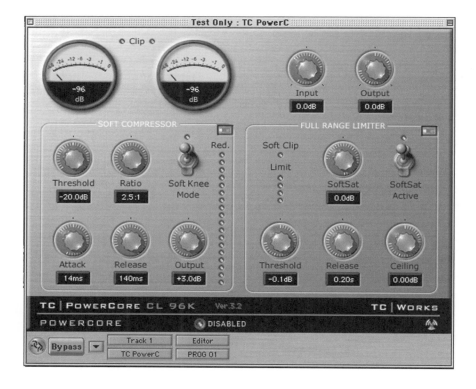

Figure 5.10 (c): Compressor plug-in

Figure 5.10 (d): Compressor plug-in

it arrives at the gain-control section. This is known as a 'look-ahead' system, and it can help a compressor or limiter deal more effectively with signal peaks. By having a little advance warning of peaks, compressors can ensure that no overshoot will take place, and this is again very important in digital mastering applications. In most other respects, software-based digital compressors emulate the controls and parameters of an analogue compressor, though the larger area of a computer screen makes possible the use of more intuitive graphical displays. Figure 5.10 shows a selection of compressor plug-ins.

Compressor Quality

The way in which technical specifications affect the sound quality of any effect or processor varies according to the job that that particular unit does. A compressor must have low noise and distortion characteristics because the entire signal passes through it (unlike a reverb unit for example, where the 'dry' signal is added to a little of the treated signal). For this same reason, the bandwidth must equal or exceed that of the audio spectrum, which

may extend from around 30Hz to over 20kHz. If the whole stereo mix is to be treated, then the technical specifications must clearly be as high as possible as any deficiency here will adversely affect the entire production. Compressor plug-ins have whatever audio bandwidth the system sample rate will support, so there are no real concerns on that score, and most host-based plug-ins (those that use the host computer's CPU) use 32-bit floating point arithmetic, which ensures they can handle a very wide dynamic range without running into clipping problems. Hardware boxes are more likely to use DSP (digital signal processing) chips, which tend to use fixed point arithmetic. In theory, this gives them less dynamic range than a host-based plug-in, but if the algorithm is well designed this shouldn't be a problem.

There are tonal attributes of both analogue and digital compressors that cannot be deduced purely by examination of technical specifications. Nearly all compressor designs have their own characteristic sound, which may be described as warm, transparent, dull, punchy, and so on where such terms bear little resemblance to measured parameters. Ratio-type compression, for instance, differs from the soft knee or over-easy variety, and some of the early tube-based designs are still much sought after for their warm tonality.

In this respect, compressors are similar to microphones and loudspeakers in that their technical specification tells you only part of the story; you must use your ears to evaluate their overall performance. For this reason it is not uncommon for studios to possess a range of hardware compressors and compressor plug-ins so that the most appropriate type can be chosen for the job in hand. For example, a standard-ratio compressor could be used for adding punch to individual instruments, a tube design may be employed for adding warmth to vocals, and a soft knee model might prove useful in generally thickening sounds without changing the tonality too severely. A multi-band, software-based compressor, on the other hand, may be pressed into service where unobtrusive control of dynamics is necessary – such as when processing a complete mix for mastering.

Compressors And Limiters

In principle, a limiter is simply a compressor with an infinitely high ratio, but in this digital age where even very short periods of clipping may not be acceptable, a regular compressor is unlikely to be fast enough to intercept all of the peaks. Fast transients may still pass through the system before the compressor is able to react, and while in the days of analogue tape this didn't matter too much (as short periods of analogue overload tend to be inaudible), digital systems don't tend to sound good when driven into clipping for more than two or three consecutive samples. In such situations, a dedicated, fast-acting limiter is a better solution.

Because most digital systems will tolerate very short periods of clipping (just a few consecutive samples) without the distortion being audible, some digital limiters deliberately allow a certain number of samples to clip before the level is reduced This can actually make the material seem much louder and is often exploited on pop records. Research indicates that repeated clipping within a short space of time is more audible than widely spaced clips, so the final

decision on how much clipping is acceptable must be made by ear using a high-quality monitoring system. Headphones are particularly good for identifying distortion and so may be more effective than loudspeakers in this role.

Another strategy is for limiters to be made to emulate analogue soft clipping, where the top few dBs of peaks are rounded off rather than clipped. This also helps to preserve the impression of loudness, although the effect can be audibly unpleasant if the signal is forced into limiting for more than very brief periods of time.

Dedicated Limiters

A dedicated limiter would normally have the fastest possible response or attack time (see below), and in applications where absolute limiting is vital, a clipping circuit may be included to arrest any short-term peaks that are too fast even for the limiter to control. A clipper is far less subtle than a limiter: instead of trying to control the signal level, it simply clips the top off any signal waveforms that attempt to exceed the clipping level. In combination with a fast limiter, such periods of clipping would be very short, and research has shown that periods of clipping less than 1ms or thereabouts in duration are not audible. Actually it's not quite that simple as clipping becomes more audible if a number of successive clips appear in a short period of time – which is why some audio software monitors how many consecutive samples were clipped during a period of overload.

Transient Enhancers

A relatively recent addition to the compressor range is the transient enhancer – a device dedicated to using compression as an effect to modify the attack portion of a sound in a creative way. Unusually, these devices monitor the incoming signal level both for average level and peak level, then adjust an internal threshold automatically. This makes the effect largely independent of input level and relieves the operator from the responsibility of adjusting a threshold control.

Earlier I described how setting a long attack time enhances transient attacks by allowing the leading edge of percussive sounds such as drums to pass through the compressor without being processed. Transient enhancers use this principle to add snap and attack to percussive sounds regardless of their level, though there's usually a control that allows the user to reverse the effect so that percussive sounds can be given a softer attack.

Similar processing can be used to modify the release characteristics of a sound so that the natural decay can either be shortened or brought up in level. Used on a drum track, the apparent damping and liveness of the drums can be changed very dramatically, as can the degree of attack at the start of a beat.

Dedicated De-essers

Although compressors can be used in conjunction with an equaliser patched into the side chain for de-essing, a dedicated de-esser generally produces fewer unpleasant side effects. Sibilance is a high-frequency whistling sound accompanying 's' and 't' sounds and is largely caused by the way air passes around and between the teeth of the speaker. It can also be aggravated by using a very bright-sounding microphone or by compressing the vocal track. A de-esser's job is to remove the unpleasant high-frequency sounds whenever they occur without unduly changing the rest of the audio spectrum.

Sibilance generally occurs at between 5 and 8kHz, so it's fairly obvious that using a compressor with an equaliser in the side chain to pull down the level of the whole signal is going to have a noticeable effect on the sound. In fact, full-band de-essing as this is known, often gives the vocal an unpleasant lisping quality.

A split-band compressor works better as this pulls down the level of frequencies only above 5kHz or so, but it still isn't ideal as there may be non-sibilant frequencies above 8kHz that you'd like to preserve. To do the job properly requires a little more ingenuity, and different manufacturers have tackled the problem in different ways. Some use a split-band compressor, but then 'leak' very high frequencies above 8kHz around the compressor so as to preserve the top end, while other designs compress only the bands of frequencies in which sibilance occurs. Yet another manufacturer does away with a frequency control altogether and replaces it with a male/female switch, and they claim that their circuit can then lock in on only the sibilance frequencies. Rather than compress the sibilant band, this particular design extracts the sibilant frequencies, then adds them back to the original signal in anti-phase so as to cancel them out.

De-essers are also available as software plug-ins for digital audio workstations and no doubt more ingenious methods will be developed all the time. However, as always, it's better to minimise the problem at source using a suitable choice of microphone type and position rather than to try to fix a serious problem later.

Compressor Applications

Compressors are useful for reducing the dynamic range of both signals being recorded onto a multitrack machine and signals being mixed from a multitrack to a master recorder.

The only real difference between a compressor and a limiter is in the compression ratio and there is no hard-and-fast figure that divides the two, though to ensure no overshoot under any circumstances, a dedicated peak limiter is required as a general-purpose compressor may not respond quickly enough. Strictly speaking, a ratio of infinity:1 would be needed to ensure that the signal never exceeds the threshold but, in practice, a compressor set with a ratio of over 10:1 has much the same audible effect.

Always be prepared to experiment with the compressors at your disposal: not only do ratio types sound somewhat different to soft knee types, but one make or model will usually sound quite unlike another – even when set up in a similar way. The subtle harmonic distortion created by tube compressors, for example, has led many engineers to favour them for their warm sound when used on vocals. Most importantly, don't make the mistake of overcompressing: music depends on dynamics to convey its emotional message, and if you flatten the dynamics entirely, you may end up with something that's easy to record but musically unsatisfying.

The following compression settings should be used only as a guide or starting point. It is not intended that they be regarded as a set of rigidly defined rules; each situation is different and the final results must ultimately be determined by ear.

Vocal Compression

Either a standard-ratio compressor or a soft knee model can be used on vocals, though my personal preference is for a soft knee type as it is possible to apply quite a lot of compression without creating an artificial sound. However, there are occasions when obvious compression makes a vocal sound more exciting, so try your hard knee setting too. If a ratio type is used, select a ratio of around 4:1 to start with and then fine-tune it by ear, though you may want to go as high as 8:1 for a hard, compressed rock-vocal sound.

Because we don't normally want a sharp attack to the words in a vocal line, a fairly fast attack time should be used so that gain control starts immediately. A release time of around one quarter to half a second is usually a good starting point, and little or no hold time is necessary. Alternatively, use a long attack time of, say, 50ms, and a fast release time of around 100ms to emulate a vintage photo-electric compressor. Try this in both hard and soft knee modes. The degree of compression required depends on the performer and, as with any type of signal processing, it is advisable to use as little as is necessary to achieve the desired result. For pop vocals, you might find that between 10 and 12dB of gain reduction during loud sections is fairly typical, though a well-trained vocalist may need less.

Providing there is no excessive crosstalk on the vocal track from other instruments or voices, it should be possible to use the compressor's own expander/gate to clean up pauses between words and phrases (you can always use an external gate if your compressor isn't fitted with one). This cleaning-up process is desirable because the gain increase during quiet sections can often raise the level of breath sounds, lip 'smacks', teeth clicks and electronic hiss to an unacceptable degree – especially when high levels of compression are necessary. Having said

that, when I'm using a computer-based system I prefer to work without gates and instead use the level automation system's graphical capabilities to 'draw in' reduced levels where needed.

It is common practice to compress vocals as they are recorded, but to err on the side of undercompression. This is so that an otherwise perfect take isn't ruined by excessive compression; when you come to mix, a little more compression can always be applied if necessary – but it is much harder to repair the effects of overcompression.

If the vocalist has a particularly sibilant style and changing the microphone type and position doesn't cure the problem entirely, then the additional compression employed during the mix can be made frequency conscious to act as a 'de-esser'. By inserting an equaliser in the side chain peaked at somewhere between 4 and 10kHz, it should be possible to reduce the effect of overpronounced 's' sounds – but care must be taken not to make the processing obvious by overuse.

The exact equaliser frequency may be found by switching the compressor to 'side chain listen' and then tuning the equaliser until the sibilance is most pronounced. For this reason, a sweep or parametric equaliser is preferable to a graphic as the frequency needing attention may fall between the slider frequencies, making precise tuning impossible. As stated earlier, a dedicated de-esser or split-band compressor will generally produce better results.

De-popping

By setting the side chain equaliser frequency to around 50Hz, the compressor can also be used to reduce the level of 'popping' on a vocal recording. However, this is one area where prevention is far better than cure. A simple pop shield made from a pair of nylon tights stretched over a wire frame, or even a frying pan mesh splashguard placed between the singer and the microphone, normally eliminates all traces of popping without otherwise affecting the sound. If de-popping is necessary, a split-band compressor with a split point at around 200Hz will usually produce fewer objectionable side effects than using a full-band compressor.

Acoustic Guitar

Steel-strung acoustic guitars may be given a denser, more even tone through the use of compression – the settings, with the possible exception of attack time, being somewhat similar to those used for vocals. To give the guitar a nice zingy attack, the compressor's attack control should be set to anything from 10 to 40ms so that the attack of each note or chord passes through unsuppressed. Release time can be from 0.1 to 0.25 seconds depending on the effect you want to achieve, and for a really glassy tone, try an opto compressor. Incidentally, a brighter-than-life sound can also be created by using an aural enhancer or exciter after the compressor (this was described in chapter 4 on enhancers). As with vocals, compression can be added both at the recording and the mixing stage.

Bass Guitar

Again you can use either a ratio or soft knee type of compressor set up much as you would for the acoustic guitar (to emphasise the attack of each note). Here, however, the release time must be adjusted to match the individual's playing style. Slap and pull bass playing may need a lot of compression to keep the level even and some of the notes could be quite short, so it will be necessary to set the release time as fast as you can without causing the sound to 'pump'. With very fast release times, you'll also need to set the hold time to 50ms or so in order to prevent distortion of the low frequencies. But this, of course, assumes that this type of distortion isn't regarded as artistically viable – again, let your ears make the final decision – you might find a little low-frequency distortion suits the sound.

It may also be necessary to increase the compression ratio to 5:1 or more to keep tight control of the louder notes, and as previously stated, a compressor with auto attack and release setting may be better if the playing style varies greatly during the course of the song. With slower playing or melodic fretless styles, the release time may be longer, say, up to half a second or more, and if the attack of the note doesn't need to be emphasised, set a faster attack time so that the level is brought under control more quickly. If the playing style changes so much

that there is no optimum attack and release time setting, try the auto mode.

Electric Guitar

The electric guitar is such a versatile instrument that you really have to think about the sound you're after and then decide on the compressor settings on that basis. For example, a heavily distorted guitar sound tends to have fairly tightly controlled dynamics due to the characteristics of the distortion circuitry, so little or no extra compression may be necessary. On the other hand, a clean rhythm guitar would need to be treated very much like an acoustic in terms of compressor settings: EQ before the compressor for a smooth sound or after the compressor for a brighter, more open tone.

If a sustained sound without undue distortion is desired, the compressor may be used as an artificial sustain device simply by compressing the input heavily and setting a fast attack time with a release of 250ms or so. Depending on the degree of sustain needed the ratio can be set anywhere from around 4:1 upwards, and you may want to apply gain reduction of anything up to 20dB. As a guitar sound dies away, the compressor will increase the gain to compensate, thus creating the sustain effect. Remember, though, that the more compression you apply, the more you will emphasise any background noise, so you may find the expander/gate section useful if you have one. (In any event, locating the guitar away from any hum-inducing equipment such as transformers, computer monitors or fluorescent lighting would help keep this interference to a minimum.) If the attack of the note needs a little more emphasis, then slow the compressor attack down while listening to the result until the desired effect is achieved.

Synthesisers

Most synthesised signals can be recorded without any compression, but analogue filter sweep sounds with a lot of resonance can contain peaks well above the average signal level and these may cause overload distortion. A standard ratio compressor set at 4:1 or greater can be used with the threshold set high enough so that gain reduction is applied only to the troublesome peaks. With a slow filter sweep sound, you can actually see where the peak occurs and how high it is simply by watching a VU meter on your mixer.

The output from samplers doesn't usually need compressing, but a compressor is invaluable when treating sounds prior to sampling. This is particularly important if you intend to create sample loops, as even apparently steady sounds can fluctuate in level quite dramatically as the harmonics 'beat' with each other, and any change in level is likely to cause an audible looping glitch. In this instance, the compressor should be set to match the character of the instrument being sampled and you may need to use more compression than you would when making a straightforward recording.

Drum Compression

In rock and pop music, drums are often recorded with very little dynamic range and so some compression is normally applied – especially if the player's technique isn't very even. This is particularly true in the case of bass drums and toms, but in dance music, the snare drum is often kept at a fixed level too. For this task, either type of compressor will suffice – the starting point for the ratio type is somewhere around the 4:1 to 6:1 mark. Set an attack time of around 10ms to emphasise the start of each beat and adjust the release to be faster than the time delay between successive beats if at all possible – try settings between 20 and 100ms. The threshold may then be set so that a small amount of compression is registering on the quieter beats, which means that all louder beats will be compressed harder.

Because of the crosstalk present, due to the proximity of the various drums in a drum kit, gating is often employed to maintain separation. Cymbals would not usually be compressed as they sound unnatural, but this has been deliberately done on some rock records to create a sense of high energy.

When ambience mics are being used to create a larger-than-life drum sound in a reverberant room, it is common practice to compress the output from these mics. When gates are to be used on the ambient signal to give the popular gated drum sound, heavy compression ensures that the ambience doesn't decay significantly before the gate closes.

Mix Compression

Some engineers always compress a complete stereo mix while others would never dream of it. The advantages of doing so are that the average loudness of the track is increased and that the slight 'pumping' adds to the sense of energy and excitement. By increasing the average level, a song can be made to sound louder, even though the peak levels are identical. It's an effect often used when mixing songs and jingles for radio to maintain maximum impact. Soft knee, or, better still, split-band compressors are best suited to this application as they don't tend to dull the sound as much as fixed-ratio models, and an auto-setting compressor may be more successful in dealing with complex dynamics than a purely manual model. If only the latter is available, try a short attack time of between 0 and 10ms and set the release time as fast as you can without pumping becoming obvious. A hold time of between 20 and 50ms may be an advantage if the release time is very fast.

In order to preserve the stereo left/right balance, the compressor must be set for stereo operation so that the same degree of gain reduction is applied to both channels. Failure to observe this requirement will result in undesirable image shifts whenever one channel is significantly louder than the other.

Though you can compress a mix in the same way as any other source, I find it useful to set a very small compression ratio of around 1.1 or 1.2:1 combined with a low threshold – say -35dB. This means compression is applied most of the time, but very gently, and it can have a useful homogenising effect on the sound. In the majority of cases, split-band compression is best for use at the mastering stage, though gentle full-band compression while mixing can help knit together the elements of a mix. If you intend to have your mix professionally mastered, it is safest not to add overall compression.

Time-Code Recovery

This tip was included in the first version of this book when recording with analogue tape was far more common than it is now. However, I've left it in because you never know when you might run into a situation that needs it. One of the more unusual applications

I found for compression was to recover a time code track that had fallen victim to analogue tape drop-out. I've had some success using the fastest possible attack and release times with the threshold set so as to give around 10dB of gain reduction. Watch the gain reduction LEDs during the drop-out periods and if they all go out, apply more compression until they just come on. By experimenting with the output level from the compressor, even quite serious situations can be rescued. (Before trying this of course, you would be well advised to thoroughly clean the tape heads as dirt can lodge on the outside track portion of the head and be quite difficult to remove.)

Hard Or Soft?

Given that soft knee compressors generally sound smoother and more transparent than straight hard knee ratio compressors, why don't we use them all the time? As you've probably guessed, it's partly because we sometimes like to hear a compressor working – a little deliberate gain pumping can give the impression of loudness and hard knee compressors pump more readily than soft knee types. Another

reason is that at higher ratio settings, the hard knee compressor provides a firmer degree of gain control, so if a signal is varying in level to an excessive degree, a soft knee compressor may not produce the required degree of levelling. The choice of which type of compressor is most appropriate must be made by ear, especially as every compressor behaves differently. For example, some soft knee designs have a relatively small knee where the ratio increases over an input range of just a few dBs, whereas some start compressing at very low signal levels and then gradually increase the ratio over a range of 20 or 30dB.

Laws And Curves

In a theoretically perfect compressor, once gain reduction is applied – after the input has passed the threshold – the response is reasonably linear, so no matter how much the input exceeds the threshold by, the output level will increase by that amount divided by the ratio. However, there are some compressor designs that don't exhibit a linear response above the threshold, and it's not uncommon for the amount of gain reduction to reduce at very high signal levels.

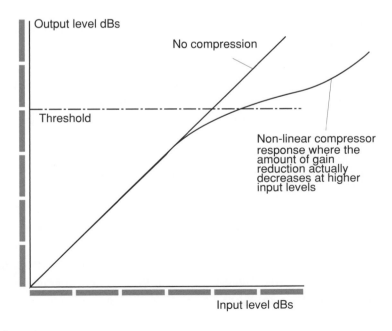

Figure 5.11: S-shaped compressor curve

In effect, this means that at high signal levels, the compression ratio tends to fall to a lower value, as shown in the graph of Figure 5.11. Compressors that use lamps and photocells are notoriously non-linear, which is part of the reason for their distinctive sound. Compressors using tubes within the gain-control circuitry may also be non-linear. It's not important to know the technicalities of compressor control curves but you should be aware that this factor contributes to audible differences between models, and in many cases the less technically perfect designs sound the most musical.

Dynamic Control

It's well known that you need a lot more energy to make a loud bass sound than a loud high-pitched sound, so it follows that most of the sound energy in a mix is dominated by the kick drum and bass instruments. When you compress a mix, the compressor will respond mainly to the levels of these instruments, as explained earlier in this chapter. For example, whenever a loud kick drum beat occurs, the level of the whole mix will be reduced for the duration of the beat, fading back to normal at a time set by the release control. Unless the amount of compression is low, this can lead to an audible dulling of the mix, as high-frequency sounds are reduced in level along with the louder bass sounds. Setting an attack time long enough to allow high-frequency transients to pass before the gain reduction occurs will certainly help in many cases, but when dealing with complex mixes the best solution to this problem is often to use a multi-band compressor. However, the designers of conventional full-band compressors have come up with some ingenious solutions to lessen the problem without the expense and complexity of a split-band design. For example, in some designs, special circuitry allows a small amount of high-frequency signal to bypass the compression process, so that when the level drops in response to a loud bass sound, the high end doesn't get killed. Others may apply a small amount of high-frequency enhancement during periods of high-gain reduction – the principle is unimportant as long as the desired sonic result is achieved. When you're trying out a

compressor, listen to the way the high end changes when heavy compression is being triggered by low-frequency sounds, and if you're planning to compress mixes as well as individual tracks, pick one that doesn't choke the brightness out of a recording when heavy gain reduction is being applied.

Peak Or RMS?

Going back to the 'compressor as a fader' analogy, remember that the side chain of the compressor is that part of the circuitry that listens to the incoming signal to see if it needs turning down or not. Most often, compressor side chains are designed to respond fairly like the human ear, which means that short-duration sounds aren't perceived as being as loud as longer sounds of exactly the same level. This is called an RMS response and is an abbreviation for 'root mean square', a mathematical means of determining average signal levels. The implication of using an RMS compressor is that the compression may sound natural, but short-duration, high-amplitude sounds can pass through unchallenged. Where peak levels also need to be managed, you could use a fast-acting peak limiter after the compressor.

Some compressors offer switchable RMS/peak operation (or indeed a continuously variably peak to RMS response), and in peak mode, the side chain responds far more accurately to brief signal peaks, ensuring they are more accurately controlled. On the other hand, this degree of 'rapid response' control creates more risk of other sounds occurring at the same time as, say, drum hits being pushed down in level more than necessary. For this reason, it is often most effective to use peak compression when treating individual drum and percussion tracks but sticking to RMS for mix compression.

More About Lookahead

Just like our hypothetical engineer controlling levels with a fader, a compressor can't take action until it 'hears' something that's too loud, so any level corrections come slightly late. Wouldn't it be better if the compressor knew a peak was about to arrive shortly before it happened? To do this in real time would require circuitry that could see into the future,

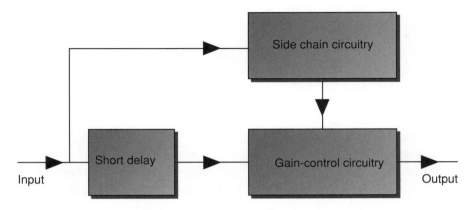

By delaying the signal slightly prior to the gain control stage, the side chain has time to react before the signal reaches the gain-control stage, the advantage being that overshoots can be prevented.

Figure 5.12: Lookahead compressor

so a more practical strategy is to delay the audio passing through the gain-control stage by just a two or three milliseconds while not delaying the audio feeding the side chain. In normal situations, a delay of this magnitude is musically insignificant, but you should be aware that any hardware lookahead compressor will introduce a tiny delay. Figure 5.12 shows the block diagram of a lookahead compressor.

Software plug-ins used to process audio that has already been recorded fare somewhat better than hardware because it's easier to arrange for them to read the audio file slightly in advance of playback to implement lookahead – alternatively all of the tracks will be delayed to compensate for any timing difference. It's for this reason that lookahead is far more common in software compressors than in hardware ones – an analogue compressor needs to include a short digital delay to make lookahead work, and in most cases that isn't cost-effective. Lookahead compressors don't give the same subjective result as normal analogue compressors and often impose more gain reduction than with lookahead switched off, but in situations where transients with extremely fast attack times are present, using a lookahead compressor may be the best way of bringing them under control quickly.

Mix Compression

During recording and mixing, we tend to use mainly full-band compressors, where the entire audio signal is processed via a single gain-control element. The disadvantages of this system have already been discussed but, in essence, the gain control is always determined by high-energy, low-frequency sounds, often to the detriment of mid and high frequencies. If the compressor is acting on a solo kick drum track, then this needn't be a problem, but if the whole drum kit is being compressed, the high-frequency sounds, such as hi-hats and cymbals (which carry relatively little acoustic energy), will be compressed along with the kick drum whether they need it or not. The more instruments in the mix, the less satisfactory this situation becomes. For mastering and other critical applications, multi-band compressors provide greater flexibility without introducing serious side effects.

Compressor Sound

Designing gain-control elements that don't distort the signal can be a difficult task, and in the days before dedicated VCAs (voltage controlled amplifiers), the most common gain elements were tubes, FETs (field-effect transistors) and photo-resistive devices. Some of these distorted more than others and became associated with a particular sound that was deemed musically useful.

Photo-resistive devices are particularly interesting because they actually add very little direct distortion to the signal. Being purely resistive, they can be hooked into a circuit much like any other gain-control potentiometer. However, while they don't add distortion to the signal being processed, the non-linear control law of a combined photo-resistive device and light source gave them a unique sonic signature. The very first such compressors were designed before the invention of the LED and used regular filament light bulbs. Compared to the dynamic of audio, light bulbs have a pretty slow on/off rate, so big attack overshoots could be expected. Modern photo-electric compressors use LEDs along with compensation circuitry to speed up the gain-change response, but there are still non-linearities in some designs that produce a musically interesting result. Modern opto compressors are made by companies such as Joe Meek and Focusrite (the Platinum range). You can approximate the sound of a vintage opto compressor using a regular VCA or FET compressor by setting a fairly long attack time (around 100ms) and a faster release than normal.

Using a tube as a gain element tends to add distortion that is subjectively similar to soft limiting. Transients that are not caught by the compressor still tend to be softened by the non-linear characteristics of the tube circuitry, which is one of the reasons that tube designs are often felt to be more musical than their more accurate VCA counterparts. Their control law is also somewhat non-linear. Some modern hybrid compressors combine a solid-state gain-control element with tube amplification stages, often designed to emphasise the soft limiting characteristic of tubes. Properly designed, these too have a warm, musical sound.

When field-effect transistors were invented, they found applications as gain-control elements and being solid-state devices they could be used in much more cost-effective designs. FETs have similar non-linear transfer functions to tubes and so tend to distort the signal in a similar way. Compressors made by LA Audio are known for their vintage FET sound.

While some compressor designs deliberately play on the musicality of vintage-style distortions, other manufacturers, such as Aphex, often concentrate on the purity of sound and develop highly sophisticated VCA chips with ultra-low distortion and linear control responses. Ultimately, the choice of a compressor that flatters or one that controls dynamics as transparently as possible is an artistic one.

Digital compressors and plug-ins can be designed to emulate all types of hardware compressor, though how good they sound depends on the designer's understanding of the distortion and control law mechanisms of the original. Even today experts argue over which aspects of a tube's electrical characteristics have the greatest influence on 'musicality'. Compression keeps the peak under control but without changing the level in the other frequency bands as heavy compression will only ever be occurring in one of the bands at any one time.

Multi-Band Compressors

I've already introduced the idea of split-band and multi-band compressors but three- or four-band compressors are perhaps the best compromise between versatility and ease of setting up. With a full-band compressor, low-frequency sounds in the mix determine the compression applied to everything else, so what tends to happen is that the kick drum and bass line dictate how the mix will be compressed. For mastering and other critical applications, multi-band compressors provide far greater flexibility as well as fewer side effects.

A typical multi-band compressor comprises a set of filters similar to a PA system's active crossover that splits the audio signal into the required number of frequency bands (three bands being a common format). After passing through the filters, each frequency band is fed into its own compressor, after which the signals are recombined. Figure 5.13 shows the block diagram of a multi-band compressor. From the viewpoint of side effects, perhaps the main advantage of multi-band compression is that a loud event in one frequency band won't trigger gain reduction in the other bands, so if a track includes a very loud kick drum, instead of pulling the whole mix

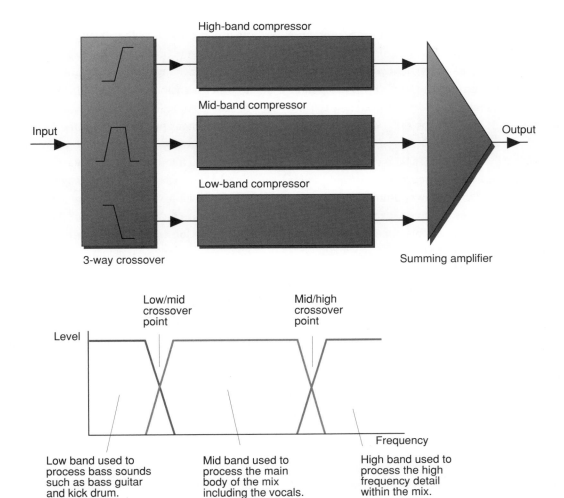

High-band compressor

Mid-band compressor

Input

Low-band compressor

Output

3-way crossover

Summing amplifier

Low/mid
crossover
point

Mid/high
crossover
point

Level

Frequency

Low band used to
process bass sounds
such as bass guitar
and kick drum.

Mid band used to
process the main
body of the mix
including the vocals.

High band used to
process the high
frequency detail
within the mix.

**Figure 5.13: Multi-band
compressor**

down on each kick drum beat, only the low-frequency sounds (kick and bass instrument) will be compressed leaving the mid-range and high frequencies unaffected. There are however, other less obvious advantages.

With a full-band compressor, whatever settings you apply affect the full frequency range, but by using a multi-band compressor you can use different compressor settings in each band if necessary. Furthermore, if the effects of compression change the overall tonal balance unfavourably, you can restore it by adjusting the levels of the three compressor bands relative to each other.

Multi-Band Stereo

Conventional stereo full-band compressors comprise two audio channels plus a stereo link control. The link system sums the two side chain signals and then uses the result to control both compressor channels so that the same amount of gain reduction is always applied to both channels. In the case of compressors with two sets of mono controls, control of the compressor parameters is handed over to just one set of the front-panel controls to avoid the necessity to set up two channels identically.

Without stereo linking, there could be audible

image shift on signals that are (even occasionally) significantly louder on one channel than another. A multi-band compressor works in a similar way except that each frequency band has its own side chain, so a three-band, stereo compressor would have three stereo-linked sections: high frequencies, mid frequencies and low frequencies.

Crossover Frequencies

Commercial multi-band compressors usually allow the user to adjust the crossover points, so if we take a three-band compressor as an example, where is the best place to set them? This depends on the type of material being processed so, as an example, let's assume we're processing a typical pop mix. Setting a crossover point in the middle of the vocal range can compromise the vocal sound, especially if you use radically different compression settings each side of the crossover frequency. In my experience it's best to set the low crossover point below the vocal frequency range and set the high crossover point no lower than 2.5kHz. A sensible low-frequency setting might be 120Hz, as this is below the vocal range but above most of the deep bass and kick elements going on in the rhythm section.

These are only suggested starting points and, as a rule, I'd suggest moving the high crossover point higher than this if you plan to do more than very subtle high-end processing as it's easy to over-emphasise the 2 to 4kHz area of the spectrum to the point of harshness. By contrast, if you restrict heavy processing to above 6kHz, you can significantly enhance the sense of detail and 'air' without disturbing the mid range, which is so important for the natural reproduction of vocals and many acoustic instruments.

Multi-Band Settings

How do you set up the compressor parameters in each of the three bands? There are two very different ways of using compressors, the first of which is the approach normally outlined in text books. This is the application of compressors in which they are set to control only those signals that are too loud, in which case we set the threshold at the 'loud enough' level, then set a compression ratio so that gain reduction is applied to anything exceeding that level. Below the threshold, no gain reduction takes place, so the signal passes through unchanged. If you need to tame vocal peaks or other occasional excesses, this is the usual way to set the compressor.

The other approach – and one I often use myself when mastering – is to set the threshold fairly low and also to use a low ratio (typically less than 1.2:1 with a threshold of -30 to -40dB). This way, instead of applying a lot of compression only to the signal peaks, a little compression is applied to all but the quietest signals. This is a good way of adding density and energy to a mix that's already well balanced, but it won't help you control peaks in poorly balanced material.

Fine Tuning

These two strategies, and any settings between, can be applied to multi-band compression, but what makes this approach so flexible is that you can use different compression settings for each band. For example, when working on a track where the bass end is lacking in weight, you may choose to use a higher threshold and a higher ratio to bring up the average bass level, but still use subtle low-ratio settings for the mid range and high end. The make-up gain in the bass band can be used to restore any tonal imbalance caused by the difference in compression settings. Similarly, by applying heavier compression to frequencies above, say, 6kHz, it is possible to increase the high-frequency density to create an effect similar to that produced by an enhancer.

That leaves the mid range, and in a mastering situation that's the area I tend to process least. Often a ratio of 1.1:1 and a threshold of -35dB is enough to produce an improved sense of integration, and when this is combined with the other two bands (which may be more heavily processed if they need it), the whole mix should sound more vibrant, clear and punchy. For maximum loudness and to control any remaining peaks, you could then process the finished mix via a peak limiter set to trim around 6dB off the loudest peaks so that the overall level can be increased by 6dB without clipping.

The attack and release settings again depend on

the material being treated, but for typical pop mixes I might use a moderately fast attack time on the bass end (try between 5 and 25ms) because very low frequencies have no fast transients to compromise. This brings the level under control reasonably quickly without 'snatching', which is what occurs when very fast attack times are used in conjunction with more severe compressor settings, and I'll set the release time as short as I can get it without any audible gain pumping being evident. As a rule, the busier the music, the faster the release time you need to ensure the compressor's gain resets itself between notes, but low frequencies tend to hang on longer than high frequencies, so you may need a longer release time at the bass end than in the mid range. As a starting point, setting twice the release time as for the mid band might be reasonable, though if you prefer to keep it simple, you'll probably get reasonable results by starting off with the attack and release times for all three bands set the same.

The mid band covers the majority of what we perceive in a musical mix, so this can be set up much as you'd set a full-range compressor. In other words, ease up the attack time if you need to enhance transients, and use a fairly short release time, but not so short that you hear pumping.

If the aim is to increase the density of the high end, then a fast attack may be necessary to prevent the transients from becoming too pronounced and you can use a higher ratio setting to push up the energy. High transients tend to decay faster than low frequencies, so you may be able to use a faster release time than you did in the mid range, but listen carefully for any pumping effects or other unnatural gain changes, and increase the release time as necessary to tame them. If you're using a compressor that allows you to solo each of the frequency bands, setting the release time may be easier, but try half of the mid-range release time as a starting point.

Compressing Tracks

I seldom use multi-band compression on single tracks because the side effects of full-band compression are often musically flattering to single sounds, but where you need gain control without obvious compression, a multi-band model is more likely to deliver the results you need. In this case, I'd tend to start with identical settings for all three bands and set the values in a similar way to using a full-band model. The main difference is that you won't have to set an artificially long attack time to keep transients intact.

While compressing mixes, we tend to keep the crossover point away from the mid band, but different instruments may require different settings. For example, a bass guitar might benefit from a low crossover point set to around 50 or 60Hz so you can control the really deep bass more precisely. At the same time, the upper crossover point could be reduced to just a few hundred Hertz as the 50 to 800Hz band is quite critical to the way a bass guitar sounds. Above that, the energy tails off quite significantly, so the high band (800Hz and up) is quite capable of looking after the rest. As with any conventional compressor, the more compression you apply, the more make-up gain you need to get the peak level back to where it was, but you have the option of using less make-up gain in a specific band if you want to suppress the contribution of that band to the overall sound. In other words, the make-up gain controls for the various frequency bands can be used almost like equaliser level controls.

Multi-Band For Synths

In some cases, multi-band compression will yield better results on synthesisers than full-band compression, specifically in the case of a sound based around a resonant filter sweep. If you apply full-band compression to moderate the increase in peak level at the sweep's centre frequency, the whole sound may be reduced in level quite dramatically.

Level peaking may also occur when two sounds are beating with each other or where a flange effect is being applied. Though full-band compression will control the level, a multi-band compressor may do so with fewer side effects. Similarly, when you have a bass synth sound that also has a lot of higher harmonics, a multi-band compressor will keep the bass end under control without the level of the higher frequencies being adversely affected.

Multi-Band Compression And Vocals

There are occasions when using a multi-band compressor on vocals can be useful for controlling or shaping timbre. For example, applying a higher ratio of compression to the high band can add sizzle and definition to an otherwise bland vocal recording. Conversely, heavier compression applied to the bass band can contribute to the thickness and richness of the voice.

You may also find that you want to accentuate the rasp of a voice, in which case try to identify the frequency area you're interested in, then set the crossover points fairly close on either side. By applying more compression to the band of interest, the characteristic will be emphasised.

6 DEALING WITH NOISE

Unwanted noise is a problem in all areas of recording. Electronic equipment generates hiss, magnetic tape generates hiss, and quantising errors in digital systems generate hiss. Poor screening, ground loops and single-coil guitar pick-ups can all cause hum problems, and then there are those noises which, though not electronically generated, are still unwanted: the rustle of sheet music, squeaking chairs, microphone spillage from other instruments, audience noise, wind, traffic and so on. Though it is good practice to keep recordings as noise free as possible, it is frequently necessary to try to 'clean up' an existing recording. In order to do this effectively, it's first necessary to understand a little more about noise.

Even in the light of some of the amazing de-noising technology available to us, it still holds true that once noise has been added to an electrical signal there is no perfect way of removing it later. Though there are digital processes that are surprisingly effective at significantly reducing the level of random noise such as hiss, or repetitive noise such as air-conditioning noise, hum or video camera whine, they still cause undesirable side effects. True, the very best digital systems introduce relatively minor side effects, but these processes tend to be expensive and are generally reserved for the post-production stage. As far as multitrack recording is concerned, it's safest to assume that any noise you collect along the way is going to be a permanent part of the recording and that all possible steps should be taken to minimise it. This means you should always optimise gain structure, unroute unused mixer channels and take all other practical measures to reduce noise at source rather than assume you can fix it later. Despite your best efforts, some noise will always remain – noise is a fact of physics, but the less there is, the fewer side effects you'll incur when trying to clean up your recording.

There are numerous fairly straightforward strategies for combating noise on recordings, which is fortunate as it isn't generally practical to reduce the noise level using a sophisticated digital de-noising process every time you record a new track. Even when working in a sequencer, where de-noising algorithms are available, processing every track would be time consuming and may compromise the overall audio quality. In most situations where the background noise is at a relatively low level, you don't need to remove the noise at all, you simply hide it!

Noise Masking

Unless the noise contamination is quite severe, the chances are that it will be obtrusive only during quiet sections of the music – the rest of the time it will be masked by the wanted signal. This gives a clue as to how to deal with noise on individual tracks, because if we can silence the pauses, any other noise present when the track is playing will be hidden by the wanted audio material.

A complete mix is very difficult to treat because periods of complete silence are infrequent, but separate tracks within a multitrack recording generally include some periods of silence. Consider a vocal line: there are inevitably short pauses between words and phrases as well as longer gaps during instrumental passages. If the signal level could be turned down during these pauses, the background hiss would also be turned down. You've probably tried something like this already during a mix where

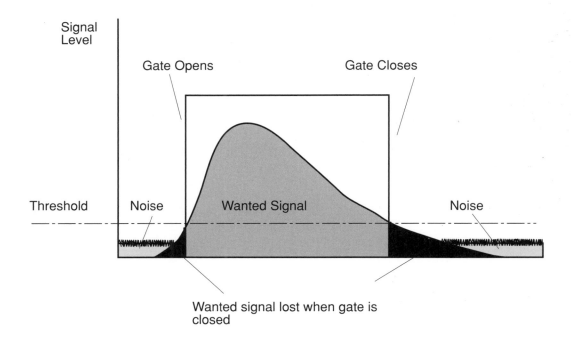

When the gate is open, both the wanted signal and the noise pass through, but the noise will be masked by the wanted signal

Figure 6.1 shows how the threshold system operates

you keep the faders down until the song is just about to start to create a clean intro. To manually perform this task during every pause on every track, however, would be quite impossible.

The answer is to use a gate and, to the best of my knowledge, these were first developed for the film industry to improve the quality of dialogue recorded on location. These early gates were based on an electronic switch that was turned on or off according to the input signal level. Like a compressor, there is a threshold set by the user, but this time, when the signal falls below the threshold, the electronic switch operates to mute the signal. A compressor processes signals above the threshold, while a gate treats only signals below it.

Figure 6.1 shows how the threshold system operates in this case. Even the most basic gate will

have some kind of indicator to show when it is open and when it is closed. At its simplest, this could be a single LED, but it is not unusual to find two or more LEDs on more sophisticated gates so that you can also see when the gate is in the process of closing.

A basic gate using a simple switch can only be on or off (there is no in between state), so quiet sounds are in danger of being muted along with the noise. Sounds with natural decays are particularly vulnerable to this effect. What's needed is a more sophisticated kind of gate action.

Attack And Release

To get around the problem of chopping off low-level sounds, later gates were fitted with a release time control, so that instead of simply switching off when the signal falls below the threshold, the sound was faded out over a period of time set by the user. To achieve this, the electronic switch was replaced by a VCA (voltage controlled amplifier) or other electronic gain element similar to those used in compressors. This represents a dramatic improvement and prevents the noise from being turned on and off too abruptly – an effect that is far more intrusive in most instances than the continuous background noise the gate is trying to hide. A more progressive gate closing action allows decaying low level sounds to fade naturally rather than being cut off abruptly.

Release is certainly the most important parameter after threshold, but it is also an advantage to include an attack control to determine how long the gate takes to fully open once the input signal exceeds the threshold. If the gate opens too quickly, low-frequency sounds may be distorted due to the gate operating part of the way through a cycle – an effect that can produce an audible click. By slowing the attack time down slightly, this problem can be overcome.

On the other hand, a sound like a snare drum beat will be robbed of its impact if the gate opens too slowly, so provision has to be made for very fast operation in these circumstances. At its fastest, an attack time of no more than a few tens of microseconds is desirable, whereas at the slower end, several tens of milliseconds might be ideal. As is often the case, however, users were not slow to recognise the creative potential of gates where an even longer attack time could be used to modify the envelope of a percussive or picked sound to create a bowing effect. Consequently, designers now tend to give their units a wider range of attack time than would be necessary for purely corrective work.

Range

So far, we have threshold, attack and release controls, and, in many cases, these parameters are all we need, but some units have an extra control called floor, range or attenuation. What this does is to allow a certain amount of signal to pass, even when the gate is closed. For example, a range setting of 10dB would mean that in the gate closed position, the signal would be attenuated by 10dB rather than muted completely. A useful application for the range control might be during a recording session where the room ambience is required in the mix but there is too much of it. By using the gate to attenuate by a few dBs rather than completely switch off, the ambience can be allowed through during pauses, but at a lower

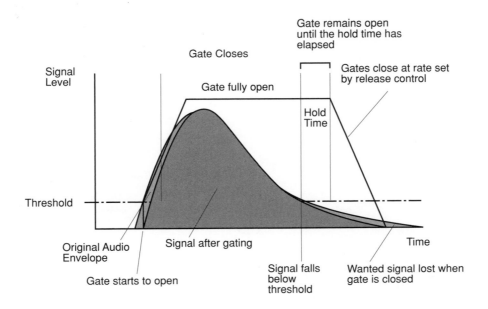

Figure 6.2 shows how the attack, release and hold times work together

level. The same goes for film or TV soundtrack work where you may be recording a conversation in a busy street and wish to retain a little street noise for atmosphere, but at a level that won't detract from the main dialogue.

Hold Time

One further control that you might come across is hold. Hold stops the gate entering its release phase for a predetermined time after the input falls below the threshold. In conjunction with a fast release setting, this can be used to gate reverb or room ambience abruptly to create the well-known gated

drum sound. A shorter hold setting may be useful to prevent the gate 'chattering' – where the input signal is rapidly fluctuating in level – though selecting a longer release time is also effective against chattering in most circumstances. Figure 6.2 shows how the attack, release and hold times work together.

Hysteresis

Chattering can be a serious problem when the sound being gated has a slowly undulating decay waveform, so the best gates tend to be designed with a degree of hysteresis built in. Put simply, this means that whatever threshold level is set to open the gate, the

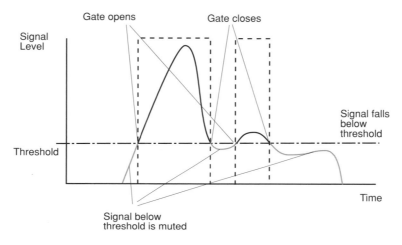

Figure 6.3a: Gate without hysteresis

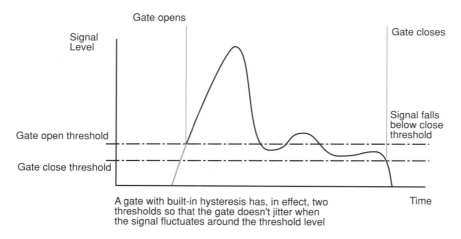

Figure 6.3b: Gate with hysteresis

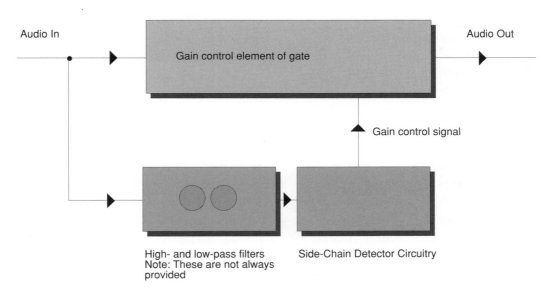

Audio In

Gain control element of gate

Audio Out

Gain control signal

High- and low-pass filters
Note: These are not always
provided

Side-Chain Detector Circuitry

The gate only reacts to the signal that passes through
the filter. Note, as the filters are not connected in line
with the gain control element, the audio passing
through the gate is not affected by the filters

Figure 6.4: Block diagram of a typical gate

signal must fall a few dBs below that threshold before the gate will start to close again. This has the same outcome as having two thresholds – one for opening the gate and a lower one for closing it – and in practical terms, it means that the input signal would have to waver in level by more than the difference between the two thresholds before retriggering could occur. An example of a waveform that might cause problems if the gate did not exhibit hysteresis would be a decaying synth tone with LFO amplitude modulation. Figure 6.3 shows how this type of signal would be handled: a) by a gate without hysteresis, and b) by a gate with hysteresis. The amount of hysteresis is generally fixed so the user doesn't have any extra controls to set. Indeed, most manufacturers don't mention hysteresis at all so the user may have no knowledge of its existence. As far as the user is concerned, the way hysteresis and hold is implemented generally means that gates from some manufacturers seem to behave more controllably and predictably than others.

Side Chain

As with a compressor, the gate has a side chain circuit that measures the level of the incoming signal and compares it with the threshold set by the user. When the threshold is exceeded, the circuit generates a control signal to open the gate at a rate set by the attack control. When the signal falls below the threshold, the gate closes according to the settings of the hold and release controls.

The gate part of the circuit is usually designed around a voltage-controlled amplifier, though some circuits use a voltage-controlled attenuator based on a type of semiconductor known as a FET (field-effect transistor). Gates within digital consoles or presented as software plug-ins are, of course, all digital, but their control philosophy is exactly the same as the analogue gate just described. The actual mechanism of operation is unimportant as long as it does the job quietly, quickly and without adding distortion. Figure 6.4 shows the block diagram of a typical analogue gate.

Like the compressor, a two-channel gate will normally have a linking switch that ensures both channels switch on and off at the same time when stereo material is being processed, even if the signal is louder in one channel than in the other. As with the compressor, this is necessary to prevent the image shifting, which could occur if both channels were operating independently.

External Key Input

For special applications (again like the compressor), it may be desirable to drive the side chain from a signal other than that being fed into the gate. To achieve this, the gate needs an external side chain key input. This way, one signal can be used to gate another – the typical example is the bass drum that opens the gate to allow the bass guitar through in order to tighten up the timing of the track. If the bass guitar is played early, it won't be allowed to pass through the gate until the bass drum beat occurs. The bass sound will then decay at a rate set by the hold and release controls so it can be made shorter than the original if so desired.

This same arrangement is used to create a rhythmic chopping effect on many dance records. In this instance, the gate is triggered from a rhythmic signal, such as a drum machine, and this rhythm is then imposed onto a sustaining sound such as a rhythm guitar part or keyboard pad.

Master Slave Mode

Multi-channel gates sometimes have a linking system so that all the gate channels open and close at the same time as the master. This is achieved by link buttons (if fitted) between the channels, where the master channel is usually the left most channel in the group. This facility is often useful where you have a group of backing vocalists who aren't working tightly enough together. By gating each singer and controlling the gate's opening and closing time from the singer with the best timing, nobody will be heard before they should, and no notes will last longer than the controlling vocalist's.

Gate Ducking

Some gates have a ducking mode that enables them to perform the same ducking functions as can be achieved by using a compressor. In fact, ducking can be easier to arrange with a gate than a compressor because the range or attenuation control can be set to determine precisely how many dBs of attenuation are applied during ducking. The attack and release times set the speed at which ducking starts and stops, and, as with the compressor, the signal controlling the process must be fed into the side chain key input at line level. The signal being ducked passes through the gate's main signal path in the usual way. As a rule, a fairly fast attack time is combined with a fairly long release time to give the most natural result.

On some gates, if the ducking mode is selected, but no external side chain input is connected, the input signal effectively ducks itself. In practice, the gate behaves as though its threshold operation is reversed, so that signals exceeding the threshold cause the gate to close. By using the floor control to set the amount of attenuation, a dynamic reversal effect can be created whereby the loudest sounds are turned down dramatically while quieter sounds are left untreated. For example, it's possible to process a drum loop to attenuate the level of the loudest beats rather more radically than you could with a compressor, and if the gate has side chain filters (see below), it may even be possible to attenuate, say, only the snare drum beats without affecting the kick drum level. This can be useful if you plan to replace one of the drum sounds with a sample, for example, but in practice requires very careful adjustment.

Side-Chain EQ

Equalisers inserted into the side chain can make the gate respond more readily to some frequencies than to others – the practical use of such a combination is best illustrated by example. If you are using a snare drum to trigger the gate, it is possible that the snare mic will pick up enough of the nearby hi-hat sound to open the gate between snare beats. Using the equaliser to filter out the high-frequency hi-hat from the side chain can significantly reduce this tendency to false trigger. Most gates with side chain access have a listen switch, which enables you to hear the signal feeding the side chain via the gate's output so that you can set the filter controls by ear to reject those sounds that are causing mistriggering problems.

It is not uncommon for gates to have built-in side chain filters to save you the trouble of patching in an external one, and these usually take the form of a pair of variable-frequency high-pass and low-pass filters with fairly sharp cut-off characteristics, usually 12dB per octave. It is important to realise that these filters do not directly affect the sound of the output in any way, they only affect the way in which the gate's triggering circuit responds. However, it is unwise to cut too much top end from the side chain signal where the sound being triggered has a fast attack as this can slow down the opening of the gate slightly.

Applications

Of all signal processors, the gate is probably the one that most makes its presence known most dramatically when it is set up badly. If the threshold is set incorrectly or if the decay is too short, the sound may be gated on and off in a spurious manner that can produce an effect like a faulty connection or even gross distortion. The correct procedure is to set the threshold as low as possible, without false triggering from noise being a problem, and then work on the release time so that the natural decay of the sound being gated is not affected. Don't set the release time longer than you have to, though, otherwise you'll still hear noise after the wanted sound has died away. Generally the attack time should be as fast as possible but not so fast as to cause audible clicks when the gate opens. Slower attacks can be used as a special effect.

If a signal is hopelessly noisy, then it is unreasonable to expect a gate to improve it without introducing unacceptable side effects, but if you take care with recording levels and do your utmost to minimise noise at source, then gating can help to turn a good recording into an exceptional one. It is common practice to employ several gates when mixing a multitrack tape, and in professional circles one gate for each track is not uncommon. Twenty-four tracks of audio can contribute a significant amount of background noise to a mix, even when the tracks heard in isolation seem fairly quiet, so it is useful to be able to mute them during pauses in the recorded signal. This applies equally to analogue and digital recording systems because in both cases it's common

for most of the unwanted noise to be recorded from the source (noisy instruments or noise added in the analogue amplification chain) – tape hiss or digital converter noise is rarely a problem providing the recording levels are properly set.

Other Applications

The creative trick of gating reverb on drums is less applicable than it used to be because most digital reverb units now have the effect built in. Nevertheless, it is still used where the reverb is natural in origin as in the case of drums recorded in a live room. Here the gate may be triggered via its side chain from the dry drum sound and the ambience mics passed through the gate, usually in stereo. By using a hold time of up to half a second and a very fast attack and release, the easily recognisable hard-gated drum sound is produced. Figure 6.5 shows how this might be set up in practice. The effect may be stronger if the ambience signal is heavily compressed before being gated.

Other valid uses of gates include cleaning up sampled sounds, modifying the envelopes of sampled sounds, and reducing acoustic crosstalk between instruments miked separately but located in close proximity to each other. The gate is not a universal panacea for noise problems but, used properly, it is a most valuable tool.

MIDI Gates

MIDI gates are essentially conventional analogue gates that also output a MIDI Note On message when the gate is open and a MIDI note off message when the gate closes. This can be useful in a number of creative situations where, for example, a MIDI sound source is used to double up the sound triggering the gate. An example of this might be a kick drum, which is arranged to trigger a kick drum sample at the same time.

The same technique can be used for drum replacement, where the originally recorded tracks are arranged so that each drum can be reasonably isolated by means of a gate. It's fairly common recording practice for kick drums and snare drums to be recorded on separate tracks, so if the recorded sound isn't good enough, or you'd like to try something different, it's often possible to use the original sound to trigger a

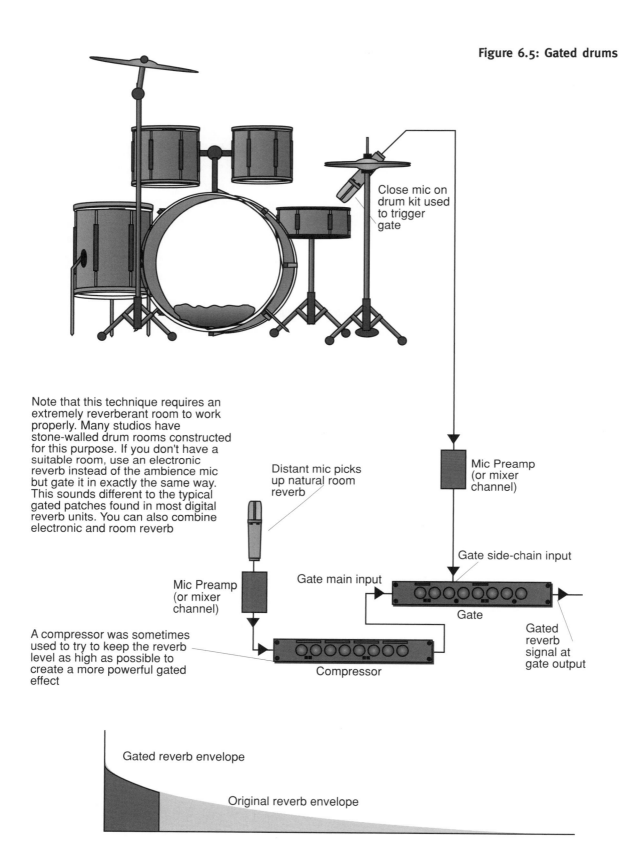

Figure 6.5: Gated drums

Close mic on drum kit used to trigger gate

Note that this technique requires an extremely reverberant room to work properly. Many studios have stone-walled drum rooms constructed for this purpose. If you don't have a suitable room, use an electronic reverb instead of the ambience mic but gate it in exactly the same way. This sounds different to the typical gated patches found in most digital reverb units. You can also combine electronic and room reverb

Distant mic picks up natural room reverb

Mic Preamp (or mixer channel)

Gate side-chain input

Gate main input

Mic Preamp (or mixer channel)

Gate

A compressor was sometimes used to try to keep the reverb level as high as possible to create a more powerful gated effect

Compressor

Gated reverb signal at gate output

Gated reverb envelope

Original reverb envelope

MIDI gate, which in turn triggers a sampler or drum-sound module. A more advanced MIDI gate may also output a MIDI velocity proportional to the level of the incoming signal, otherwise the MIDI-triggered sound will always be at a fixed level.

Providing it's possible to separate out the original drum sounds using the MIDI gate, there's no reason not to substitute sampled drum sounds for live ones, though you have to keep in mind that MIDI is not an instantaneous system and that some MIDI sound modules may take a few milliseconds to sound after they have received a MIDI command. In extreme cases, this may be enough to upset the feel of a drum part, although in most situations the delay will be too small to perceive. Figure 6.6 shows a MIDI gate being used to trigger replacement drum sounds. Where the delay is long enough to be a problem, it's easiest to work with the MIDI parts recorded to a sequencer and then advance the MIDI track triggering the drum replacement parts by however many milliseconds it takes to cancel out the triggering delay. The sequencer may be synced to an audio recorder or the audio tracks may be transferred to the audio tracks of the sequencer.

If you're working with analogue tape synced to a sequencer, this will still work providing you have a spare track for time code (assuming you have the necessary sync hardware). Simply record the MIDI drum triggers into the sequencer, then apply a small negative delay to the MIDI track to slide everything back into time. Recording into a sequencer also has the advantage that you can edit out any false notes caused by other drums accidentally triggering the gate. You can optimise the negative delay time by ear by monitoring both the recorded drum sound and the MIDI drum sounds, then adjusting the delay to minimise any flamming or doubling effect.

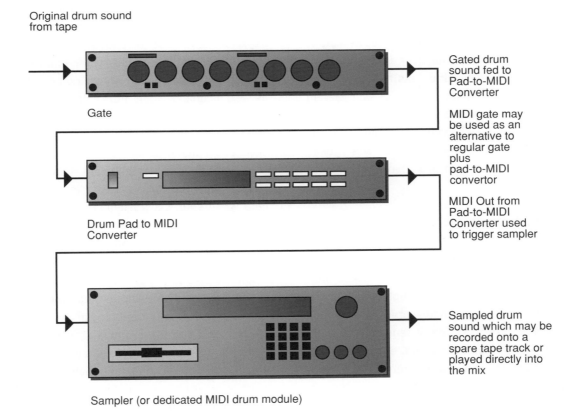

Original drum sound from tape

Gate

Gated drum sound fed to Pad-to-MIDI Converter

MIDI gate may be used as an alternative to regular gate plus pad-to-MIDI convertor

Drum Pad to MIDI Converter

MIDI Out from Pad-to-MIDI Converter used to trigger sampler

Sampler (or dedicated MIDI drum module)

Sampled drum sound which may be recorded onto a spare tape track or played directly into the mix

Figure 6.6: Drum sound replacement

Expanders

Some gates work on the expander principle, which is best visualised as being exactly the opposite mechanism to that of a compressor. When a signal falls below the threshold, it is not switched off as in the case of a simple gate, but is instead subjected to gain reduction. If, for example, the input signal was present all the time just below the threshold level, a normal gate would give no output at all – it would never open. The expander, however, does give some output, but at a reduced level. The further the input falls below the threshold, the more the gain is reduced. For example, a 1:2 expander ratio would mean that for every dB the input fell below the threshold, the output would fall by 2dB. An expanded signal sounds rather odd as the peaks remain loud while the quiet sections are all but inaudible, but gain reduction happens only below the threshold level (which would normally be set only a little way above the noise floor) and sounds less obvious than simple gating. The overall result is not much different from that of a conventional gate but the switching on and switching off points are less obtrusive, especially when using short release times.

Expanders of a lower ratio (less than 1:1.5) may be used to subtly increase the dynamic range of signals falling below the threshold, and if the threshold level is set to be very high, then the whole signal is expanded. This may be useful when trying to restore the natural dynamics of an overcompressed piece of music.

Dynamic Noise Filters

Another related device – although not a gate in the strictest sense of the word – is the dynamic noise filter, which is sometimes used in combination with an expander or gate to form a single-ended noise reduction system. All that single-ended means in this context is that unlike tape noise reduction systems (Dolby, DBX and so on), the signal doesn't have to be encoded on record and decoded on playback. A single-ended system takes any signal, live or recorded, and processes it to reduce the subjective noise content.

What a dynamic filter does is progressively reduce the high-frequency content of the signal being processed as its level drops. To put it simply, as the signal gets quieter, the device automatically turns the treble down using a variable-frequency high-cut filter. This might sound drastic but, providing you don't overprocess, the reduction in high-frequency noise can be dramatic, with no apparent loss in brightness. As with most other processors, any side effects are likely to be less noticeable if you process individual tracks rather than complete mixes, though with care, complete mixes can be improved to a useful extent.

The reason that dynamic filtering works as well as it does is that most natural sounds are richer in high-frequency harmonics at the start where the amplitude is highest, so the filter is wide open, allowing most or all of these harmonics to pass through unattenuated. As the sound decays, the high frequencies tend to die away more quickly so the filtering effect of the dynamic equaliser isn't obvious. When the input signal falls even further, the expander gate steps in to silence it completely. Usually the expander and filter sections have independent threshold controls and, unlike the usual type of gate, this system is reasonably effective on complex mixes as well as on individual tracks or instruments.

The low-level expander section of these single-ended-noise reduction devices is used simply to silence the signal completely during pauses. When you're processing a complete mix, this can be useful to clean up the start and end of a song, but won't help when sound is present. Figure 6.7 shows the block diagram of a typical single-ended noise reduction system based on a dynamic filter teamed with an expander.

At one time, dynamic noise filters were extensively used to clean up recordings taken from cassette or analogue tape, but in the light of more sophisticated modern-day digital noise-removal technology, they are more likely to be used for processing individual sources such as noisy vintage synthesisers or guitar amplifiers. Most models these days have two channels and stereo linking facilities so that they may be used to process either mono or stereo signals.

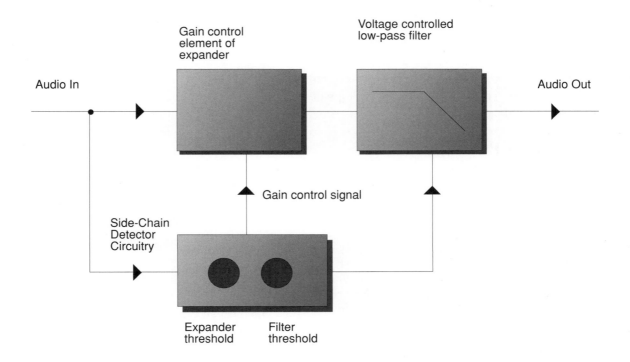

Figure 6.7: Block diagram of single-ended noise reduction system (based on a dynamic filter teamed with an expander)

Signal Quality

As with the compressor, gates and expanders, single-ended noise reduction units based on dynamic filters treat the entire audio signal passing through them, so the quality of the signal path is very important; any shortcomings will adversely affect the whole of the output signal. Obviously, the electronically generated noise and distortion must be low, otherwise there would be no point in having it there in the first place, and given the wide range of uses to which a gate or expander is likely to be put, its frequency response must be flat over the whole audio range. Dynamic filters are designed to have a variable frequency response by their very nature, but when the filter is wide open, the upper limit should exceed 20kHz and the overall frequency response should be flat. A good test whenever you're checking out a gate, compressor or noise filter is to set the controls so that no processing is being applied, then check that the quality of audio passing through the unit is indistinguishable from the original audio source.

It is also important that the gain-control circuitry of gates or expanders doesn't cause clicks when the gate opens or closes rapidly. Clicks will always occur if a signal is abruptly switched on or off, but if the gate is made to switch with no signal present (by feeding a signal into the side chain or key input), no clicks should be audible.

Connecting Up

Gates are processors and are always placed in line with the signal being treated, never (under normal circumstances) via the aux send or return loop. Signals may be gated during recording, or they may be gated during mixing – the advantage of gating during the mixing stage is that you can also gate out any noise that may have accumulated during the recording process. Furthermore, an inappropriate gate setting during recording can ruin an otherwise perfectly good take, whereas an incorrect gate setting at mixdown simply means readjusting the settings and trying again. However, when several signals are recorded on the same track, as is often the case when recording large drum kits, some application of gating while recording may be necessary.

Gates And Reverb

If at all possible, don't attempt to gate a signal that has had reverb added to it (except to create deliberate gated reverb effects), as you may 'chop off' some of the reverb decay. It's far better to gate the signal prior to adding reverb (or delay) effects as not only will the reverb remain intact regardless of the gate setting, the reverb will also help disguise any breaks in continuity in the original signal caused by the gate action.

Gate Applications

Most vocal sounds tend to have a fairly fast attack followed by a slower decay, though some words can cut off abruptly, especially those that end with hard consonants. If the gate is set to open very quickly, there is still the chance of introducing a click on those words that have a slower attack than others, so increasing the attack time to one or two milliseconds helps reduce the risk of clicking in general-purpose vocal applications. This is still fast enough to allow the attack of the word to pass through without any of it being lost, but slow enough to avoid audible clicking. In situations where the background noise is high, resulting in a higher than usual threshold setting, it may be necessary to further increase the attack time to avoid clicks. In any event, always listen carefully to ensure that the start of the word isn't being cut off.

A release time of between a quarter and half a second should be enough to avoid truncating the ends of words, yet it should still be fast enough to fade out the noise quickly at the end of an abrupt sound. If noise is still audible after the ends of words, try shortening the gate release time further. On a sustained note that fluctuates in level, the gate may open and close rapidly resulting in a chattering effect, in which case the hold time should be increased until

the chattering stops. If there is no hold parameter, extend the release time. Chattering is normally only a problem at shorter release times, but if the release time is extended too much in an attempt to alleviate the effect, the sound being gated may end before the gate closes fully, leaving any background noise unmasked. Inevitably, all gate settings are a compromise and part of the engineer's skill is finding the best settings for a particular job.

There's a similar problem with the threshold level: the lower you set the threshold, the less obtrusive the result will be, but then if it's set too low, there is a danger that background noise or unwanted sounds will trigger the gate. It is therefore important that good recording practice is observed to keep noise as low as possible at all stages of the recording process rather than expecting gates to perform miracles.

If you are compressing vocals at the same time as gating them, it is generally better to put the gate before the compressor; if it comes after, the reduced dynamic range will make it more difficult to set the threshold control correctly. Finally, don't feel you have to gate out all vocal breath noises as removing these completely can detract from the natural feel of the performance. Attenuating such noises by a few dBs using the gate's range control may be more appropriate.

Electric Guitar

Noise is often a problem when recording electric guitars, especially instruments with single-coil pick-ups. These pick-ups also tend to be very susceptible to hum from computer monitors, so always keep guitar players and computers as far apart as possible. Unlike humbuckers, which are designed to cancel interference, single-coil pick-ups are susceptible to all forms of electromagnetic interference, primarily hum, present in the room. To some extent this can be minimised by rotating the instrument's position until a point of minimum hum is found. This happens because the position of the pick-up coil relative to the interfering magnetic field varies the degree of coupling between the interference source and the guitar pick-up. There will always be one angle at which the hum is a minimum and another at which it is a maximum.

Another common source of guitar noise is the instrument amplifier or overdrive pedal – overdrive effects are created by using large amounts of gain prior to a non-linear circuit of some kind, and the extra gain amplifies hum and hiss as well as the wanted signal. In many situations, a properly set-up gate prior to the overdrive stage will eliminate the worst effects of guitar noise. Be aware, however, that most studio gates are not designed to take guitar signals directly. Either buy a dedicated guitar gate or use a DI box with a high input impedance at the input of a regular gate.

A guitar, particularly one being used with an overdrive effect, has a fast, biting attack, which means the gate needs to be set near or at its fastest attack time. The release time depends on the style of the piece of music being played, but as a general rule, the gate release should be set as fast as possible without allowing the tail ends of decaying notes to be clipped off. The release setting may range from a few tens of milliseconds for staccato, distorted guitar to half a second or more for slow, clean passages.

Because electric guitars tend to have a limited frequency response (due to the speakers traditionally used in guitar amplifiers) I often find that a dynamic noise filter produces better results than a gate and quite a high degree of processing can be applied without compromising the tone. Excessive hum is harder to deal with than noise, and short of using sophisticated digital hum filters (banks of narrow notch filters set to the frequency of the hum and its harmonics), avoidance is invariably better than trying to solve the problem after the event.

Keyboards

You might think that electronic keyboard instruments don't need gates; they are usually DI'd into the mixer and so can't pick up noise. This is true to an extent, but many keyboards actually create noise of their own, particularly low-cost digital synths or older models. This is sometimes evident only between notes or during the decay of notes, so an improvement can often be effected using a gate. However, because synthesised sounds can have virtually any envelope, the attack and release times

of the gate must be set accordingly; there is no 'one-size-fits-all' setting. Apply the general rule of the fastest attack you can get without clicks and the fastest release you can get without chopping off the decay of the sound. With some sounds, you may get retriggering during the decay, but increasing the hold time will help eliminate this.

A dynamic noise filter type of single-ended noise reduction unit will give even better results as it will reduce the noise during the decay portion of the synth sounds, not just in the pauses. Indeed, because these work well on complete mixes, it may be worth creating a stereo subgroup of all the keyboards (or at least the more noisy ones) and patching this through the dynamic noise filter using the subgroup insert points.

Drums

Gating is used on drums not only to clean up the sound but also to modify it by giving a fast, clean decay. With bass drums or toms that tend to ring, for example, a gate would close down, cut out the ring and give a tighter sound. Because drum sounds are by nature very transient, the fastest possible attack time should be set and the release time adjusted by ear.

In the case of a close-miked drum kit, gating is generally employed to improve the separation, but as there is likely to be a significant amount of spillage between microphones, the threshold level might have to be quite high and there is the attendant risk of missing quiet beats. For this reason, frequency conscious gates are nearly always preferred in this application as they can be tuned to the sound of the drum keying them, whilst rejecting (to some extent) the sounds of other differently pitched drums and cymbals. This is particularly important in the case of the snare drum, where hi-hat spillage might otherwise be a serious problem. A word of warning, though: setting the filters to give a lot of top cut will delay the opening of the gate slightly and may affect the attack of the instrument being gated.

Another problem is that when the gate does open, sound spillage from any other drums or cymbals playing at the same time as the wanted sound will be allowed through the gate. And this, in the case of the hi-hat and snare drum, will make any hi-hat beat falling on a snare beat slightly louder than it should be as it will be picked up by two mics instead of one. This may not be noticeable, but some engineers go to the trouble of using the other channel of the gate for the hi-hat mic, setting it to duck instead of gate and triggering it from the same source as the snare drum gate. If both sets of controls are identically configured and the floor control correctly adjusted on the gate handling the hi-hats, the signal level from the hi-hat mic will drop by a preset amount whenever the snare drum gate opens, thus keeping the combined hi-hat level reasonably constant.

Although not a perfect solution, careful setting of the floor control should enable the increase in hi-hat volume on the snare beats to be 'tuned' out – though there may be some image shift in the hi-hat sound if the snare drum and hi-hat are panned to radically different parts of the soundstage. However, the contribution of the overhead mics generally helps to even this out. This crosstalk problem also applies to crash and ride cymbals, but here the problem can be minimised if the drummer can be persuaded to mount the cymbals at a reasonable distance above the toms rather than right over them.

Special Effects

The previous technique of setting one side of the gate to act as a ducker may be used in conjunction with a long attack time to create automatic panning every time the input exceeds the threshold. The way this works is that both sides of the gate are fed from the same signal and the two outputs panned hard left and hard right. If the floor control is set for maximum attenuation, the signal on one channel will fade out at the same rate as the other fades in. The same applies to the release time settings.

If this setup is further modified by keying the gate from an external low-frequency oscillator running at anything from 5 to 50Hz, the input signal will be rapidly panned from one side to the other at whatever speed the oscillator is running. With fast attack and release settings, the signal is chopped into bursts coming from alternate sides and this too can be effective in small doses, especially on vocals or electric guitar.

Gate Chopping

Most gate applications are concerned with fixing problems, but it's also possible to use a gate to produce very creative effects, perhaps the most impressive being the chopping effect touched upon earlier in this chapter. Here the gate is triggered via the key input and is set up with a fast attack and release time. The key input is often derived from a drum machine or sequenced MIDI instrument with a constant envelope, for example an organ patch, and this is programmed to play a simple rhythm. At its simplest, this could be on for an eighth of a bar, off for an eighth of bar, on for eighth of a bar and so on. The note played is irrelevant; you only need a sound to trigger the gate. Now, if you put a completely different sound into the gate's main input, for example, a distorted guitar played continually, this will be chopped into four bursts per bar. You can try any rhythmic sequence you like, and the chopped sound will always follow it. This trick is used extensively in dance music production, and the patch for doing it is illustrated in Figure 6.8.

Further variations on this technique include leaving the original sound untreated, but chopping its reverb to create a rhythmic feature. Any sound can be chopped effectively providing it is continuous.

MIDI sound sources can be chopped without requiring a gate at all. Because most MIDI devices respond to Controller 7 as a master volume controller, it's possible to create control tracks in your sequencer where Controller 7 is set to 127 when you want to the sound on and 0 when you want it off. A sequencer with a graphical editing package makes this easier as you can draw in the controller information as a series of straight lines as shown in Figure 6.9. Favourite chopping sequences can be stored in a dummy song and then pasted into any song you are working on. You could also combine level and panning information so that sounds jump from side to side as they are chopped. Any MIDI sound source can be chopped in this way, but continuous pad sounds, strings and organs work best because of their relatively constant levels.

MIDI sequencers with audio recording capabilities sometimes allow standard MIDI commands to be used to control the audio level and pan positions, in which

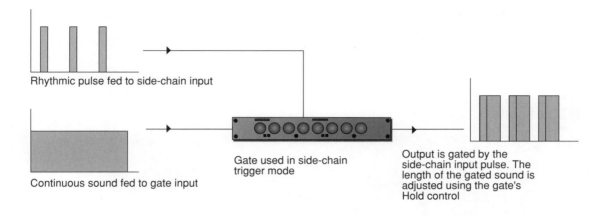

Rhythmic pulse fed to side-chain input

Continuous sound fed to gate input

Gate used in side-chain trigger mode

Output is gated by the side-chain input pulse. The length of the gated sound is adjusted using the gate's Hold control

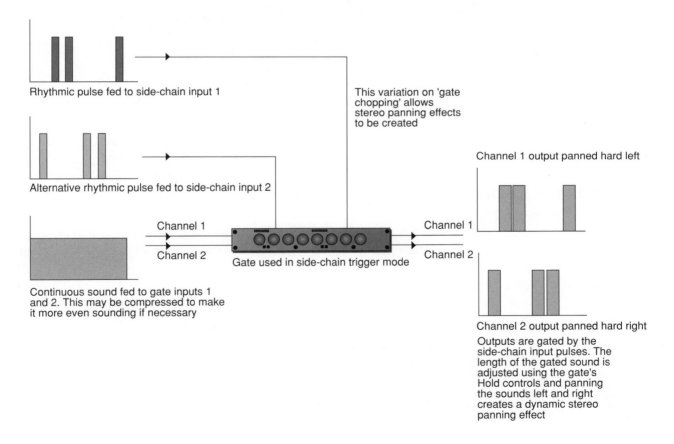

Rhythmic pulse fed to side-chain input 1

This variation on 'gate chopping' allows stereo panning effects to be created

Alternative rhythmic pulse fed to side-chain input 2

Channel 1 output panned hard left

Channel 1

Channel 2

Gate used in side-chain trigger mode

Channel 1

Channel 2

Continuous sound fed to gate inputs 1 and 2. This may be compressed to make it more even sounding if necessary

Channel 2 output panned hard right

Outputs are gated by the side-chain input pulses. The length of the gated sound is adjusted using the gate's Hold controls and panning the sounds left and right creates a dynamic stereo panning effect

Figure 6.8: Gate chopping

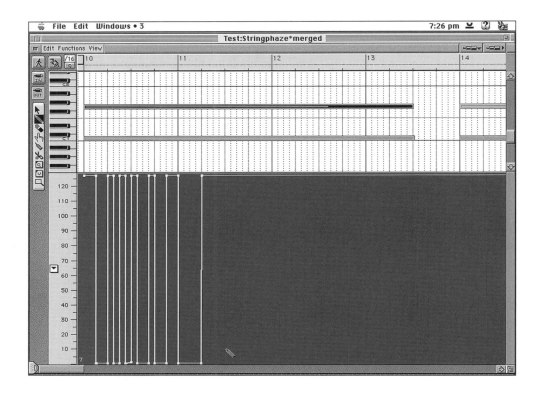

Figure 6.9: MIDI chopping

Digital Noise Reduction

Digital de-noising systems, which may be implemented in both hardware and software, are far more sophisticated than gates or expanders, and generally work by first splitting the incoming signal into a large number of separate frequency bands. Most systems split the audio into 512 or more different bands, where each band is equipped with the digital equivalent of its own expander. When the signal within the band falls to a threshold set just above the noise floor, the signal within that band is attenuated. Done properly, this can significantly reduce the side effects that beset simple gating or expansion because only those bands in which nothing is happening are attenuated. In any band showing 'above-threshold' activity, the signal is unaffected, as is the noise within those bands, but in most cases,

case you can try all these techniques without needing any additional equipment.

the wanted signal will mask noise occurring within the same frequency band.

The trick is figuring out how to set several hundred different thresholds to the right level. Having a common control is fine if the noise spectrum is flat, but in real life, the noise energy tends to increase at low frequencies, and with certain sources, there may be peaks in the noise spectrum.

Most affordable systems rely on there being a short section of background noise with no signal present directly before or after the recording of the wanted material. A short section of this noise, usually less than one second long, is selected and then the software is asked to 'learn' the noise characteristics. In effect, the software performs a spectrum analysis of this noise sample, so it is vitally important not to clean up the start and end of tracks or mixes that may need de-noising until after the de-noising has been done.

The information from this 'learn' scan is then used

to automatically set the thresholds within the different frequency bands to just above the noise floor, though most systems allow further manual adjustments to be made if required. Most of the time, it is only necessary to move the overall threshold up or down by a fixed amount to achieve optimum results. Figure 6.10 shows a screen shot of a commercially available software plug-in package. As a rule, computer-based systems have more adjustable parameters than hardware de-noisers, but most are relatively simple to operate.

Although it is possible to completely mute the contents of any frequency band where the signal has fallen below the threshold, to do so often results in unpleasant side effects. As individual filter bands cross through the threshold (due to fluctuating noise levels), when the adjacent bands are muted they tend to 'ring' or 'chirp' at the characteristic frequency of the band, producing an unnatural tinkling sound. This sound occurs at a very low level, but in the absence of noise the effect can be quite disconcerting. A better compromise is reached by attenuating rather than muting the 'below threshold' bands, and in most commercial systems this value is user-adjustable. In practice, an improvement in noise of several dBs is possible with virtually no side effects, though much depends on the type of material being processed and the quality of the noise-removal software. Pop music with limited dynamics may sometimes be processed much more heavily with no ill effects, whereas a solo piano or similar recording will be the first to show up any shortcomings in the system. My own method of adjustment relies on starting with a high level of attenuation, then reducing the amount of attenuation until the residual noise just hides the tinkling. If too much processing is applied, low-level detail such as reverb tails may also suffer, so it is very important to listen critically while adjusting this kind of system.

More Advanced Digital Systems

One reason a basic multi-band noise reduction system can only bring about a limited improvement in noise performance without audible side effects is partly due to the fact that noise doesn't have a constant spectrum, but may change throughout a recording as

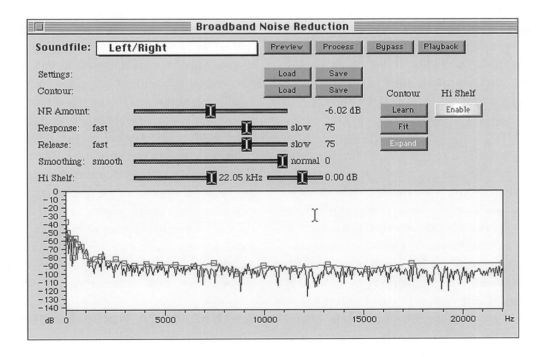

Figure 6.10: Multi-band digital noise reduction

noisy sources are faded in and out of the mix. Also, noise, being statistical in nature, tends not to be as predictable as perhaps we'd like it to be. It is this changing noise spectrum that causes the levels in each band to jitter either side of the threshold causing ringing or chirping. Raising the overall threshold may reduce the chirping effect, but then other audible side effects become apparent, such as a loss of low-level detail in the signal being processed, or a 'choked', lifeless sound. Advances are constantly being made in this area and even inexpensive systems tend to include intelligent threshold management designed to reduce the magnitude of ringing or chirping.

A more advanced approach is to use a system that can mathematically differentiate noise from wanted signal on a continual basis so that, in effect, the thresholds within the bands are updated several times per second. Such systems don't require an isolated noise sample to analyse, which is an advantage when you're dealing with a master tape where all the recordings have been topped and tailed to remove all traces of noise prior to the start and end of the tracks.

By constantly adapting to the changing noise spectrum, these systems are able to provide around twice as much noise reduction before side effects again become apparent. They are, however, very expensive, and often their use is confined to professional studios or audio restoration facilities – for example, they are often used in restoring old analogue tape recordings for digital release.

De-clicking

Another process that can be done effectively in the digital domain is de-clicking, a process designed to reduce or remove the annoyance of clicks in a recording caused by such things as digital glitching or scratches on records that have been transferred from vinyl to a digital format. De-clickers use elaborate algorithms that analyse the behaviour of the wanted signal and also use stored information about the characteristics of clicks and scratches to identify the sections where problems are occurring. This isn't easy as some naturally occurring sounds can sound very much like clicks, so there's usually some kind of adjustable user threshold as well as a system for

auditioning just that information the system is set to remove. For example, you may be able to audition just the clicks to make sure no wanted audio is being mistakenly identified.

Once the parameters have been set up, the file can be processed, and in the case of both de-noisers and de-clickers, slower computers do this off-line while faster machines or those with DSP assistance can do the job in real time. Hardware de-clickers work in real time.

In the case of de-clicking, removing the clicks isn't enough as this would leave gaps in the waveform. Part of the software's job is to make an educated guess as to what the missing piece looks like and reconstruct it. Though the reconstructions may not be entirely accurate, they're usually of such short duration that any momentary increase in distortion is not audible. At worst, there may still be a very low-level click where once there was a loud one!

De-crackling

A further process used almost exclusively for the recovery of vinyl recordings is de-crackling. Vinyl records and acetate 78s pick up dust in the grooves, which eventually causes the groove to become scratched. These scratches sound like crackles when played back, but unlike background hiss, crackles are very definite events. Unfortunately, because the crackles are continuous in most cases, using a de-clicking algorithm won't help as it would attempt to remove virtually the whole file, leaving little or none of the original recording from which to calculate the missing sections. The only solution is to use elaborate modelling techniques to identify what is real signal, and as few companies build successful de-cracklers, the precise working of these algorithms is a closely guarded secret.

For high-quality record restoration, separate de-noising, de-clicking and de-crackling processes are needed, though given enough hardware or processing power, these could all be carried out simultaneously.

Cutting-Edge Noise Removal

If audio is examined as a simple time-domain signal, noise removal is very difficult, but if it can be converted into the frequency domain, then lots of new possibilities become available. One of the newer technologies uses frequency domain analysis to show unwanted noises as coloured areas on a computer screen where the operator can correlate the visual image with what's heard over the monitors. Specific sections of the audio spectrum may then be 'selected' (for the duration of the unwanted event) on screen for processing, allowing seemingly impossible tasks to be achieved such as the removal of a page-turn noise or cough. Once the problem area has been selected for removal, the software synthesises the missing frequency components based on what was happening either side of the problem area. To date, impressive results have been achieved using this technology and it is inevitable that it will eventually become available in lower-cost plug-ins.

7 PANNING AND POSITIONING

In the recording studio, the usual way of creating a stereo perspective is to use pan pots to position essentially mono sound sources across a stereo soundstage. By varying the balance of the sound coming from the left and right speakers, the apparent source of the sound can be positioned anywhere between the speakers. However, the human hearing system uses rather more than the amplitude differences between the two ears to determine the position of a sound source. It also compares the phase of the sound arriving at our ears, so that if a sound reaches the right ear slightly before the left, it is perceived as coming from the right-hand side. This latter principle can be demonstrated by splitting a signal into two and delaying one side of the split by 10ms or so using a DDL. If the delayed and undelayed signals are then panned left and right respectively and set at equal levels, the sound will still appear to originate from the speaker fed from the undelayed signal. This is sometimes referred to as the Haas, or precedence, effect.

The purpose of this short chapter is not to give a thorough discussion on the principles of stereo sound, but to investigate some of the less obvious ways of using everyday signal processing to create the illusion of stereo width or movement. Given that most of the effects discussed are available as software plug-ins, experimenting with the ideas put forward in this chapter is much simpler than it was when this book was first written.

Autopanning

An autopanner is, at its simplest, a kind of electronic pan pot controlled by an LFO (low-frequency oscillator) such as you might find in a chorus or vibrato unit. A mono signal is fed into the unit and there are two outputs between which the signal is panned in a repetitive, cyclic manner. This is achieved in the analogue domain by placing a VCA (voltage controlled amplifier), in each signal path and feeding them from a common LFO. The control signal from the LFO is inverted in phase before being applied to one of the VCAs, so that its rise and fall is a mirror image of the signal fed to the other VCA. Figure 7.1 outlines this arrangement. The digital equivalent works in much the same way.

Such a simple autopanner might be fed into two mixer channels, panned left and right, to make a sound within the mix move back and forth across the soundstage. This was popular in the '60s (and much used by artists such as Jimi Hendrix), but would probably be considered unsubtle by modern standards, though it might have applications in dance music. With the LFO running slowly, the sound would drift in a leisurely fashion from left to right, while at a higher rate, say 5 to 10Hz, it might sound a little like a Leslie cabinet (a mechanical means of producing a chorus effect by placing rotating baffles in front of the speakers).

MIDI Control

A more subtle use for this type of panner is to move an effect such as echo or reverb back and forth while the untreated sound remains in a fixed position. Ideally this movement should be timed to relate to the tempo of the music, but with a simple free-running panner this can only be approximate. A number of multi-effects units include MIDI controllable panning as one of their effect options, so if you're working

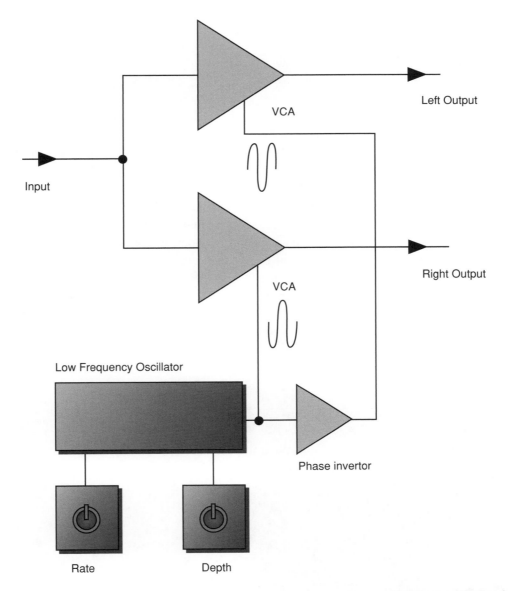

Input

VCA

Left Output

VCA

Right Output

Low Frequency Oscillator

Phase invertor

Rate

Depth

Figure 7.1: Electronic panner

alongside a MIDI sequencer it should be possible to use MIDI clock to synchronise the pan rate to the tempo of your track, even if the sequence includes tempo changes. It's also common for software plug-in effects, including panning, to be tempo syncable, which makes setting up these effects much easier than when using hardware.

The next refinement comprises two panner circuits in one unit and is configured so that instead of one sound moving from left to right, a stereo signal can be fed in and the two channels made to change places at a rate set by the LFO. Again this is something that may be possible using a multi-effects unit, and as with the previous example, the pan rate could be controlled by MIDI if required.

All the above effects can be achieved manually using a digital console with dynamic automation as pan movements are stored along with EQ changes and levels. You may not be able to trigger the pans via MIDI, but you can operate the controls manually while in automation record mode and, in some systems you can copy pan data from one part of a song to another.

Most sound sources, such as MIDI synths or audio tracks, that are recorded into a MIDI sequencer may also be panned automatically using MIDI controller data for the MIDI tracks and mix automation data for the audio tracks. The majority of sequencers allow you to draw in your pans graphically rather than having to enter strings of numbers. One useful tip is to create a dummy song, and within it create short sequences of pan data, for example, one pan to the bar, two pans to the bar, four pans to the bar and so on. You can also create rhythmic pans. Use this song to store all your pan ideas, then when you want to use one in a new composition, cut and paste it into your current song then copy it for as many bars as you need it. The tempo will always match that of your current song because your pan information is stored as so many pans per bar of a sequence, not as a specific pan rate. Figure 7.2 shows a screen from a MIDI sequencer where pan data has been drawn in.

Triggering

Although dedicated autopanners are rare because of the low cost of digital multi-effects units, there are still a number of analogue units to be found on the second-hand market, and just occasionally you'll find one that can create effects that the average multi-effects unit can't handle – although, to be fair, just about any panning effect can be set up using a MIDI sequencer with audio tracks.

Some analogue autopanners have a synchronising function, which enables an external pulse (from a drum machine, for example) to be used to initiate a sweep from left to right. In this case, the LFO speed control might well set the rate at which the sound moves from one side to the other, but once the sweep is complete, no further movement takes place until another trigger

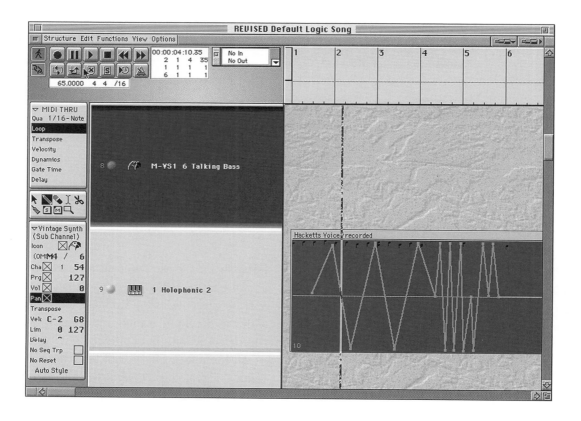

Figure 7.2: MIDI sequencer showing pan data

pulse is received. When the next pulse comes along, the sound moves back to the other side. This is useful in systems where there may be no MIDI source to trigger the panning, though you still have to record a separate audio track of clicks (drum machine side – sticks are usually fine), to act as triggers.

A panner with a sync function, either analogue pulse or MIDI, is far more versatile than one without because it can be synchronised to the beat of the music. As the sweep occurs only when triggered, you could have, for example, one sweep per beat in the first bar of a song followed by two sweeps per beat in the second; you could even arrange for each note in a sequence to come from alternate sides. Once again, this effect is best used sparingly and it is often sufficiently dramatic to pan only the effect returns.

Musical Applications

Apart from the more obvious effects already mentioned, it is possible to connect additional signal processors to create completely new effects. One technique is to patch the two outputs from the panner to a stereo graphic equaliser and then set both channels of the equaliser to give radically different tones. As the panner moves the signal from side to side, the tone will change, and depending on the rate of pan you can simulate phasing, rotary speaker cabinets, tonal morphing and so on. You can even pan both signals to the same part of the soundstage and produce the cyclic tonal change without the movement if that's more suitable.

Getting a little more adventurous, you could try patching the two outputs into different effects entirely, giving you the opportunity to crossfade from one effect to another – with or without left/right movement. You might try flanging on one output and a short, slap-back echo on the other, two flangers set to different sweep rates or even echo on one side and fuzz on the other. The effects that can be created in this way are limited only by the imagination, though

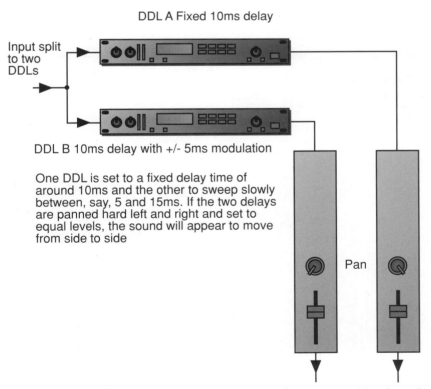

DDL A Fixed 10ms delay

Input split to two DDLs

DDL B 10ms delay with +/- 5ms modulation

One DDL is set to a fixed delay time of around 10ms and the other to sweep slowly between, say, 5 and 15ms. If the two delays are panned hard left and right and set to equal levels, the sound will appear to move from side to side

Pan

Mixer channels set to equal levels and panned hard left and right

Figure 7.3: DDL panning

a synchronised pan would work best for most types of music. It can be interesting to pan the affected sounds left and right while positioning the untreated sound near the centre of the mix, though in some applications you may prefer to dispense with the dry sound altogether.

DDL Panning

If you don't have an autopanner or a panning facility within your multi-effects unit, you can achieve some interesting psychoacoustic panning effects by using two DDLs (either hardware or plug-ins). Figure 7.3 shows the arrangement: here a signal is split and fed through two DDLs, one of which is set to a fixed delay time of around 10ms and the other to sweep slowly between, say, 5 and 15ms. If the two delays are panned hard left and right and set to equal levels, the sound will appear to move from side to side as the modulated signal first lags, then leads the signal with the fixed delay. This effect is called psychoacoustic panning because it works on the Haas

effect discussed earlier and not by changing levels. When this effect is being created using plug-ins, the audio tracks may be advanced by the requisite number of milliseconds to cancel out the delay introduced by the static delay.

Pseudo Stereo

As stated earlier, there is more to creating a sense of stereo perspective than positioning a mono sound somewhere between the left and right speakers. In real life, reflections from our surroundings mingle with the direct sound, and even if these are too brief to create the impression of reverberation they can still create a sense of space, which our brain manages to interpret. This can be simulated using a stereo digital reverb set to a very short room or ambience setting, but there are other methods that can produce more out-of-the-ordinary results.

Figure 7.4 shows a patch that can be set up to process a mono signal to provide the impression of stereo width. Notice that three mixer channels are

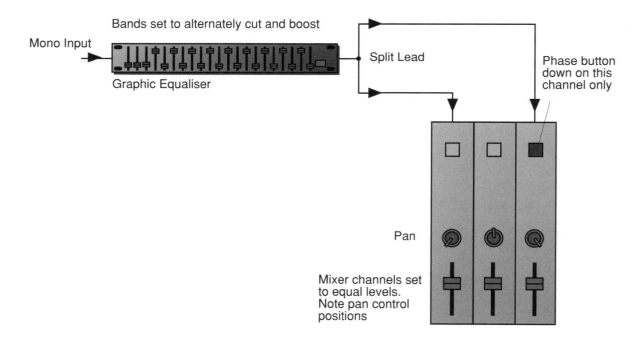

Figure 7.4: Pseudo stereo using graphic EQs

used. The original signal is split with one part fed directly to the middle channel and panned to the centre. The other part of the signal is then fed to a graphic equaliser set up to produce a pseudo-random frequency response by positioning alternate faders to heavy boost and heavy cut. The output from the equaliser is again split and fed to the other two mixer channels – one panned left and the other right. Finally, the phase button on one of these channels is depressed. Check the diagram if this sounds confusing. The resulting effect is a right-hand signal, which is the sum of the centre and the equalised signals, and a left-hand signal, which is the difference between the two (because of the phase inversion caused by using the phase button).

In practice, this patch goes some way towards simulating the comb filtering produced when direct and reflected sounds interact in a real environment, and though it doesn't create a specific sense of direction, it does produce a definite illusion of width and depth.

It is also possible to replace the graphic equaliser by a DDL set to a fixed delay of between 5 and 15ms. If the mix control is then adjusted to give even levels of direct and delayed sound, the output will be coloured by the 'comb filter' effect caused by adding the delayed sound to the undelayed sound. The delay is too short to sound like an echo but is long enough to ensure that some frequencies are shifted enough to cancel while others add – according to their frequency.

A graph of this filter effect would show a whole series of peaks and troughs, which because of their spiky appearance gave rise to the name 'comb filter'. In practice, this kind of filtering is just as effective as a graphic equaliser in creating the illusion of a stereo image and it has the advantage that a very shallow, slow modulation can be applied to create a sense of movement as well as of depth.

A number of software plug-ins utilise these principles to create a sense of stereo width and space from a mono source, but in practical applications it may be best to avoid processing frequencies below 100Hz as bass sounds can be changed quite drastically by phase/EQ tricks of this kind. Furthermore, because we tend to extract less of a sense of direction from low frequencies than we do from higher frequencies, there's little benefit to processing very low frequencies. At one time, such methods of generating pseudo-stereo sounds from mono sources were used for repurposing mono recordings for stereo release but are now more likely to be used on mono components within a mix, such as the output from an analogue synthesiser.

3D Panning

A number of multi-effects units include 3D panning algorithms that attempt to make the sound source appear as though it is either circling in front of the listener or, in some cases, actually circling around the listener as shown in Figure 7.5. The mechanism for doing this is explained more fully in the chapter on enhancers, but in essence these devices attempt to simulate the auditory cues that occur in nature when a sound is moved around the listener. These cues mainly comprise left/right level differences, left/right arrival time differences (due to the distance between the ears), and spectral filtering to simulate the change in perceived frequency response caused by head masking and the shape of the outer ear. None of these systems is completely successful because no two people have exactly the same shape outer ears, and to some extent we rely on head movement to identify sound direction. Even so, these treatments can be used to add considerable interest to a mix if they are confined to what I call secondary sounds, such as additional percussion, special synth effects and so on. It is generally best not to treat the main elements of the mix as 3D processing tends not to translate very well to mono.

In my experience, 3D effects work best when the sound source is kept moving, so a 3D panner is probably the most effective way to employ the effect. Harmonically rich sounds of the type that respond well to flanging seem to work best, especially when you're after the effect of a sound passing behind or closely in front of the listener, with tonally neutral sounds (such as vocals), being least successful. Bright percussive sounds such as bells, triangles and similar instruments can also respond reasonably well. To avoid the effect becoming repetitive or boring it may

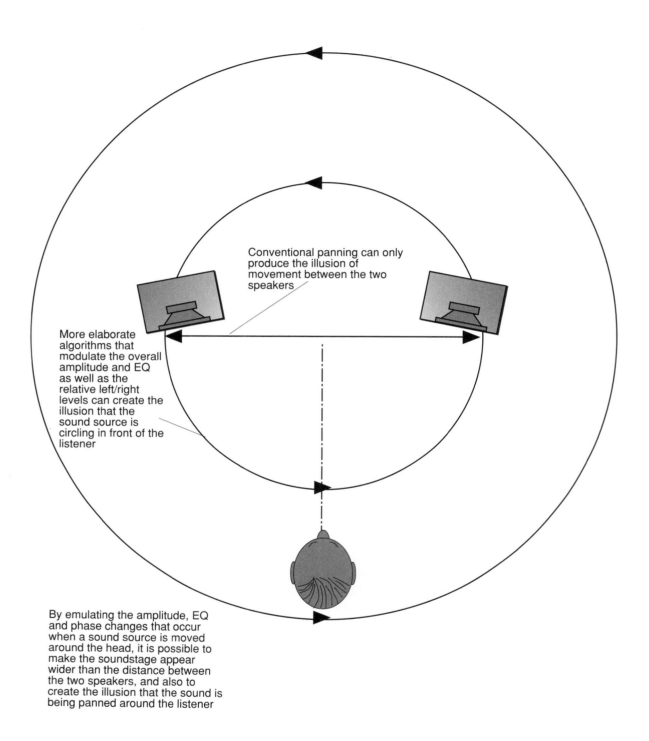

Conventional panning can only produce the illusion of movement between the two speakers

More elaborate algorithms that modulate the overall amplitude and EQ as well as the relative left/right levels can create the illusion that the sound source is circling in front of the listener

By emulating the amplitude, EQ and phase changes that occur when a sound source is moved around the head, it is possible to make the soundstage appear wider than the distance between the two speakers, and also to create the illusion that the sound is being panned around the listener

Figure 7.5: 3D panning

be worth confining it to short sections of your mix such as intros, bridges or solos.

It's also wise to bear in mind when mixing any kind of dance music that most people will hear this over a club PA system, and very few people will be in the ideal position to benefit from the true stereo perspective of your mix. What sounds like a true pan from midway between the speakers may simply sound like level modulation to somebody standing close to one speaker or the other.

A number of software plug-ins are available for creating both conventional and 3D panning effects, some of which also include doppler shift simulation so that the pitch of sources apparently moving away from you drop in pitch slightly while those moving towards you increase in pitch. The musical usefulness of such doppler effects is questionable but there's undoubtedly an application for them in film soundtrack work where they can enhance 'moving' sound effects.

Quality Issues

Because a panner processes the complete signal rather than being an effect added to the untreated sound, it must work over the full audio bandwidth and have low noise and distortion. Also pay particular attention to the different ways the panner may be triggered as this is the key to its flexibility. Obviously a panner is a processor rather than an effect as it treats the whole of the signal passing through it, so connection should be via insert points, not via effect sends and returns.

8 DIGITAL DELAY EFFECTS

While most standalone compressors, equalisers and gates still use analogue circuitry, virtually all effects that involve time manipulation in any form – delays, reverb units, pitch shifters and so on – rely on digital electronics. Before looking at any specific processors, however, it is advantageous to have at least some insight into how digital systems work – if only to help in interpreting specifications sheets when evaluating equipment.

All digital signal processors designed to work with analogue input signals, such as music, must first convert the input into a digital format. An analogue signal is one where the voltage varies in proportion to the original event; in the case of sound, the signal voltage varies in proportion to changes in air pressure. A rapidly vibrating string, for example, will create rapid air pressure fluctuations, which a microphone can convert into variations in voltage. A digital system, on the other hand, works on binary numbers – 1s and 0s – which are represented in the circuit by the presence or absence of a nominally fixed voltage. Converting an analogue signal into digital information involves measuring the analogue voltage at regular intervals and from this producing a series of binary numbers.

Every second of sound may be represented by several tens of thousands of numbers, each relating to a particular instant in time. If this concept is difficult to grasp, think of it like a cine film, where each frame is slightly different from the next. By running these through the projector in quick succession, the illusion of smooth movement is created. So it is with sound: if you have enough instantaneous measurements per second, the original sound can be recreated. The real

question is: how many measurements or samples do we have to take to capture the full human hearing range? That's where sampling theory comes in.

Sampling Theory

This process of measuring and digitising minute sections of the input signal is known as sampling. Figure 8.1 shows a rather simplistic view of what happens when a signal is sampled: it is cut into slices rather like a loaf of bread and the height of each slice is measured. As you can see, the slices or samples have 'flat tops' (corresponding to the voltage measured during the sampling time), so they don't accurately follow the curve of the waveform. From this, you might deduce that the thinner the slices, the more accurate, or less distorted, the sound will end up, and this is indeed the case.

Sampling theory states that you must sample at a minimum of twice the frequency of the highest harmonic you are likely to encounter if the output is to be reconstructed accurately. If the sampling frequency is less than twice the highest frequency, additional frequencies will be introduced based on the difference between the sampling frequency and the audio frequency. These frequencies were never originally present and sound musically unpleasant. This effect is known as aliasing and, to prevent it, we need to filter out any frequencies in the original signal that are above half the sampling frequency. However, because no filter is perfect, the sampling may be a little higher than twice the maximum audio frequency, which is why for an audio bandwidth of 20kHz we have ended up with a minimum sampling frequency of 44.1kHz, not 40kHz.

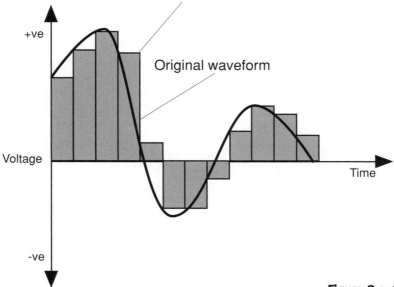

The signal voltage is sampled at regular intervals so that the original signal can be reconstructed by, in effect, 'joining the dots'. The sample levels are converted to binary numbers for digital storage and manipulation

Original waveform

+ve

Voltage

Time

-ve

Figure 8.1: Sampling a waveform

The other factor affecting audio quality is the accuracy with which our samples are measured, and the more digital bits used to represent each sample, the more accurate the measurement. CDs and DAT tapes use 16-bit sampling, though many digital multitrack recorders, sound cards and signal processors now use 20- or 24-bit conversion.

Digital numbers go in steps, there are no halves or thirds of a bit, and the number of steps depends on the resolution of the analogue-to-digital converter used. Eight bits will give you only two to the power of eight steps – which works out at 256. That means that your loudest signal could have 256 steps but quieter ones will have considerably fewer. This gives a rather poor level of resolution and causes what's known as quantisation distortion. Nowadays, 8-bit sound is rarely used other than in some non-demanding computer applications.

Quantisation distortion actually sounds like noise – the main difference being that it disappears in the absence of a signal (unlike most other sources of noise). Using more bits gives a vast improvement in resolution and all serious digital processors now use a minimum of 16-bit sampling (as do CDs) with 24-bit being common for tapeless recorders, sound cards and digital outboard equipment. A 24-bit system divides the audio level into more than 16 million steps, which makes 8-bit's 256 steps look a little sad!

Each bit used in linear sampling (where the sampled step sizes are the same) yields a maximum of 6dB of dynamic range, so an 8-bit system can give you a dynamic range of only 48dB – about as noisy as a cheap cassette recorder. 16 bits, on the other hand, yields a maximum dynamic range of 96dB, which for most audio purposes is more than adequate. Even though 24-bit systems aren't perfected yet in terms of realising their maximum theoretical dynamic range of 144dB, they can still give practical dynamic ranges in excess of 120dB.

To recap: the higher the sampling frequency, the higher input frequencies the system can cope with – which, in turn, means a better frequency response. The trade-off is that the faster you sample, the more samples per second you have, so the more memory you need to store the sound – and that means either higher cost or shorter delays (in the case of digital delays or samplers). Fortunately, both random access memory (RAM) and hard drive space is considerably cheaper than it was when digital recording first became available, so data storage is no longer a major cost concern. This may be one reason that high resolution sample rates such as 96kHz and 192kHz are being explored more seriously.

Digital Delay Effects

To create a digital delay, you have to find somewhere to store one delay time's worth of samples before outputting them, so to create a mono delay of one second with a 20kHz upper sampling limit and a 44.1kHz sampling rate, you have to find somewhere to store 44,100 samples. This is done using random access memory similar to that used in computers. By continually updating and outputting the contents, a one-second delay can be created, and for more delay you simply need more RAM. While hardware effects use their own RAM chips, plug-in effects use the RAM of the host computer.

Early DDLs – or digital delay lines, to give them their full title – compromised both on-frequency response and on-delay time to keep the cost down, but most modern machines, even budget multi-effect models and simple plug-ins, offer a full 20kHz bandwidth with several seconds of delay time. Once you have the capacity to create a long delay, it is a simple matter to set up a shorter one by switching out some of the memory. A basic, dedicated DDL uses memory switching, often connected to a coarse range switch and a fine control. Though such basic DDLs are fairly primitive by modern standards, they are still in demand because of their intuitive control interfaces.

Digital reverberation is very much more complex than digital delay and involves high-speed microprocessor or DSP manipulation of the digitised data to synthesise the thousands of individual echoes that go to make up natural-sounding reverberation. It is due to the complex nature of this process that the early digital reverb units were phenomenally expensive, though they're now available to suit virtually any budget. Natural digital reverberation does not require the kind of audio bandwidth encountered in delay technology and the frequency response may be as low as 10kHz without affecting the sound, though virtually all modern reverb units and plug-ins have a full 20Hz to 20kHz bandwidth.

A Practical DDL

Originally conceived as a successor to tape loop echo machines, DDLs soon acquired modulation controls that allowed them to produce a wide range of effects – from echo and doubling to chorus, flanging, ADT, vibrato and phasing. All these effects are available from a modern multi-effects unit and from many plug-ins, but it helps to understand how these are created by looking at the elements of a dedicated DDL.

Figure 8.2 shows the block diagram of a typical DDL. The input signal is first passed through a gain control, usually accompanied by some kind of metering system so that level can be properly adjusted to avoid clipping, yet still use as much of the dynamic range of the converters as possible. As with analogue, failure to set the input level correctly may result in either excess noise or, in the case of clipping, audible distortion. Just after the gain control, the signal splits and a proportion of the unprocessed signal passes directly to the output mix control, where it can be combined with the delayed sound.

The input to the delay line first encounters the ADC (analogue-to-digital converter) where it is turned into a continuous sequence of byte-sized numbers before being passed to the memory for short-term storage. The reading into and writing out of this memory is controlled in most cases by a microprocessor, which receives instructions from the range control so that more or less memory can be brought into play according to the amount of delay required. Also interacting with the memory part of the system is the sampling clock and the modulation oscillator. These are shown as separate blocks for the sake of clarity, but are more likely to be incorporated into the microprocessor section in an actual production model.

By varying the sample clock rate, the delay can be modulated to set up a cyclic change in pitch at the depth or speed required for the creation of chorus, flanging or vibrato effects. The shape of the

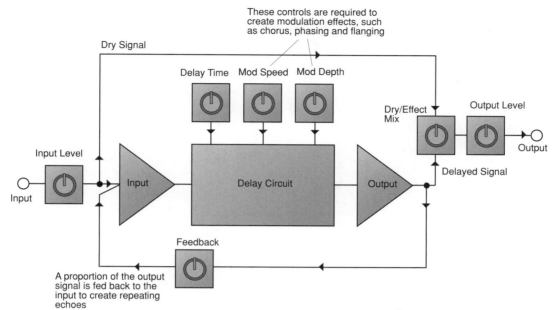

These controls are required to
create modulation effects, such
as chorus, phasing and flanging

Dry Signal

Delay Time   Mod Speed   Mod Depth

Dry/Effect
Mix

Output Level

Input Level

Output

Input

Input   Delay Circuit   Output

Delayed Signal

Feedback

A proportion of the output
signal is fed back to the
input to create repeating
echoes

Figure 8.2: Block diagram of a DDL

modulating wave is usually triangular or sinusoidal, both of which are capable of giving a fairly smooth sweep, though the sinusoid is generally considered to be the more natural-sounding of the two. Elaborate techniques (such as linear interpolation) are necessary to make the modulation effects sound as smooth as they did when everything was analogue, but that is (fortunately) a concern of the designer, not the user.

A short time later, the digital representation of the signal emerges from the memory and is subsequently mixed with the desired proportion of the undelayed signal. Originally, the undelayed signal tended to remain in the analogue domain, whereas in more modern effects units and in plug-ins the clean signal path is also fed via the digital converters as this simplifies the design and places the signal level under digital control. However, guitar players in particular tend to prefer the sound of an analogue signal path for the untreated portion of the sound, so some specialised guitar processors maintain an all-analogue direct signal path.

DDL Feedback

Another major DDL control adjusts the amount of output signal fed back into the input so that repeating echoes can be set up. Feedback gain must be less

than unity however, otherwise the echoes will build up in level rather than decaying, resulting in an uncontrollable howl. On some models there is a phase invert switch in the feedback path, which gives a subtle change in sound at very short delay times – particularly with flanging effects. Its use determines whether the flanger cancels or accentuates odd or even harmonics, and the choice of setting is entirely a matter of taste.

Creating Delay Effects

Perhaps the easiest effect to set up is the single delay. For this, modulation depth and rate and the feedback controls should be set to minimum and the range control adjusted for the length of delay required. You can then use the fine control to match the delay time to the speed of the song you're working on – the effect is usable from a short slap-back echo around 20ms to a distinct repeat occurring a second or more after the original sound. To convert this single repeat into a true repeating echo it's simply a matter of advancing the feedback control. Whatever appears at the output is then fed back to the input and so goes through the delay again – the time taken for the echoes to die away being set by the amount of feedback. With the feedback full up, the echoes may

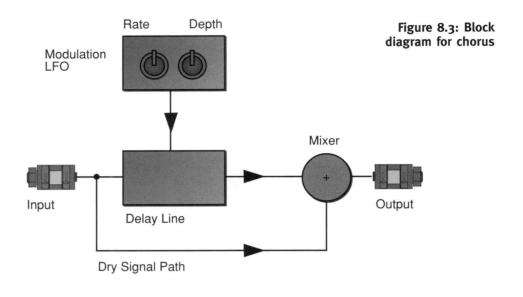

Figure 8.3: Block diagram for chorus

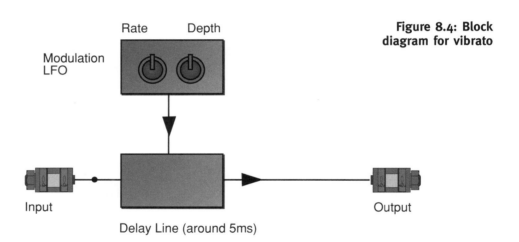

Figure 8.4: Block diagram for vibrato

go on indefinitely or even build up uncontrollably, so care must be taken when adjusting this control if you're working near the maximum setting.

Chorus is instantly recognisable (it sounds a little like two instruments playing the same part) and is frequently applied to guitar, bass and keyboards. It is obtained by setting the delay to a few tens of milliseconds and then introducing a little modulation at around 3Hz. For optimum results, the direct and delayed sound should be mixed equally and restraint

must be shown in relation to modulation depth, or the subtlety of the effect will be lost. As a rule, the correct settings are easy to determine by ear.

The reason that chorus is so named is because it creates the illusion of two or more instruments or voices playing together by simulating the difference in timing and pitch that always occurs when two or more people try to play exactly the same thing at the same time. Additionally, it has the effect of making certain electronic instruments (specifically string machines and synthesisers) sound more realistic. This is because synthesised waveforms tend to be far more rigidly structured than they would be in naturally occurring sounds – a cheap electronic organ, for example, can be made to produce a good impression of a pipe organ simply by adding a little chorus. Figure 8.3 shows the block diagram of a chorus effect.

By further shortening the delay to only a few milliseconds and then removing the untreated portion of the sound using the mix control, it is possible to produce true-pitch vibrato for instruments or vocals. Figure 8.4 shows the block diagram for vibrato. Adding the direct sound again will give an effect something like phasing, and gently increasing the feedback will produce flanging. Flanging produces a heavily comb-filtered whooshing sound and, like many effects, is difficult to describe to those who have never heard it before, but it is instantly recognisable and found favour in the '60s and early '70s as a 'psychedelic' treatment for pop records. It enjoyed a bit of a comeback with dance music where unsubtle effects are one of the main ingredients of a successful mix!

Flanging tends to sound best using a slower modulation frequency – around one second – and a little more depth than would be used for chorus. Changing the delay time will affect the notes and harmonics that the flanging picks out, while the

feedback phase switch, if fitted, provides a further sound option. Take care not to overload the input when using high levels of feedback, because the input signal is added to the fed-back sound before the ADC – so there's more going through the system than just the original signal. Ignore what the input level meter says and use your ears to decide when the input level is too high. Figure 8.5 shows the setup for flanging.

One extra feature that you will find on a good many DDLs is the hold button. This freezes any sound currently stored in the random access memory and recycles it rather like a tape loop; once the button is pressed, no new sounds are added to the memory. Of course, on its own this is of limited creative use, but a further feature available on some machines is a single-shot trigger facility whereby the sound stored in the hold mode can be played back once each time a trigger pulse or MIDI signal is received. This forms the basis of a very crude sampler, which, for example, will allow short percussive sounds to be triggered by a drum machine or similar trigger source. You'll find this facility in many multi-effects units as well as in dedicated DDLs.

Delay Applications

Simple delays and echoes are always popular both on vocals and instruments, but it's generally considered to be more useful if the delay time of the

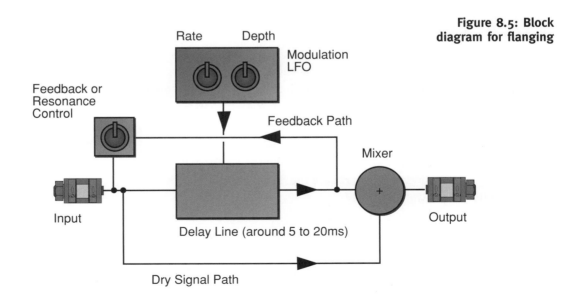

Figure 8.5: Block diagram for flanging

Rate   Depth

Modulation LFO

Feedback or Resonance Control

Feedback Path

Mixer

Input

Delay Line (around 5 to 20ms)

Output

Dry Signal Path

effect is matched to the tempo of the track so that you get one, two or four echoes per bar. You can also arrange your delay time to produce triplet measures. In this way, the repeats reinforce the beat of the song rather than detracting from it. However, it is possible to experiment with the delay time to create new and more complex rhythms by timing the repeats to occur in unexpected places – especially if you are treating drums or some other percussive sound source. Plug-in delays make this kind of effect very easy to set up as they tend to include the ability to sync to tempo.

One much-used trick is to add echo only to certain words or phrases, usually at the end of lines or verses. This is accomplished by turning up the echo or aux send control just before the phrase occurs and shutting it down again immediately afterwards. This ensures that the only words echoing are the ones you want. If you try to do the same thing using the effect return level control instead, you'll find you can't control exactly which words have echo and which don't. Again this is really easy using a sequencer or digital mixing console as the effect send return levels can be automated.

One problem to be aware of is that some DDLs distort more readily on high pitched sounds than on low ones, especially older models with less well-designed anti-aliasing filters. For this reason, it would probably be worthwhile doing a few tests (just as you might with an analogue tape recorder), to see what meter reading you need to give a clean result. You'll probably find that your input signal needs to be around 10dB less when treating tinkly DX synth sounds or real bells and cymbals, for example, than when treating vocals. Level setting can also be misleading with brass and sampled brass instruments, which tend to produce a spiky waveform where the peaks are much higher than the average figure indicated by a VU meter or where a peak meter reads only one half of the input waveform. Ironically, plug-ins, which tend to be cheaper than hardware, often produce the best-quality results for delay.

Most of the early rock singers used liberal amounts of vocal echo, and the famous John Lennon 'trippy' vocal sound relied heavily on short, 'slap-back' delay. At very short delay times, (1–50ms) increasing the feedback will give a resonant cardboard-tube or tunnel-echo sound, the pitch of the resonance being set by the delay time. This effect is useful in creating new sounds or modifying existing ones beyond recognition, and used with a synth, it can create the illusion of ring modulation or phase sync.

Using Chorus

Chorus is a wonderfully fluid effect and providing it is kept fairly subtle it can be used extensively without sounding gimmicky. It works well in mono but is much more impressive if the dry sound is panned to one side and the chorused sound to the other. This simulates one of the psychoacoustic tricks our ears produce in real life, creating a very wide, dynamic sound, which is particularly suited to string parts, textural keyboard sounds, electric guitar and electric bass – especially fretless. Because of the regular modulation, the electric chorus effect isn't entirely authentic compared with real life, but has gained acceptance as an effect in its own right. You can also use very gentle modulation on longer delays to create a combined chorus and echo effect.

If you have access to two mono chorus units and pan one to each side, you can create an even more dramatic effect, and fine-tuning the modulation controls to get them running at slightly different rates will improve things still further.

Modern multi-effects units and many plug-ins tend to provide a number of stereo chorus treatments, often using multi-tapped delays to give a more complex effect, so experimentation isn't as important as perhaps it once was. However, it's still possible to produce something interesting and unusual by patching together two or more discrete effects units (or plug-ins) rather than by using a single multi-effects box. When using plug-ins, try combining two different chorus plug-ins – ideally from different manufacturers – as this is more likely to produce a musically interesting variation.

ADT

Similar in many ways to chorus is ADT (artificial double tracking). This effect can be created by setting up a delay of around 100ms and then modulating the delayed signal so that there is a hint of pitch wavering. When added to the dry signal, this treatment gives the illusion of two instruments or voices playing together. It isn't as good as the real thing but it provides an acceptable alternative.

Bear in mind that when using the effects send circuit on your desk to create any of the effects that rely on a mix of the dry and delayed sounds, it is necessary to balance the 'delay only' output from the DDL with the untreated sound passing through the channel in order to obtain the optimum depth of effect.

Vibrato

Vibrato is essentially the same process as chorus but without any of the dry sound added, so it would be more appropriate to connect the DDL to the mixing desk via the channel insert point in this application, or to switch off all the routing buttons on the channel being treated so as to keep the dry sound out of the mix. The only advice here is to exercise discretion and not overdo the vibrato depth as the results tend to be quite extreme. Also, because there is no dry signal, the time delay must be kept short so as not to introduce a perceptible delay. Less than 7ms is ideal.

Phasing

The effect of phasing was originally achieved by simultaneously running two identical tapes on two tape recorders and then mixing the outputs together at equal levels. By manually slowing down one or other of the machines by simply using the hand to brake first one and then the other tape-supply reels, the two pieces of music would drift in and out of sync and the characteristic 'whooshing' phasing effect would be produced.

To approximate this effect using a DDL, it is important to ensure that the delayed and direct sound are as near equal in level as possible. The actual delay time is normally between 3 and 10ms, with a slow, shallow modulation applied to create the sweep effect. No feedback is used, but depending on the type of delay the tone colour of the effect will vary, so there is plenty of room for experimentation.

If you don't want a regular sweep, the modulation may be turned off and the sweep generated manually by slowly turning the delay time 'fine' control. This gives a more exact simulation of the original tape

effect – though it isn't quite authentic as the delay time can never pass through zero as it would when one tape recorder overtook the other.

If you are really keen on experimenting, you can use two DDLs, set to equal delays of 5ms or so and fed from the same input signal. The mix controls are both set for delayed signal only and the two DDL outputs mixed to mono – again with equal levels. If one of the DDLs is now modulated, either by its sweep oscillator or manually, true through-zero phasing is achieved, which is very similar to gentle tape flanging. As with all phasing this works best with instruments that produce a lot of upper harmonics such as distorted guitar, string synth or reverbed drums. The arrangement for doing this is shown in Figure 8.6. Increasing the feedback slightly will produce a stronger flanging effect.

Try changing the rate control from a slow sweep to a fast modulation and you'll see that the range of effects is quite wide. A very slow modulation rate generates a nice, evolving sweep, which can sound great on pad keyboard sounds while faster rates can sound similar to a rotary speaker cabinet.

You can also 'tune' which harmonics are affected by changing the basic delay time: the shorter the delay time, the higher the frequencies that are affected and vice versa. A delay time of between 1 and 3ms gives a thin, whining phase sound, whereas longer times sound fatter or smoother.

Tape Flanging

If you have an analogue open-reel tape machine (or a cassette player with varispeed) and a DAT machine, you can try to recreate the original effect by making a copy of the recording you want to process onto analogue tape. Next, copy this analogue recording onto DAT and mix the outputs of the two machines together at exactly the same level. Start both machines together (a little trial and error will be needed here), and use the varispeed control on the analogue machine to get the timing as close as you can. As you adjust the varispeed so that the analogue machine alternately overtakes the DAT machine, then falls behind again, the familiar tape-phasing sound should be produced. Using hand friction on the analogue machine reel to slow it down slightly is a good way to control the effect.

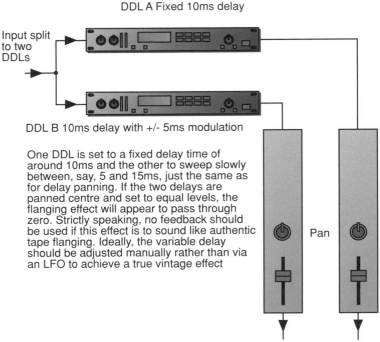

DDL A Fixed 10ms delay

Input split to two DDLs

DDL B 10ms delay with +/- 5ms modulation

One DDL is set to a fixed delay time of around 10ms and the other to sweep slowly between, say, 5 and 15ms, just the same as for delay panning. If the two delays are panned centre and set to equal levels, the flanging effect will appear to pass through zero. Strictly speaking, no feedback should be used if this effect is to sound like authentic tape flanging. Ideally, the variable delay should be adjusted manually rather than via an LFO to achieve a true vintage effect

Pan

Figure 8.6: 'Through-zero' phasing

Mixer channels set to equal levels and both panned centre

Delay Flanging

Flanging relies on a precise balance between the direct and delayed sounds to create the optimum effect so it may be as well to experiment first with the channel insert points on your desk rather than the aux sends. Once you've got the hang of it, you can try using the aux sends, but it is trickier to get the balance precisely right this way. Again, if you arrange it so that the flanged sound (an equal mix of dry and delayed signal) is panned to one side and a dry version of the signal is panned to the other, you'll find that the effect is much more dynamic and gives the illusion of movement as the flange sweeps through. This is a useful alternative to the ready made stereo flanging you get on most multi-effects units.

Flanging can be applied to any instrument or voice, but because of its distinctive nature, it is not appropriate in all contexts. Leaving a sound dry and flanging its reverb send provides a more subtle alternative, and this is used by a number of producers

to make the reverb shimmer. The more feedback is applied, the more aggressive the effect.

Essentially, flanging is similar to phasing, although it may use slightly longer delay times – say up to 50ms – and the feedback control is advanced to give a dramatic, swirling effect. In general terms, the slower the modulation rate, the more depth you can get away with using. The higher the feedback setting, the more 'whooshy' the sound.

Phase Invert

And now that mysterious phase invert button or parameter that your delay unit may or may not have; the effect of this is most noticeable on effects that use a very short delay time, particularly flanging. At delay times where you can hear the delay as a discrete echo, it will have virtually no effect. By inverting the phase of the signal fed back to the input, it allows different harmonics to be accentuated by the filtering process, providing a choice of two types of tonal colouration, one usually sounding 'thinner' than the other. Which one you use is entirely a matter of personal choice in context with the song you are working on.

Delay Panning

One aspect of the digital delay that is still much under-utilised is its ability to create panning effects, though this was touched upon in the chapter on panning where I described a phenomenon known as the 'precedence effect' that is related to the way in which our ears interpret the direction from which a sound is arriving. As our ears are physically spaced apart, a sound will arrive at one ear slightly before the other, and even though the time difference may be less than a millisecond or so, our brains are capable of deciding from which side the sound came first and from this determining its direction.

If we simulate this condition using a delay line and feed an undelayed signal into the left speaker and the same signal, delayed by a few milliseconds, into the right, we sense that the sound is originating from the left. To experiment with this effect, pick a sound with plenty of mid- and high-frequency information and ensure that the level feeding each speaker is the same. A delay of around 10ms is ideal because it is too short to give the sensation of an echo, yet too long to create serious phasing problems if the signals should be summed to mono at any stage.

You can also try dynamic delay panning using two delay lines, one with a fixed delay time and one modulated, as described more fully in the chapter on panning.

Freeze Looping

If you have a DDL or multi-effects unit that offers several seconds of delay and has a freezer/trigger function, you can store short vocal phrases in the machine, which can then be mixed in with your tape tracks by hitting the trigger button whenever the sound is needed. If you have the option to trigger replay via MIDI, this can be triggered from a sequencer for greater precision and repeatability. This is known as 'spinning' or 'flying in' and is a useful ploy if you have only one correctly sung version of the phrase

on analogue tape and you don't have access to a sampler. By hitting the trigger button before the sample has finished playing, it can be made to re-trigger to produce the much-used scratching effect. The effect is much like a conventional sampler but with the exception that only one sound can be played back at any one time.

If the unit has an external trigger input that can be triggered from a drum machine, then some interesting rhythmic echoes can be set up by programming one of the drums in the pattern to trigger the delay. A simple bass or synth pattern can be given a very tight, sequencer-like feel using this method and, though not all modern DDLs have the facility, you can get the effect from most DDLs that have either an audio trigger, a pulse trigger or a MIDI trigger facility. Fortunately, when working with a sequencer that can also record audio, most of the results that used to rely on triggered delays or samplers can be achieved by using simple copy and paste editing.

Stereo Delays

Most hardware DDLs and multi-effects units on the market offer a stereo mode of operation where a different delay time can be programmed for the left and right channels. Careful choice of delay times can give the impression of a sound bouncing back and forth between the speakers, and, for ADT effects, both channels can be set to different delays to give the impression of three instruments playing together rather than just two. If it is possible to modulate the two delays, the effect will be further enhanced, supporting the illusion of slightly different performances from left, right and dry signals.

The more advanced multi-effects units provide a number of stereo delay options, including ping-pong delay, where the echoes appear to bounce from speaker to speaker. There are also numerous multi-tap delay options that can sound similar to a multi-head tape echo unit, and by taking feedback from each tap, the delay quickly builds up into a very complex pattern. Essentially, a multi-tap delay is one that simultaneously produces two or more delays of different delay times.

Useful Initial Settings

- Slap-back delay: 20–80ms, no feedback.

- Tunnel echo or resonator: 2–10ms, feedback as high as possible without going unstable.

- Tempo delay: 60 beats per minute gives you the delay time of one bar in seconds. Divide this delay time by four to give you the delay time per quarter note.

- Echo: 100–300ms with feedback. The higher the feedback level, the more repeat echoes will be generated.

- Vibrato: 3–10ms delay time, dry signal off, modulation rate between 3 and 8Hz, depth set by ear.

- Phasing: 3–10ms delay time, mix control set to 50/50, modulation rate between 3 and 8Hz, depth set by ear. Try the feedback invert facility if you have it.

- Flanging: 5–50ms delay time, mix control set to 50/50, modulation rate between 3 and 8Hz, depth set by ear. Increase feedback in order to make the effect more dramatic. Try the feedback invert facility if you have it.

- Chorus: 30–100ms delay time, mix control set to 50/50, modulation rate between 3 and 8Hz, depth set by ear. Apply little or no feedback. Increasing the feedback creates a rotary speaker-type of sound.

More DDL Applications

We've learned what a DDL is and some of things it can do, but what exactly is a delay when you think about it in musical terms? A delay device repeats the original sound one or more times, so the musical outcome is to add more notes to the performance at time positions later than the original. This highlights a potential problem: if you have a very pronounced delay and the delay time doesn't fit in with the tempo of the music, the delay may upset the musical timing

of the piece. If the song is a fixed tempo, then it's easy enough to calculate the delay time needed to get the repeats to fall on the beat (for example, if you're working at 120bpm, you need 60/120, or half a second), and you can double up or halve the delay time without going out of time with the song. Even so, you can occasionally run into trouble when a delayed note clashes musically with the new note it coincides with.

Part of the reason this is a problem is that digital delays produce almost perfect copies of the original sound, whereas tape delays had a spectacularly poor frequency response that, fortuitously, made the delays seem more like natural echoes. If a delay is quieter and duller-sounding than the original, then we accept it as an echo, but if it's equally loud and just as bright, then it may simply be heard as a note in the wrong place. Echoes that occur in nature get duller every time they reflect from a new surface, so to get the same result from an electronic delay line, we need to try to emulate this.

Simply feeding the delay return back through a mixer channel with the top rolled off doesn't produce exactly the same effect because every delay will be equalised in exactly the same way, but it's still a lot better than nothing. However, to really do the job properly, the EQ needs to go after the delay line, but before the feedback path used to create multiple repeats. Some of the better multi-effects units provide a delay damping parameter to simulate this, but there is a trick you can use if you're using a very basic DDL.

Instead of bringing the DDL output back into an effects return point on the mixer, bring it back into a spare channel and roll off the appropriate amount of top as described, but instead of using the feedback within the DDL to create multiple echoes, turn the feedback completely off and instead use the aux send control on the FX return channel. For example, if your DDL unit is being fed from send aux 1, then use the aux 1 control on the channel you're using as a return to feed some of the signal back to the DDL input. This is illustrated in Figure 8.7. Every time the signal is fed around the loop, it will pass through the channel EQ again, so each repeat should be slightly duller than the last. The return channel fader is used to

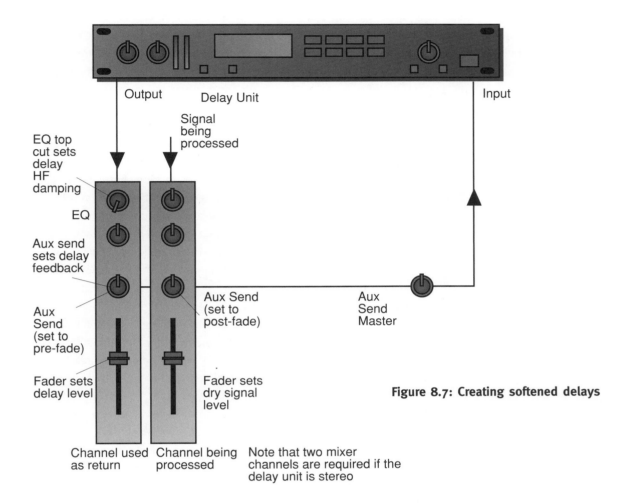

Output   Delay Unit   Input

Signal being processed

EQ top cut sets delay HF damping

EQ

Aux send sets delay feedback

Aux Send (set to pre-fade)

Aux Send (set to post-fade)

Aux Send Master

Fader sets delay level

Fader sets dry signal level

Figure 8.7: Creating softened delays

Channel used as return   Channel being processed   Note that two mixer channels are required if the delay unit is stereo

control the overall FX level in the usual way. However, if the aux 1 send on your return channel is set to post-fade, as effects sends usually are, then the amount of feedback will change as the effect return level is adjusted, which is not ideal. A better option is to use an aux send that is switchable for either pre- or post-operation so that you can use it in post-fade mode on the channels carrying your mix, but set it to pre-fade on the channel that's handling the effect return. This way the effect won't change as you alter its level. This probably makes more sense when you study the figure than it does just reading about it. It's also important not to make the echoes too loud in the mix or the brain will no longer accept them as natural. Where a stereo effects unit is being used, two mixer channels (panned hard left and right) will be needed for use as returns.

Multi-Tap Delays

Multi-tap delays are useful in situations where you don't want to be forced to make the delay time match the tempo of the song. By setting the various delay taps to times that aren't exact multiples of each other, the delay pattern should be complex enough that the listener's brain gives up on trying to match it to the pace of the music. For a good example of this, listen to the echo used on '60s instrumental guitar music. The echo gave the guitars a big sound, but there was enough apparent randomness in the effect not to upset your perception of the tune's timing. By feeding the output of all the delay taps back into the DDL input, the repeat pattern rapidly builds in complexity as it decays, rather like a very coarse reverb effect. By the same token, if you need to create a multi-tap delay that does reinforce the tempo of a piece of music, all the tap times must be set to multiples of the tempo, though of course you could set some taps to straight time (4ths, 8ths and 16ths) and others to triplet time (6ths, 12ths and 24ths).

Delay And Tempo

What happens if your song contains tempo changes? Obviously if you have a fixed delay time, this will throw out the synchronisation between the delays and the music, but using a programmable effects unit you can create a new patch at the new tempo and switch to this – either manually or via MIDI – at the appropriate time. Unfortunately, many effects units fail to change patches smoothly, so how well this works depends a lot on the make and model of your effects unit. Ironically, the cheaper ones often change patches quicker than the more expensive ones as they're running less complex algorithms.

A more elegant way to tackle the sync problem is to use one of the multi-effects units that allow you to sync delays, LFOs and so on to an incoming MIDI clock. Providing that you have a sequencer running, you can actually force the delay timing to precisely match any tempo changes you might choose to make.

Best of all is the software plug-in that can be set to a multiple of the tempo rate rather than a fixed delay time. Not only does this ensure the echoes are exactly in time with the song, but also that any tempo changes will automatically reset the plug-in's delay time accordingly. However, strange pitch effects or other artifacts may be audible in the event of a sudden delay time change, so in some cases it's best to set up two separate plug-ins to handle the two tempos used by the song, then use mix automation to fade from one to the other at the appropriate times.

More About Tape Echo

The early tape delays had terrible technical specs, but they still produced a wonderfully warm sound (albeit with more noise than was comfortable), and

the limited bandwidth aspect was only one of the reasons. Another reason was the rather poor stability of the tape transport – musicians would leave their echo units in the band's van for days, all the time with the rubber pinch roller pressing against the capstan. Often this would put flats on the pinch roller resulting in a little speed unevenness in the transport, so instead of getting completely clean repeats, they'd all have a tiny amount of vibrato applied. You can simulate this by putting chorus or vibrato before your DDL, but keep the effect very subtle otherwise the chorus effect will be too obvious. In a real tape echo, every time a repeat is fed back and re-recorded more vibrato is added, making each repeat less accurate than the one that went before. To emulate this exactly using a digital DDL, you'd need to put the chorus effect between the feedback loop and the delay line input, but many algorithms don't permit you to do this. That being the case, just a little chorus before the DDL will get you close enough.

Patching together effects using plug-ins can be difficult if you want to do something out of the ordinary, even if you're using a routing system such as the TCWorks FX Machine. Fortunately, there are some very good tape emulation plug-ins that incorporate all the right sonic ingredients, though passing the delay through another plug-in that adds mild distortion sometimes helps make the effect sound more realistic.

Echo And Psychoacoustics

In real life, there's rarely no such thing as a clean echo – each echo will include some ambience because of multiple reflection paths, so to recreate this electronically it's necessary to add a hint of reverb to each echo. The easiest way to do this is to place a reverb after the delay block, but you don't necessarily need a very long reverb (or a very elaborate one at that) to make the effect work. As a special effect, reverbs of up to three of four seconds can sound quite spectacular, but as a rule, a reverb time of between 0.8 and 1.5 seconds should be fine. By varying the reverb mix parameter, you can adjust the balance of reverb added to the delays, and in music that has enough space to let you appreciate these subtleties, the added sense of space can be very worthwhile. For a more natural effect, pick a short ambience reverb type. Because the reverb doesn't need to be anything too elaborate, this technique lends itself to the use of host-powered plug-ins.

Reverse Delay

One studio trick that is impossible to replicate live is that of reversing the audio so that everything plays backwards. This technique was used to great effect by artists such as The Beatles and Jimi Hendrix during the psychedelic era (currently enjoying something of a revival), but although the laws of physics prohibit real-time reversal, a number of delay units now have a reverse delay feature that, when used with care, can create the illusion of reversed audio. The means by which this apparently impossible trick is achieved is that the audio is genuinely reversed, but only in short sections of two or three seconds, and these are delayed by the length of the reversed segment. Essentially, the audio is played into a RAM buffer, then when the buffer is full, the audio is played out in reverse order while the next section of audio is filling up the buffer again. Each reversed section is crossfaded into the next, and if you set the RAM buffer size to correspond to a whole number of musical bars at the current tempo, the way in which the sections are rejoined can seem quite natural. In live performance, using a tap tempo facility to set the reverse delay buffer time, then playing a bar or two ahead is all you need to do to create the effect. You could do this in the studio, but it's easier just to reverse the audio if you are using either open reel analogue tape or a computer-based multitrack recorder. Nevertheless, in studios based around recording systems that don't have a reverse facility (such as ADAT tape machines), reverse delay can be used to good effect.

Programmable Delay Effects

Virtually all but the very cheapest digital effects units are now programmable and offer MIDI control over patch selection as well as some form of dynamic MIDI control over the effect parameters. MIDI control is a very important subject and will be discussed in detail later in the book. Digital reverb, which is also a vital part of any multi-effects unit, will also be examined in depth in the next chapter.

Programmability allows the user to set up several effects of each type, and in the cases of chorus, flanging, ADT, vibrato and other DDL-based effects, the programs, once created, will probably be useful in a number of different contexts with little or no further modification. Pure delay, on the other hand, often needs to be fine tuned, simply because a lot of delay effects are tempo related. Various delays can be stored to suit all the more popular tempos, but a more satisfactory solution is to use the tap tempo facility now found on the majority of effects devices. Here, the user taps the tempo of the song using a front panel button or footswitch and the delay time automatically matches itself to this tempo. It is only necessary to tap twice, though if the song contains tempo changes, these can be tapped in at the appropriate places.

Plug-ins invariably include the ability to save user patches and in most cases, effect parameters can be automated simply by recording movements of the on-screen controls in real time. Of all the methods of working, plug-ins are perhaps the most convenient as all the settings are automatically saved with the song file, and if they have been set to lock to tempo, they will automatically adjust if the song tempo is changed.

Delay Specifications

Digital delays are very flexible devices – some effects are created by adding the delayed sound to the original, but others, such as vibrato, require only the delayed part of the signal. Because of this, the ideal DDL should encompass the full audio bandwidth of 20Hz to 20kHz. For most echo, phasing, flanging and chorus effects, a 12kHz bandwidth is more than adequate, and indeed, some believe it produces a warmer sound, but unless you buy second hand, you're unlikely to find a device with such a limited frequency response. However, some units include a dedicated tape echo mode, which filters the delayed sound and may also add a small amount of pitch variation to simulate worn mechanical parts.

16-bit circuitry will produce a low enough level of noise and distortion for professional use, though a good 20- or 24-bit machine is better for discerning applications as it provides more operating headroom.

Connections

A great many delay effects are created by adding the delayed signal to the untreated sound so the auxiliary send system on the mixing desk is the obvious connection point – especially if you want to add the same effect in different degrees to several tracks. In this case, the DDL would be set up to give a 'delay only' output, which would then be fed into the desk via an effects return input or via an unused input channel. The pan position of the delayed signal is a matter of taste.

9 REVERBERATION

Reverberation is one of the few studio effects with a direct counterpart in nature, and is based on our real-world perception of audio in an acoustically reflective environment. Everything we hear is a mixture of the sound travelling directly from its source to our ears reinforced by thousands of echoes of the same sound reflected from the ground, walls, objects and so on. Even in apparently dead-sounding environment, reflections still account for the greater part of the sound we hear. Because sound has a finite velocity – in the order of 335m (1100 feet) per second – these reflections arrive later than the original sound and also from different directions depending on the locations of the surfaces they've been reflected from. Our brains make use of all this sonic information to subconsciously evaluate the environment.

Deprive a sound of these reflections by conducting an experiment in an anechoic (totally sound-absorbent) room and it will sound dry, unnaturally quiet and lacking in character. It is understandable, then, that multitrack recording, which often involves close miking (a technique that substantially excludes all but the direct sound), requires some form of artificial reverberation to be added in the studio. Without reverberation, the sound may appear one-dimensional and detached from reality, giving it the impression of being 'stuck on' when it is added to the rest of the mix.

In real life, the character of reverberation varies depending on the physical layout and composition of the surroundings. In a cavern or large cathedral, for example, the reverberations may take a considerable time to die away and are also likely to be rich in both high-frequency and low-frequency content (though high frequencies are absorbed by air, so the high frequencies tend to decay faster than the low frequencies). A more familiar environment such as a room or office, produces such a short reverberation that often it is not even perceived as being present. Nevertheless it is present to a significant degree, and it affects the way that we interpret sound and also the way in which we make our psychoacoustic evaluations concerning the nature of the space in which the sound is being heard. That's why you can hear a sound in a large hall in darkness and still know that you're in a large space.

Reverb Parameters

So, exactly what are the important parameters that must be simulated in order to convince the ear, or more accurately the brain, that an artificial source of reverberation is genuine? To find out, it's necessary to consider what happens when a real sound is created in a confined space. The newly created sound moves out from its source in the form of spherical wavefronts travelling at the speed of sound. This, for sake of convenience, can be approximated to around 0.3m (1 foot) per millisecond. The effect is often likened to ripples in a pond, but in fact sound travels in all three dimensions whereas water ripples effectively exist only in two. Sound waves consist of rapid fluctuations in air pressure and keep moving away from the source until they encounter an obstruction, whereupon some of their energy is absorbed and some is reflected back into the room.

Any reflected sound subsequently re-reflects from any further obstacle it encounters as it travels through the air – the amount of energy reflected and the amount absorbed depending on the nature of the surface. The sound waves get progressively weaker every time they are re-reflected and finally die away altogether. For practical purposes, this decay period – known as the reverberation time of a room – is usually defined as the time taken for the level of the reverberation to decay by 60dB. This time is sometimes referred to as the RT60. Some of the sound energy is absorbed by the air itself, especially the higher frequencies, but this effect can be ignored for most small rooms. However, it's one of the reasons that large buildings produce a warm reverb sound, even those made of hard material such as stone.

The spacing between the reflections at the start of the reverb build-up is an important factor in our perception of room size. The larger a room, the further the sound will have to travel before it is reflected, and the spaces between the individual reflections become longer as a consequence of this. After a very short time, the series of reflections will become too dense and too complex for the ear to separate, but the first few, known as early reflections, provide vital auditory clues about a room's geometry both from their spacing and pattern.

While it is true that a single sound in a room will give rise to a certain early reflections pattern, another sound source a small distance away will give rise to a different set of early reflections because it will be closer to some surfaces and further from others compared to the original source. In the case of an orchestra, choir or other large musical ensemble, each player is in a different physical location and so will set up a different set of early reflections. When all these are added together they become much more complex and less definable than the reflections from a single sound source. For this reason, it may be wise to reduce the level of early reflections (if your reverberation unit allows this) when trying to recreate the sound of a large number of players in a natural acoustic environment. A very strong early reflection pattern simply creates the illusion that all the instruments are located in the same place.

Initial Delay

Of course, no reverberation at all is heard until the sound has reached the nearest obstruction and bounced back to the listener. This initial delay between the direct sound and the first reflected sound provides an even more powerful auditory clue as to room size. Excluding the first reflection from the floor (which follows the original too closely to create any sense of space), the greater the delay between the sound

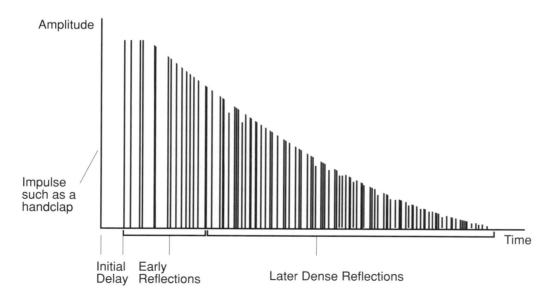

Figure 9.1: Reverb development

and its first reflection returning to the listener, the larger the room size is perceived to be. We have so far isolated three stages in the development of reverberation: the first reflection, the early reflections and the dense reverberation that follows. Figure 9.1 shows how these reflections might appear following a single, short impulse of sound such as a handclap or bursting balloon in an enclosed space.

The Nature Of Reflections

The next important area to consider is the mechanism of reflection. Virtually all materials reflect sound more efficiently at some frequencies than at others and most of the materials we use inside buildings reflect low frequencies far better than high ones. As you might expect, this produces a longer reverberation time at low frequencies than at high ones. In very large or very reflective spaces, we may witness a spectacularly long reverberation decay time due to the fact that the sound has to travel a great distance before it finally dies away. In this case, the viscosity of the air further shortens the high-frequency reverberation time by absorbing high-frequency energy, giving the reverb a bassy, almost thunder-like quality.

Because of this high-frequency absorption effect, it is hardly ever necessary to create an artificial reverberation with the same high-frequency response as the original sound if our intention is only to generate a convincing natural effect. A bandwidth of 8kHz is more than adequate for most natural simulations. However, as many recording engineers refuse to be confined by the laws of nature, most modern reverberation devices offer a full 20Hz to 20kHz bandwidth to allow for the creation of special effects that are not intended as exact replicas of a natural process. Moreover, many reverberation units are capable of producing a number of non-reverb effects that may benefit from a wider bandwidth.

Note that although we discuss reflections in much the same way as we might discuss light bouncing from a mirror, audio tends to be scattered from room surfaces rather than being reflected as a perfect replica of the incident sound. The practical outcome of this is that the early reflections are diffused to some extent producing the audio equivalent of a 'soft focus'

treatment. How well this effect is emulated in a digital reverb unit plays a large part in how natural it sounds.

Artificial Reverb

Before the advent of affordable digital reverberation in the early '80s, recording studios relied on either live rooms or so-called 'echo plates' to create the effect. Live rooms, while capable of sounding spectacularly good, present a problem in terms of the studio space they occupy, and, perhaps more significantly, the effect can be varied over only a limited range by introducing damping material into the room. Live rooms remain popular for treating vocals and drums because of the quality of sound that can be achieved, although only major studios tend to have good live rooms and often these studios will be booked more for the acoustic qualities of their rooms than for their equipment.

The Reverb Plate

The principle of the reverb plate is quite straightforward, but these devices need to be carefully isolated from other sources of sound due to their microphonic nature. A suspended thin steel plate is driven into vibration by means of a transducer (not unlike a loudspeaker), fed from the signal to be reverberated. Contact transducers attached to the plate pick up these vibrations and feed them back to the mixing console via special preamps where they are combined with the original signal. Because the vibrations within the plate closely simulate those of natural reverberation, the effect can be very convincing, though some equalisation may be required to tame the metallic ring of the plate.

The more professional plate systems were fitted with remote-controlled mechanical dampers comprising felt pads or similar, while the simpler plates could be damped by hanging a tea towel over them! In this apparently low-tech climate, a huge number of classic pop and rock records were produced. Figure 9.2 shows how a plate reverb works.

The plate has a fairly limited range of reverberation time, but some models have maintained their popularity because of their unique tonal character. During the '80s, many professional studios

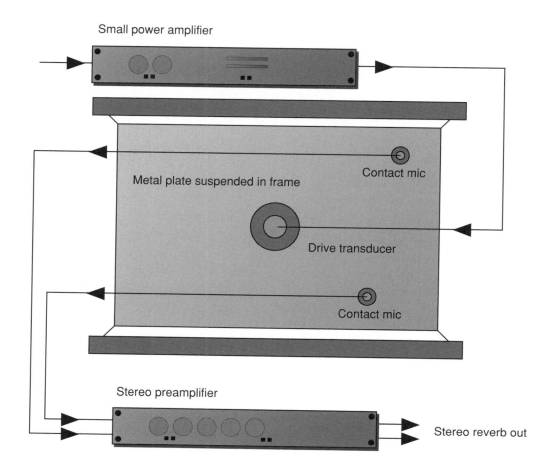

Small power amplifier

Metal plate suspended in frame

Contact mic

Drive transducer

Contact mic

Stereo preamplifier

Stereo reverb out

Figure 9.2: Plate reverb

dumped their plates in favour of the new digital reverberators, and in the '90s it was possible to pick up a very high-quality plate for just a few hundred pounds. However, many engineers now realise that a genuine plate reverberator still has a certain magic compared to its digital simulation and so prices have increased again.

Spring Reverb

Cheaper artificial reverberation systems using a spring instead of a plate are still used in guitar amplification and were at one time popular in home studios. Unfortunately, springs perform badly on drums and other percussive sounds when compared to a plate or digital reverberator as percussive sounds tend to

set the spring ringing at its resonant frequency, producing an unnatural twanging characteristic. Springs are, however, acceptable for treating vocals and other non-percussive sounds for home recording and demo applications, but now that digital reverberation is so cheap, there's little advantage in using a spring device at all (other than where built into a guitar amplifier), unless you specifically want the spring sound. Figure 9.3 shows how a spring reverb works. As with plate reverbs, the spring itself had to be isolated from mechanical vibrations.

Now that digital reverb has fallen in price to the extent that any recording enthusiast can afford it (indeed, it's now the cheapest option), the spring reverb and even the plate have become virtually

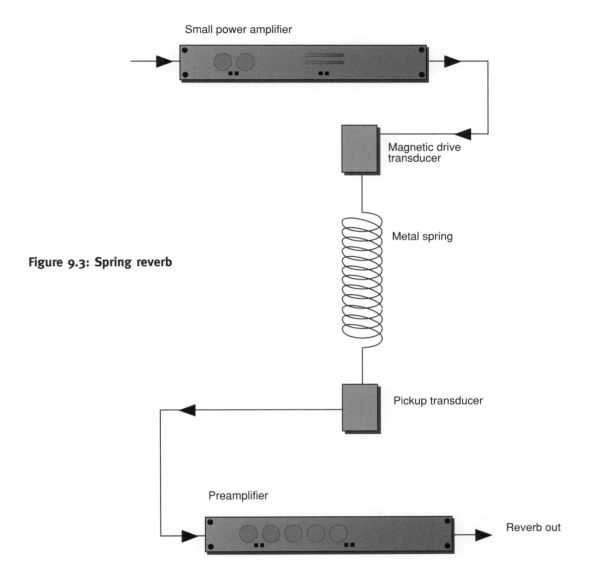

Small power amplifier

Magnetic drive
transducer

Metal spring

Figure 9.3: Spring reverb

Pickup transducer

Preamplifier

Reverb out

obsolete. The great attraction of a digital system is that the user has a far greater control over the parameters that make up a reverberation treatment so that one unit can provide a large number of room, halls and plate simulations with a huge range of decay times. Furthermore, the digital reverberator is compact, electronically quiet, and is unaffected by external sounds or vibration. While the resulting sound may not be entirely natural, so many records have been made using these devices that we now expect reverberation on records to sound this way.

Digital Reverb

Creating electronic reverb is far more complicated than combining a few digital delay units. Research has shown that somewhere between 1,000 and 3,000 separate echoes are needed every second to create the illusion of dense, natural-sounding reverberation. Additionally, the spacing between these reflections has to be chosen very carefully or the resulting reverberation will ring in a most unnatural fashion.

Because of the way in which digital reverberation works, it is easy to produce very strong early reflections patterns, something that plates and springs can't do. These reflections are an integral part of the character of any natural enclosed space, but digital systems allow us to over-emphasise them quite dramatically if we want to. The early reflections in a typical digital reverb system often sound more distinct than those that occur naturally, which can be both a curse or a blessing depending on the application. Over-emphasised early reflections on percussive sounds, for example, can result in a very grainy sound that is quite unlike real life. On the other hand, smooth sustained sounds can be considerably enhanced by using a reverb patch with strongly pronounced early reflections.

Getting the reflections right is only part of the story: digital filtering is needed to impart the right frequency characteristics to the reverberant sound, and the software needs to be sophisticated enough to create a number of different simulated environments without making setting up too complicated for the user. Good digital reverb units can produce excellent approximations of real acoustic spaces, but they also have the capacity to create reverberant characters that simply could not occur in nature. For example, what bizarre set of natural parameters would result in a reverse or gated reverb sound? Gimmicks aside, digital systems also allow us to produce reverbs that are longer and brighter than anything normally encountered in the real world.

Of course, the microprocessor and DSP technology involved in the production of reverberation is very complex and only mass production has enabled units to be built as cheaply as they now are. Hardware models tend to fall into two types: fully programmable and the less costly preset-based machine, where there may be only one user-variable parameter per preset. Software-based reverb plug-ins follow a similar pattern but because of their need to economise on processing power, hardware units still tend to sound better. As a rule, plug-ins and low-cost hardware produce less dense reverb than high-end hardware.

If we first examine the programmable type, it is then easy to understand the compromises that must be made in a preset machine. Both types have stereo outputs and may either have mono or stereo inputs

depending on the manufacturer. In either case, the reverb is generally derived from a mono mix of the inputs – only the dry signal remains in stereo throughout. This, in practical terms, is quite acceptable since reverb comes from all directions, regardless of the stereo positioning of the original sound, so for natural-sounding reverb, a mono-in/stereo-out system is all that is needed.

However, a number of machines also offer true stereo-in, stereo-out operation for the production of special effects, and dual-reverb modes are also common – the same processor can function as two independent reverb units where one is fed from the left input and one from the right. These may be mono, in which case the processes are quite separate, or they may be stereo with the outputs from both virtual reverb processors summed at the output of the unit. This latter mode is useful if you need a short reverb in the mix for drums and a longer one from vocals. All you need do is feed the two inputs from different console aux sends. Only one stereo aux return is required for the effects unit.

Reverb Programming

The important parameters generally placed under user control are pre-delay time, early reflection pattern and level, overall decay time and high-frequency damping. There may be numerous others on more sophisticated machines, but these are the important ones common to most programmable units.

Pre-delay simply sets the time between the original sound and the first reflection, and may be variable from virtually instantaneous to half a second or more. This is a simple way of creating an illusion of room size and also helps to separate the dry sound from the reverb. Longer pre-delays can be useful in conjunction with medium decay vocal reverb treatments to prevent the reverb clouding the vocals.

Early reflection patterns are not usually variable by the user to any great degree; normally the user selects from a handful of stored patterns simulating various rooms, halls, chambers, plates or small room ambience, though in some cases the level and spacing of these reflections is variable. As a rule, the greater the spacing, the greater the impression of room size.

Overall, decay time simply determines how long the reverb takes to die away or fall in level by 60dB after the initial sound stops. Longer reverb times are suggestive of large environments with very reflective surfaces whereas shorter ones may be used to simulate the natural acoustics of a typical small room. Most reverb units can produce an impressively long decay time, but the real way to evaluate the quality of a reverberator is to see how convincingly it emulates small room ambience.

High-frequency damping allows the high-frequency decay time to be shorter than the overall decay time and to simulate the absorbency characteristics of real rooms. This simulates both surface absorption and air absorption. Some units also have independent control over low-frequency damping to simulate environments that reflect mainly high-frequency sounds.

By selecting the appropriate pattern for the environment you wish to simulate, then adjusting the other parameters, the available effects vary from a barely reverberant room to a huge hall or cavern where the reverb decay thunders on for several tens of seconds. In practice, most of the useful reverb treatments have a decay time below two seconds as over-long reverb tends to muddy a mix, though there are occasions when a long reverb can be effective.

Some models incorporate a room size control, which adjusts several of the parameters simultaneously to give the impression of a larger or smaller space, and this is useful in that it saves time and effort in reprogramming several parameters manually.

A typical programmable reverb provides a number of presets that the user can call up and either use as they are or use them as the basis to create new effects that can then be saved for later use. Both the factory presets can be called up for use via the front-panel controls, and on all but the cheapest units, MIDI program selection is supported. Not only does this make it possible to access patches quickly, it also makes it possible to change from one reverb setting to another automatically during a mix using a MIDI sequencer synchronised to the multitrack recorder. Where there are more than 128 presets and user patches, they are normally organised into banks so that they can be accessed using MIDI bank change messages. Note that many reverb units take a couple of seconds to change patches as a new algorithm may have to be loaded, so try to arrange patch changes when no audio is being processed.

Further Parameters

Additional parameters you might find on more sophisticated machines include chorus-like modulation within the reverb algorithm to further randomise the reflection patterns. As with chorus, there are depth and rate settings, but unless the depth is very high, the chorus-like quality is usually hidden. Instead, the reverb just seems more dynamic or shimmery. It may also be possible to control the shape of the reverb decay as in a number of real spaces, the decay isn't necessarily a simple exponential curve.

Preset-Based Machines

The preset-based reverb unit uses essentially the same ingredients to produce reverb but they are either not placed under user-control or the user may have access to just one or two parameters, reverb decay time usually being one of them. This may seem limiting, but for most applications a choice of a dozen or so different reverbs is quite adequate provided they are well chosen in the first place. An appropriate analogy would be in the wine taster's approach to wine. Tasting wine in isolation, the expert may be able to differentiate between hundreds of different types, each having its own distinct flavour and character. When it comes to wine used for cooking, however, it is debatable whether the wine connoisseur could tell exactly which was used as long as it was the right basic type. And so it is with reverberation. Test a reverb with a single handclap and various distinctions can be made: bright, mellow, metallic, coarse, and so on, with countless variations on each type. In the context of a complete mix the task becomes immeasurably more difficult. There is little point in spending hours creating a subtle variation on a specific patch when the difference would be impossible to detect in the final piece of music. My own view is that absolute reverb quality is far more important than a high level of adjustability.

At one time, preset-based machines tended to be budget models with limited processing power, so the best-quality reverb tended to be available from more expensive programmable machines. That's still true to some extent, though some of the big names in reverberation now produce very low-cost preset-based models that come very close in sound to their more expensive studio models. Simpler reverb plug-ins may also be based on selecting a preset reverb type, then adjusting a very small number of parameters compared to their hardware counterparts.

The choice of which type of reverb unit to go for is of course your own, but if finances are tight you may be better off in terms of sound quality buying a good preset model rather than opting for a functionally more sophisticated unit that sounds unnatural. Bad digital reverb can sound terrible, but fortunately most manufacturers have refined their designs to the point that there are few truly awful units on the market. Even so, listen carefully to any second-hand models dating back to the '80s and early '90s as some of these sounded unnaturally ringy. No matter what environment you dialled up, the result was always like some type of plate!

Reverbs sound different because they rely both on processing power and good algorithm design – the poorest ones are coarse or ringy and generally are unsuitable for percussion unless you're after a deliberately trashy sound to use in a dance mix. The best way to test a reverb unit for these vices is to process a snare drum or clap sound and then listen for any traces of ring or note in the reverb decay. Some ring is to be expected on 'plate' and 'small room' settings but 'large rooms' and 'halls' should be quite free from resonances and ringiness. Also check that the reverb fades into silence smoothly rather than sounding grainy or gritty.

Like the programmable reverb, it is now usual for preset machines to incorporate MIDI control so that the presets can be remotely selected from any MIDI sequencer or keyboard that provides program patch information. Many have a patch assignment system to enable the preset numbers to be allocated to the desired MIDI patch number. This way you aren't limited to calling up preset 1 with MIDI patch 1, and so on. This is useful if you are using the reverb unit connected via MIDI to a synthesiser, as you may well

want synth patch 1 to call up reverb preset 15 or whatever. Similarly, you may want to assign the same reverb patch to several different synth patches. In the studio however, it's more common to call up patches directly rather than via a keyboard, in which case it's simpler to leave the patch numbers corresponding to the MIDI program numbers.

Gated Reverb

In addition to simulating reverberation in natural and not so natural spaces, two further effects have become standard issue in the armoury of the modern digital reverb: gated and reverse.

Gated reverb was first created using the ambience of a live room (often heavily compressed), and a noise gate to produce an abrupt cut-off rather than a smooth decay. This is described in the section that deals with gates, though the effect is easily simulated in a digital unit. The effect is that of a burst of reverb following the initial sound that persists for half a second or so, then ceases abruptly. The main parameter is the gate time, which is, in effect, the length of the reverb burst following the end of the original sound. The effect was extensively used on drums in the '80s but can also be applied to other instruments with great success. It's one of those effects that keep drifting in and out of fashion, so it's up to you whether to use it or not.

Less obvious applications for gated reverb include treating electric guitars to create a 'small club' effect. Perhaps the best attribute of gated reverb is that it manages to make its presence felt without filling up all the spaces between notes or beats. Because plenty of contrast is retained between the beats and the spaces between them, the sense of loudness is exaggerated by the effect whereas most reverb has the effect of diminishing the impression of loudness.

Reverse Reverb

Electronically generated reverse reverb, does not, as the name might suggest, involve anything actually playing backwards, but rather is achieved by applying a reverse type of envelope to the reverb so that instead of decaying, it builds up in level after the original sound and then cuts off abruptly. Like gated reverb, the main parameter is the time taken for the reverb to build up and cut off. The result is very convincing, but the reverb still occurs after the original sound. Figure 9.4 shows both gated and reverse reverb envelopes.

True reverse reverb sounds quite different, and can be achieved by turning over an analogue multitrack tape so that it plays in reverse, applying conventional reverb to the desired track, recording the resulting reverb onto a spare track and then turning the tape the right way round again. The

outcome of this, when the dry and reverb tracks are played together, is that the reverb occurs before the sound that created it, producing an eerie and surreal effect that works splendidly on vocals or guitar parts, so long as it is not overused. A similar effect can be produced using a digital audio workstation by reversing the section of file you wish to process, adding reverb to the file (via a destructive edit), then reversing the file again.

In fact, both artificial or genuine reverse reverb

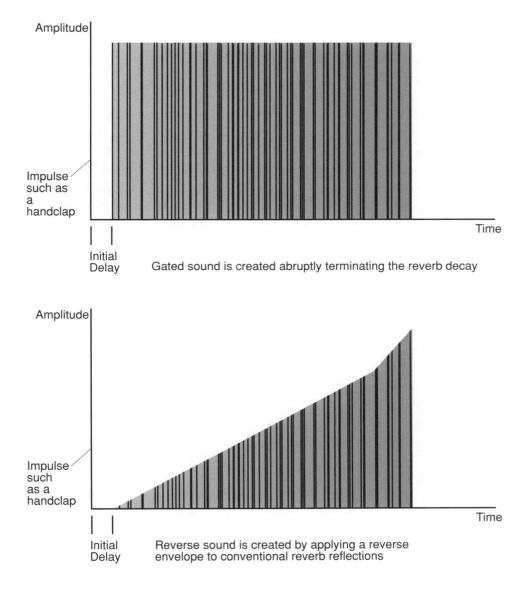

Figure 9.4: Gated and reverse reverb envelopes

can be used to good effect in this way and can also make percussive, sampled and synthesised sounds more interesting. In general, very dynamic or percussive sounds give more dramatic results than continuous voices such as synthesised strings.

Reverb Specifications

Digital reverb is an effect, and as such always has to be mixed with the untreated sound (apart from in certain special effects applications). This, coupled with the fact that natural reverb doesn't contain much in the way of high-frequency information (due to air absorption and the physical nature of reflective surfaces), means that an audio bandwidth of 10kHz is technically quite adequate to produce even bright-sounding reverberation, and some good-quality early units were made with this kind of bandwidth. However, modern units all tend to be 20Hz to 20kHz.

Obviously, low noise is a desirable feature of all recording equipment, and 18-plus-bit units (24-bit is pretty much the norm now) are to be favoured over 16-bit models as they generally produce less noise and have a smoother reverb tail. However, poorly designed circuitry can cause more noise than is necessary, so budget units that seem to offer good bandwidths and number of bits can still be hissy. For any digital effect, you can calculate the best possible signal-to-noise ratio simply by multiplying the number of bits by six. Thus, a 16-bit machine can achieve a 96dB signal-to-noise ratio, in theory, but a practical design might offer between 85 and 90dB – which is still adequate. Older 12-bit designs, on the other hand, can manage only 72dB, and this, in practice, may turn out to be between around 65dB, which is much less impressive. In theory, 24-bit designs should give you at best a 144dB dynamic range, but sadly the laws of physics prevents the real-world dynamic range of even the best converters from getting much better than 110dB.

Of course, the most important aspect of a digital reverb – the sound – cannot be quantified by specifications alone as it depends so much on the software and algorithm design used to create the effect. It is for this reason that a well-designed 12-bit reverb with, say, a 10kHz bandwidth (such as the old Klark Teknik DN780) can sound much more realistic than a poorly designed 24-bit machine with a 20kHz bandwidth.

Once you've satisfied yourself that a given unit is quiet enough and offers sufficient variation in the types of reverbs and decay times on offer, then it is really just a matter of listening. Pay particular attention to any unnatural metallic ringing on percussive sounds such as snare drums or handclaps. If you can close your eyes and visualise the room in which the sound is being played, then the reverb simulation is a good one. I also find that listening to the small room ambience programs is a good test of quality.

Connections

Because reverb is rarely used without the original sound being present, it is most commonly used in conjunction with the auxiliary or effects send system on the mixing desk. The outputs from the reverb are then fed into either two effects returns or into two spare channels and are panned hard left and hard right to create a wide stereo spread. This arrangement allows you to add the appropriate amount of reverb to each channel provided the same basic reverb type is required on each.

Alternatively, the channel insert point can be used to add reverb to a single instrument or voice if the aux sends are already fully utilised, and in this case the mix control on the reverb device must be used to set the balance between the dry and reverberated sound. Normally an insert point would limit you to mono operation but if there are any unused mixer channels you could feed the other output of the reverb processor into the insert return point of the spare channel as shown in Figure 9.5. Panning the two channels left and right would position the dry sound in the centre with the reverberated sound split into stereo.

There's a growing trend for effects units to be built with digital as well as analogue inputs and outputs to allow connection to digital mixing desks. Digital interconnection can present a number of problems regarding sample rate and clock synchronisation, so always refer to the manual that comes with your digital

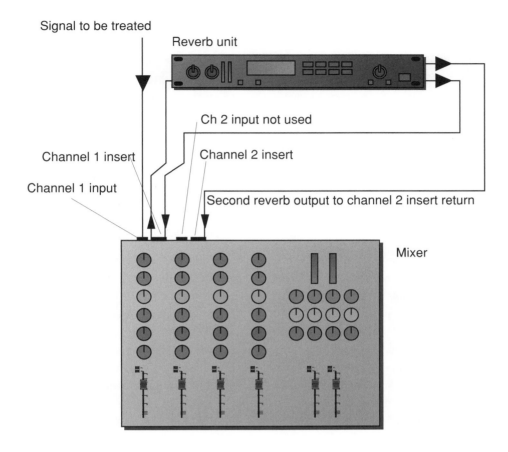

Signal to be treated

Reverb unit

Ch 2 input not used

Channel 1 insert

Channel 2 insert

Channel 1 input

Second reverb output to channel 2 insert return

Mixer

**Figure 9.5: Reverb via insert points
(stereo out using insert of next free channel)**

console to find out the best way to connect your effects units. However, if you can arrange to connect digitally rather than via analogue, you bypass the need for level matching and avoid the risk of ground-loop hum.

Software Reverb

Reverb is now available from a number of companies as plug-in software for use with both native and DSP-based digital audio workstations. Generally the parameter set will be simpler than for a programmable hardware reverb unit, but the principle of operation is the same. Though designers have made great advances in simplifying their algorithms without unduly compromising the reverb sound, it's still fair to say that the best-sounding reverbs take up a significant amount of the available processing power where they're designed to run using only the CPU of a desktop computer. DSP-based systems can afford to be a little more generous with their processing power, but reverb is still one of the hungriest effects, which is why there's a move towards specialised add-on cards that include high-quality reverb and other effects so as not to place an unnecessary burden on the rest of the system.

The flexibility of connection for software plug-ins is generally determined by the architecture of the host system, although virtual aux sends and insert points are commonly available in systems that also include mixing. Plug-in settings are generally stored within the song itself and controls may often be automated.

Applications

Reverberation can be applied to any sound, but it is most often associated with percussion and vocals in modern pop music production. The secret is not to overuse it, and this applies to both the level of reverb in the mix and the decay time chosen.

It's worth listening to some commercial recordings to see if you can pick out the different types of reverbs and how they've been used. You'll probably find at least two reverb settings used on a typical pop record – a short one for ambience and a longer one for use on vocals or snare drums. If you have only one reverb unit and you want to use the same idea yourself, record the longer reverb settings in mono as you record the individual tracks, then add the shorter setting when you come to mix. By applying a short stereo reverb to a longer mono one already recorded on tape, you'll give it some semblance of a stereo image. However, it's always nice to leave decisions concerning effects until the mixing stage, so if you already have one good reverb unit, it's worth considering a simpler (but still good quality), preset model to add to your armoury.

Drums

Close miking offers good separation between the individual drums and, to a great extent, removes the drums from the effect of their acoustic surroundings. As a result, a mix taken directly from the close mics will sound pretty dry, so some artificial reverb is generally needed. However, artificial reverb may be unnecessary if the drums are recorded in a large live room with distant ambience mics. The following suggestions assume close-miked drums.

Kick drums are usually left fairly dry or treated with a short, snappy reverb/ambience treatment such as a small room, ambience or plate setting. Excessive reverb will simply cloud the low end of the mix, so keep kicks as dry as you can. Other musical styles might need something a little more spectacular so a more obvious gated reverb might be applied to the bass drum to good effect. The abrupt cut off keeps the sound uncluttered and maintains the contrast of the beats and the gaps in between them.

Snare drums tend to benefit from more added reverb, and a plate setting is the traditional choice, partly because it mimics the rock drum sounds of the '70s, which were created using real plates. Plates also have a fast attack and a bright tonality, which helps reinforce the attack and definition of the snare drum. Longer plate settings can be used to create a very transparent, steamy kind of sound, but here it can help to roll off some of the bass to prevent the sound from becoming muddy. As a very general rule, the longer settings work best on slower pieces of music or songs with sparse instrumentation.

A typical snare reverb might range from as short as half a second for a tight, bright sound to over two seconds if an obvious effect is required. When using very short reverb settings, it is usually possible to use a higher level of reverb without swamping the sound; a useful trick is to pick a very short, very bright setting to add snap to a dull snare drum. For a bigger sound, pick a room sound with a longer decay time or hall setting, which should be warmer and have a slower build-up or attack.

If you like experimenting, try placing a graphic EQ before the reverb and then harshly boost the frequencies between 500Hz and 1kHz so that you get a sound like a champagne cork popping. This can be most effective on pop/techno recordings and is very simple to achieve.

Contrary to popular belief, toms don't need masses of reverb, as they tend to have a natural sustain to their sound anyway. Plate or small room settings work well in pop music, with longer settings being appropriate for heavy metal or ponderous progressive rock. As with the snare drum, hall settings can be used as an alternative to plate emulations to give a very 'big' sound.

As a general rule, the busier the drum part, the less reverb it will need. Gated reverb can also be used on toms if the nature of the music warrants it.

Hi-hats can benefit from a short-to-medium bright reverb/ambience setting, and one with a high level of early reflections can add interest and detail to the sound. Indeed, it's worth trying out reverb patches with high levels of early reflections (or ambience patches that are all early reflections with no reverb tail) on all the drums, just to get a feel for what can be achieved. In most cases, you'll notice a dramatic increase in the sense of 'being somewhere real' but without spreading the sound out too much. This type of setting is ideal for music that needs an intimate, club-type atmosphere. Dance music tends to use little or no hi-hat reverb in order to preserve the impact and timing of the dry sound.

Overall Drum Reverb

Being able to pick different kinds of reverb for every drum and cymbal is all very well in a top professional studio, but for those of us working at home one reverb unit often has to be used for everything. Similarly, if the drum sounds come from a drum machine or sampler, it may be impossible or impractical to separate the different sounds. For example, a drum machine with only a simple stereo output forces you to compromise between separating the kick drum from the rest of the kit (by panning the kick to one side and the rest of the kit to the other) or keeping the stereo image created by panning the individual sounds to their correct positions.

You can simply feed the whole drum kit through the reverb unit with a short plate or early reflections setting and turn down the bass on the reverb returns so that the kick drum doesn't cause too much of a mess. Used with restraint, this simple measure can actually be very effective and comes quite close to the sound you'd get miking a kit in a naturally live room, especially if you have a good reverb unit with a convincing ambience setting. This type of natural sound is currently very popular, so being forced to use it isn't too much of a compromise!

Percussion sounds also benefit from the sense of space and depth reverb can provide, though very little reverb is necessary for creating the illusion of spatial identity. Even so, ethnic and Latin percussion is an integral part of New Age and experimental music where long reverb settings can be used to fill space in an interesting way. As ever, the musical arrangement must provide the space in the first place, but it is not unusual to hear delicate instruments such as triangles or shakers treated with cavernous hall programs.

The way reverb is used on drums varies considerably according to musical fashions, so while a rock band might go for a thunderous, reverberant tom and snare sound, a dance mix might be very sparing in the use of reverb and where it is used; it may be much shorter than the treatments used in rock music. As a rule, the shorter the reverb times you intend to use, the better quality the reverb unit should be.

Vocals

For some ingrained psychological reason, vocals sound rather better with reverb than they do without it. One theory is that we humans like to be able to hear some kind of reference pitch, and by adding echo or reverb to a sound we are constantly hearing the new notes being sung, overlaid on the reverb or delay of the immediately preceding sounds. This is borne out in practice, as there's something very uncomfortable about listening to a totally dry voice, even an exceptionally good one, whereas even an average singer sounds tolerable when singing in the bath! This is one reason singers perform better with reverb in their monitor mix, even if the reverb won't be used in the final mix.

Vocal Reverb Considerations

With lead vocals, there are several conflicting factors that need to be balanced when we add reverb.

- In the case of lead vocals, it is important that the words themselves are clear, but adding reverberation tends to reduce intelligibility. The longer the reverb, the more the intelligibility is reduced.

- Bright reverbs can sound exciting but emphasise sibilance and can be annoyingly distracting if mixed too loud.

- Too little reverb may make the voice sound unattractive, and may also make it sound as though it's 'stuck on' to the backing rather than sitting comfortably in the mix.

- Long reverb times sound flattering, but they tend to fill up the spaces in a mix that create the all-important contrast; the space is just as important as the music.

- The traditional place for a vocalist is at the front of a band, so we normally try to make the singer stand out at the front of the mix. However, adding a lot of reverb creates the impression of distance, which tends to push the singer back.

As you listen to different records, you'll come across dozens of different reverb treatments, all of which create a specific effect. The following list describes some techniques you can try.

- To make a vocal sound close and intimate, you may need to choose a relatively short setting (less than one second), and depending on the kind of environment you want to create, it may need to be fairly bright to suggest an intimate club rather than a large concert hall. Be aware though that if the reverb is too bright, it will bring out any sibilance in the voice and may become annoyingly obtrusive.

- A high level of early reflections with a relatively low density (wide spacing between reflections) can help suggest an intimate environment as it fools us into perceiving the existence of nearby reflective objects. A plate or small room simulation in conjunction with a little pre-delay works well in this context, as do ambience programs that provide mainly early reflections with little or no following reverb.

- If a bigger sound is sought, then it may help to introduce more pre-delay to provide a little separation between the original sound and the following reverb. If the original sound is kept quite dry, this can still maintain a degree of intimacy providing the reverb is mixed low enough not to bury the vocal.

- Those who have the luxury of more than one reverb unit might like to try using one of them to produce an intimate, (short, bright with little or no pre-delay) effect and a second unit with maybe 200ms of pre-delay and a longer reverb time to create the sense of depth. It may even help to keep the short reverb in stereo but pan the longer reverb to one side or the other to lend a little movement to the sound.

- Really big reverb sounds can work in songs that have the space to give the reverb room to coexist with whatever else is going on, but a useful dodge is to feed the reverb output through a gate or compressor configured as a ducker. For more on ducking, see the chapter on compressors. Here, the compressor (or gate with ducking mode), is used to pull down the level of the reverb when the vocalist is singing but without affecting the level of the dry sound. This will allow the reverb level to swell back to its full level during pauses between phrases or at the ends of lines. The ducker should be set with an attack time of around 200–500ms and a release time in the same range so that the reverb level changes aren't too abrupt, and the ducking level may need to be only a few dBs. The precise release setting will need to be fine-tuned by ear depending on the material – if it is too short, the gain changes will be too abrupt, but if it's too long, the reverb will have died away before the ducker can fade it back up again. The range of the ducker should be set somewhere around 6dB to start off with, but again, the actual value depends on your taste and the style of the song.

Reverb And Backing Vocals

A somewhat different approach can be taken with backing vocals as, by definition, they don't need to sound as forward as the lead vocal.

- Using a setting with prominent, widely spaced early reflections will thicken the sound considerably, and you can usually get away with a longer reverb time than you use on the main vocal. By the same token, choosing a slightly less bright reverb will help the backing vocals sit further back in the mix creating that all-important sense of perspective.

- It can help to thicken the sound further if the feed to the reverb unit is first treated using a chorus unit or a pitch shifter set to produce a mild detuning effect. Even a flanger placed before the reverb isn't too unsubtle, as the characteristic sweep of the flanger is diffused by the reverb and the dry portion of the sound remains unchanged. The result is to add a rather nice shimmer to the sound but without making it too gimmicky.

- Another little-known technique is to connect a gate before the reverb unit and set the threshold so that only high-level sounds are treated. Alternatively, use the gate's range control to allow a low level of signal to be fed to the reverb unit when the gate is closed. I first heard of this trick being used when I interviewed Tony Visconti many years ago and he described how he'd produced a vocal effect on a David Bowie album. He'd used real acoustic reverb from the back of a large hall, picked up via ambience mics then gated, but a digital reverberation unit makes the whole task so much easier. Aside from the novelty of having reverb on only high-level sounds, there is a side benefit in that the mix becomes less cluttered. Again, the technique can be expanded upon if you have two reverb units by combining a small room sound from one reverb unit that is connected normally, with a longer setting on the second reverb unit brought in by the gate.

To create a more unnatural, eerie sound, try the reverse reverb effect I mentioned earlier – the results really can be quite fascinating. Remember though that if you're doing this with analogue tape, when you turn the tape over the track numbers are reversed. It's all too easy to accidentally record over tracks you want to keep, so check they're empty first.

For simple speech, try a very short room or ambience setting and mix in just enough to kill that 'padded cell' feel that comes from recording in a heavily damped studio or voice-over booth. A word of warning though: a bright reverb treatment can emphasise any sibilance in the voice so listen critically to the vocal sound once the reverb has been set up to make sure that none of the 's' sounds are over emphasised. This applies to both the spoken word and singing. See the de-essers section in the chapter

on compression for more advice on how to deal with sibilance. As a rule, room ambience treatments are best for spoken-word recordings.

Guitar

The electric guitar seems less critical of the type of reverb setting used; indeed, all the more subtle fine detail seems to get completely lost unless the piece of music has a lot of space. For conventional music, many guitar players prefer the sound of their amp's spring reverbs, and it's ironic that the new generation of physically modelled guitar amps and preamps tend to include spring reverb simulations, complete with all the twangy imperfections of the original.

If you pick a digital reverb setting with the right decay time and the right brightness, then you're probably pretty close to what you need, though you could experiment with pre-delay to create a little more space. It's also worth spending some time experimenting with gated and reversed treatments as these can work very well with guitar in the context of rock music.

A short, bright plate reverb can add zing to the steel-strung acoustic guitar too, but again, don't overdo it as the most natural sound is generally the most appealing.

Keyboards

To thicken synthesised sounds, again go for the brighter settings with predominant early reflections and perhaps try combining the reverb with a touch of chorus if you're dealing with a pad sound. Don't make the decay time too long as you're not trying to stretch the sounds, only thicken them. A short reverb setting used at quite a high level in the mix can create a convincing impression of massed instruments in a real acoustic space. Cheap synth sounds can be given a degree of sophistication by treating them with reversed reverb and this works particularly well on breathy wind patches and choir sounds.

Most digital synths have effects built in, though you may sometimes find it quicker to get what you want by bypassing the internal effects and using your external effects processor instead. Analogue synths tend to have no effects at all, so you'll have to add your own reverb or other effects where required.

Practical Reverb Tricks

It is well known that reverb units create a sense of stereo width and space, but they can also be used to give a sound front-to-back perspective or depth. To see how this might be done, imagine yourself in a concert hall with a solo musician playing on the stage in front of you. Because you are close to the performer, you will hear a higher proportion of direct sound than you would if you were at the back of the room. One reason for this is that reverberation in an enclosed space doesn't follow the normal inverse square law for decreasing loudness with distance but instead is at nominally the same level throughout the room. The direct sound, however, does obey the inverse square law, so the further you are from the source, the quieter the direct sound appears to be. With a good reverb unit, turning down the dry level will have almost the same effect as moving the mic further away in a live room.

At the front of the hall it's also noticeable that early reflections build up quickly and seem to be more strongly defined, whereas at the back of the room the early reflections appear to build up more slowly, giving the reverb a noticeably slower attack time. The reflections heard from the back of the hall also appear to be softer in tone, as they have had to travel further and encounter more obstacles before reaching the listener. To confirm the psychoacoustic validity of this observation, try adding a single delay with a 60ms delay time to a vocal or guitar sound. This creates a slap-back effect that immediately conjures up the image of being close to the sound source in a reflective room.

If a sound source is relatively distant, the reverb will also have less high-frequency content, as it suffers from air absorption. Not all programmable reverb units allow the shape of the early reflection build-up to be changed, but if you have one that has this facility, it's quite easy to combine this with additional high-frequency damping and a higher wet-to-dry ratio to suggest distance. Strictly speaking, the dry sound should also be attenuated using EQ to be less bright if it's supposed to be a long way off.

As mentioned earlier, the two outputs from a stereo reverb unit should normally be panned hard left and right for maximum stereo width, but some producers have created interesting perspectives by panning the dry sound hard to one side and all the reverb to the other. This state of affairs does not occur in nature but that's no reason not to use it on records if you like the sound of it. Again, there's no reason that all reverb treatments have to be in stereo, and some producers will deliberately use a mono reverb panned to the same place in the mix as the original sound to prevent the stereo image from becoming too smeared.

Another interesting avenue of exploration, if you have more than one reverb unit, is to pan a normal reverb to one side and a similar length of reverse reverb to the other. This gives an apparent shift of the stereo image as the sound decays, and with long settings might be used to add interest to ambient music.

Change As An Effect

Any good stereo reverb will create a sense of stereo width, and even front-to-back perspective, but the human hearing system will very soon decide that the effect isn't really important because it isn't changing. In other words, we tend to get used to effects that are consistently applied. Our hearing systems are far more likely to take notice of change, possibly because our hearing systems evolved as part of our survival mechanism. Obviously, a loud roar followed by the gnashing of sharp teeth right next to your left ear is going to get your undivided attention, but more subtle changes, such as a sudden silence where there was previously background noise, can also warn of possible dangers. Working on these principles, it follows that if we make changes to the expected reverb character, the listener's attention is more likely to be engaged. One way to do this may be to use a noticeably different reverb treatment for the chorus than for the verse. In most pop songs, space-creating reverb will probably be used all the way throughout a mix, but the occasional use of massive or unusual reverb settings can help create interest and hold the attention of the listener.

Creating Movement

One easy way to create a sense of movement without having to actually pan anything is to set up two different reverbs for the left and right channels. At its most basic, this could involve putting one of the outputs of a stereo reverb through a delay unit set to give around a second of delay with no feedback.

Another nice 'movement' dodge is to use a reverse type reverb in the left channel and a conventional reverb in the right. If you can match the two effects so the reversed sound reaches maximum just as the other channel decays to nothing, you get something similar to a gated reverb but with a degree of left/right movement.

Of course the most direct way to get movement is to physically move the reverb from left to right using an autopanner. Most multi-effects units now include a panning facility, and if you set the pan rate to a multiple of the song tempo you'll find the effect adds movement without interfering with the rhythm of your music. If you have an effects unit that can give you panning synced to MIDI clock, then you can have precision panning. Whereas normal panning can be gimmicky, just panning the reverb (or other effects) and leaving the dry sound in one place is far more subtle but still busy enough to be interesting. Again this is particularly easy to do using plug-in software effects.

All Wet, No Dry

Normally, reverb is added to a dry signal, but you can create interesting effects by muting the entire dry signal and using only the reverbed signal. This can work nicely on certain types of backing vocal where you want a disembodied, distant effect, and in New Age music, you can create seriously washy synth pads by using just the reverb output for certain sounds. Note that sounds treated in this way tend to move to the back of the mix, so it's a useful way of creating a sense of distance.

Another creative possibility is to crank up the reverb time to several seconds, then use a key-triggered gate to change the envelope of the gate as described in the section on using gates to create chopping effects. This is similar to the gated reverb, but instead of simply chopping off the reverb after half a second or so, you can feed a rhythmic sound into the gate's trigger input to switch the reverb on and off. For example, a percussive sound from a drum machine can be used to force the reverb to 'play' the

same rhythm as the percussive instrument. The length of the reverb notes can be changed by varying the hold and decay time of the gate, as shown in Figure 9.6. If you're more adventurous, try feeding the outputs of the reverb to two gates and panning the outputs left and right. Two different rhythmic trigger inputs can be used to create counter-rhythms that appear from the left and right channels. How well this works depends on what signal is being fed into the reverb unit, but harmonically rich sounds such as gritty synth pads or distorted guitars work well.

A similar effect can be created in an audio/MIDI sequencer by setting up rhythmic envelopes using the graphic mix automation editor. These envelopes (which can be saved in a 'library' song for future use) can then be applied to any reverb or delay effect.

Reverb Tips

- If you find a reverb patch is making a vocal appear sibilant, edit the patch so that it has more high-frequency damping. You may need to bring the HF damping right down to 3kHz or even less to clean up the sound. Alternatively, use a de-esser on the effects send feeding the reverb unit.

- During post-production, you may sometimes need to add reverb to a track that's already been mixed, in which case the bass instruments will probably get over treated and become muddy sounding. You can get around this by putting a high-pass filter before the reverb input to cut off anything below 150Hz or thereabouts. The side chain filters of a gate work particularly well for this if you're using hardware – just put the gate in key listen mode and use the filters as equalisers.

- To add interest to an otherwise static-sounding reverb, try feeding the effect send though a chorus or flange effect before feeding it into the reverb input as shown in Figure 9.7. The modulation of the chorus/flange effect will add movement and interest to the reverb patch but leave the original sound untouched so that you don't end up with a gimmicky result. This effect is great for all kinds of music from pop ballads to New Age.

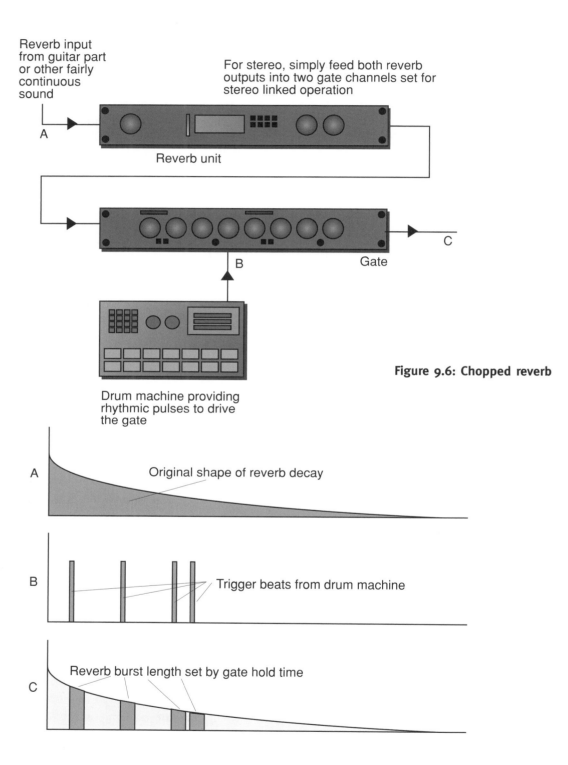

Reverb input from guitar part or other fairly continuous sound

A

For stereo, simply feed both reverb outputs into two gate channels set for stereo linked operation

Reverb unit

B

Gate

C

Drum machine providing rhythmic pulses to drive the gate

Figure 9.6: Chopped reverb

A — Original shape of reverb decay

B — Trigger beats from drum machine

C — Reverb burst length set by gate hold time

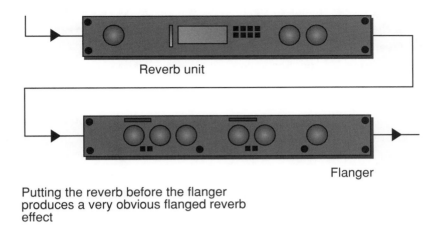

Reverb unit

Flanger

Putting the reverb before the flanger
produces a very obvious flanged reverb
effect

Flanger

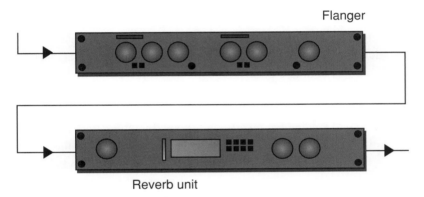

Reverb unit

Putting the reverb after the flanger
diffuses the sweep effect of the flanger
to produce a less obvious 'shimmery'
effect

Figure 9.7: Flanged reverb

- For more radical musical styles, try heavily affecting the sound before it is fed into the reverb but leave the dry sound untreated. You could use a pitch shifter, for example, to push the reverb feed up or down by an octave or even a musical fifth. You could use distortion before the reverb or even go via a multi-tap delay so that all the individual delays get transformed into their own little cloud of reverb. There's no limit to what you can try, either using discrete effects boxes, multi-effects units or plug-ins, and although some of what you come up with may be too off the wall to use, the occasional gem will emerge. Never be afraid to experiment.

- If you feel a sound needs more reverb, but adding more makes the mix sound messy, consider increasing the reverb level but shortening the reverb decay time. This increases the sense of the sound being in a real space without flooding everything in a wash of reverb. If an ambience algorithm is available, try this as an alternative to the more conventional reverb types. You can also roll off some bottom end from the reverb return to reduce low-frequency confusion.

Where you need to use long reverb sounds to create a special effect, make sure that the musical arrangement leaves space for the reverb to be appreciated. In practice, this means avoiding having too many mid-range sounds layered over the top of the reverb. As a rule, a few bright, tinkly sounds at the top end of the spectrum won't get in the way of your reverb and, by the same token, a bright reverb will still be audible over a low bass note. You'll find that in well-arranged pieces, the longer reverbs are not fighting with other sounds – it's a bit like stage lighting, where a single lamp post in the centre of a side-lit stage will cast a long and dramatic shadow, but if the stage is full of closely-spaced objects, the shadows from side-lighting will probably confuse rather than enhance.

- The majority of the energy in a pop mix is at the bass end, so avoid adding much reverb to bass sounds such as kick drums, bass guitars or bassy synth lines. If you find that a significant degree of reverb is needed on one of these sounds, then it helps to EQ either the aux send feeding the reverb unit or the reverb return to roll off the bass end.

Try to get your mix well balanced before you start to add reverb, then add it sparingly. Using less reverb invariably results in a punchier mix and you may be surprised at how little reverb is used on commercial pop records. Keep in mind that our brains interpret large amounts of reverb as distance and that nearby sounds invariably have a lower level of reverb. When we listen to a real sound source that's very close, the majority of what we hear is the direct sound, so if you want to something to sound close, don't smother it with reverb.

- Lastly, you may have an old reverb that you feel sounds unnatural by today's standards. Don't bin it because some of those trashy old sounds are great in a creative context. Some early reverbs have a nice industrial edge to them, so don't judge everything by how natural it sounds. Indeed, some software reverb plug-ins have been developed with a deliberately trashy, metallic sound as they work well in certain types of dance music.

Reverb Overview

Artificial reverberation can be thought of as the audio equivalent of lighting in photography or film making. Without light and shadow, photographs would appear very flat and two-dimensional, and the same is true of recorded music.

In the western world, we are used to hearing our music played indoors, and all buildings have acoustic properties of one kind or another. Natural concert hall reverberation could be considered as the equivalent of natural lighting – everything is illuminated by the same light source, all the shadows fall in the same direction and everything feels very comfortable and homogenous. Pop music production, on the other hand, tends to make use of a variety of different reverb treatments within the same mix – the vocals may have a long reverb, the bass may have little or no reverb and the snare drum might use gated reverb. This can be considered as being equivalent to a carefully lit film set, where different lights are used to create specific effects of light and shadow rather than emulate nature. And, just as set lighting can make or break the look of a film, the use of reverb in a mix can either turn a good recording into a masterpiece or reduce it to a swirling mess of sound.

Home-recorded demos often suffer from too much reverb, which has the effect of filling all the available spaces in a mix, and preventing it from breathing. Reverb is a powerful effect that works best when used sparingly. If you listen to a selection of well produced records, you might be surprised at how restrained the use of reverb is, and on those that use more obvious reverb treatments you'll probably find that the arrangement has been tailored to provide the space for the reverb to work.

One technique employed by pros is to combine reverb with ducking so that when the mix is busy, the overall reverb level is dropped by a few dBs. When the mix hits a quiet spot, the reverb level will swell back up to its full level. You can set this up using a stereo compressor or gate in ducking mode, then use that to process the reverb output, but an increasing number of multi-effects units include a ducked reverb algorithms, which makes setting up much easier.

My final observation is that the top-name reverbs have a distinctly more musical sound than most budget units. Specifically, the dry and reverberant sounds integrate better when you use a good-quality reverb unit and you can add more reverb to a sound without it getting smothered in reverb.

10 MULTI-EFFECTS

Initially, effects units were mainly dedicated devices: you'd buy a reverb unit that produced only reverb, a DDL for delay or echo effects, a pitch shifter for transposition effects and so on. That meant that we got to know the adjustable parameters relating to the various effects pretty well, but then along came multi-effects unit that offered all the above – and more – in a variety of configurations. With these units came presets and easy edit options, which meant a lot of newcomers to recording skipped over the essentials of effects creation. Even so, creating a multi-effects patch from the ground up is a skill worth learning – you need to know how the different effects are created, and how they interact with each other depending on their position in the signal chain.

While most software plug-ins are designed to create specific single effects, it is still possible to chain them in series to produce more complex effects. Furthermore, there are third-party software products, such as TCWorks' FX Machine, which enable software plug-ins to be connected in more complex series/parallel arrangements.

The most common individual effects found in a typical multi-effects unit tend to be based on those already discussed in previous chapters, but there are often additional effects not based on modulated delay or reverb. This chapter aims to explain how the different effects types (including the delay and reverb effects already covered) might usefully be combined. Less familiar effects will also be introduced including some that are more commonly available as software plug-ins.

Digital Delay

Digital delay is the successor to the tape echo unit, a special type of recorder using one record head and between one and four replay heads. A continuous loop of tape was used on most machines to prevent the tape running out part way through a performance, and the principle was simply that any input signal was recorded, then played back a short time later via the replay heads. An erase head then wiped the tape before returning it to the record head. The delay time was set by the tape speed and the head spacing, and by incorporating a variable speed control, and on/off switching for the replay heads, various delay effects were possible. Repeat echoes were achieved by feeding some of the output signal back to the input.

Digital delay is one of the key elements of a modern multi-effects unit and performs essentially the same task as the tape loop echo machine, but there are no tapes to wear out and the range of parameter adjustment is far greater. It may also be possible to modulate the delay time as described in the chapter on digital delay to create effects such as chorus, vibrato, flanging and phasing.

Whereas the original tape echo units were mono, today's digital effects are usually stereo. A typical DDL effect offers variable feedback to produce multiple decaying repeats, and many offer multi-tap delay, where several repeats at different delay times can be created. This is directly analogous to the multiple heads of the tape loop echo, and by feeding back some signal from all the taps the density of the repeats builds up very quickly into a kind of pseudo reverb. Occasionally there are alternative arrangements for feeding back some of the output – for example, feeding some of the left-channel output to the right-channel input and vice versa. These different strategies affect the way repeat echoes build up in complexity and you should take time to experiment with them so that you know what differences to expect.

The various delay options (given names such as delay, echo, multi-tap and ping-pong) are usually presented in the form of 'algorithms', where the routing within the effect is fixed but the user has control over the values of various parameters, including delay time (often individually adjustable for the two channels) and feedback. There's also a mix parameter or control allowing the original and delayed sounds to be balanced. In more advanced systems there may also be a means to filter out some of the top end from recirculated delays so that successive repeats become duller sounding, just as they did with tape loop units. Some may also offer a means of modulating the signal to emulate the wow and flutter of a mechanical tape echo unit as well as a means of introducing distortion into the feedback path to replicate the signal degeneration that occurs in analogue tape-based systems. This isn't simply a nostalgic fad as these 'side effects' have the subjective effect of making the repeat echoes seem to disappear into the distance.

Delay Effects

The simplest DDL effect is a single repeat using no modulation and no feedback. Short delays of between 30–100ms are used to create slap-back echo effects while longer delays tend to be used with feedback to create multiple, equally spaced echoes. As the delay time is shortened you'll notice that the echo effect disappears and is replaced by a metallic resonance, sometimes called tunnel echo. The frequency of resonance depends on the delay time: for example, a 5ms delay time will resonate at 1000/5 = 200Hz. Increasing the feedback will maximise this resonant effect.

Using a multi-tapped delay enables a less rhythmic echo effect to be created, and ideally the delay times of the various taps should not be set to exact multiples of each other. Adding feedback to a multi-tapped delay causes the echo decay to become quite complex, and this effect is popular on electric guitar, synth lead lines, sax or flute. Delay is also useful for treating synthesised sounds. Delay units and plug-ins designed to imitate tape echo units will usually offer multiple delay taps and include both high-cut filtering and distortion in the feedback path with the more authentic-sounding ones also including simulated wow and flutter.

Resonant Chords

Though not covered before in this book, the resonant chord effect is closely related to delay and is achieved by using several delay lines, each set to a very short delay with feedback and each tuned to resonate at one note of a musical chord or scale. The higher the level of feedback, the more pronounced the resonance. Any harmonically rich or percussive sound fed into these resonant delays will make the delays 'ring' at the appropriate pitches creating an eerie, almost vocoder-like effect. By using MIDI control from a keyboard or sequencer to input MIDI chords (and hence change the pitch at which the delays resonate), the ringing chord effect can be 'played' in a musically useful way. The effect has to be heard to be fully appreciated and, depending on the input source, the results can range from ethereal to disturbingly mechanistic. Perhaps the most impressive demonstration of this effect is to impose a musical chord structure onto a drum loop or other percussion track. Hardware effects that offer this facility include the Lexicon PCM80/81 and the original Alesis Quadraverb.

Resonant Filter

Closely related to EQ, the resonant filter is sometimes included so that synthesisers or samplers with no internal filtering can be treated to produce the familiar analogue filter sweep effect. In principle, a highly resonant filter, often a low-pass type, is linked to an envelope generator that controls the filter frequency. This envelope may be triggered via MIDI note ons or it may follow the envelope of the signal being processed, and there's often the means to invert the sweep direction. Multiple filter types (high-pass, low-pass and bandpass) may be offered as well as control over resonance and starting frequency. These filters generally work best on single-note lines or on block chords.

A number of synth manufacturers are now producing separate add-on filters, which can be used to impart their filter sound to instruments from other manufacturers. Depending on the model, these may be triggered by MIDI or by the analogue input signal. Most synthesisers use filters with 6, 12, 18 or 24dB/octave slopes coupled with variable resonance or Q. If a filter is to be useful in approximating most of the major synthesiser filter types, it should offer at least 12 and 24dB/octave filter settings.

Note that a single filter won't affect a musical chord in the same way as a true polyphonic synth filter unless the notes of the chord are played and released together, hence the earlier stipulation concerning single notes and block chords. If other playing styles are used, the filter's behaviour will be less predictable and, though the results may still be musically valid, they will be very different to the way a true polysynth would behave.

Vocoder

A vocoder is a special type of multi-band filter that automatically mimics the frequency spectrum characteristics of a signal being fed into a second control or analysis input. You can visualise it as a graphic EQ that's able to listen to any signal and constantly adjust its fader settings to match the spectral content of that signal. When a signal is passed through the vocoder's filters (called the synthesis signal), it takes on the same spectral characteristics as the control or analysis input. Traditionally the analysis input is a human voice and the synthesis input some form of sustained musical sound.

That's how the effect of talking or singing keyboards is produced, because no matter what pitch the vocal input, the vocoder output will always follow the pitch of the synthesis input. Fortunately, there are far less clichéd ways of using vocoders. For example, you can trigger them from more rhythmic sounds to turn a pad synth into a melodic rhythm. Some of the better sample CDs make extensive use of vocoders in unusual and interesting ways, so check these out if you need inspiration.

In order for the output of a vocoder to be intelligible, the 'unvoiced' elements of human speech such as 't' and 's' sounds need to be considered as they have no musical pitch as such – they are

essentially filtered noise. If these are omitted, vocal clarity suffers, so some way has to be found to add them back into the final signal. One method is to use a so-called voiced/unvoiced generator that recognises these 'fricative' sounds and replaces them with some kind of electrically generated noise. Another option is to extract the very high frequencies from the analysis input and add these to the output. In either case, the user has a control to set how much of these unvoiced sounds are mixed into the vocoder output.

Although it is difficult to make analogue hardware vocoders that offer much user adjustment, software vocoders can include such facilities as offsetting the analysis and synthesis (synthesis input) frequency bands (the vocoder equivalent of format shifting), making the filter bands resonant and so on. While hardware vocoders can work in real time, software plug-in vocoders tend to use pre-recorded audio tracks as their inputs. One tip when using vocoders is to ensure that the two inputs are kept at as constant a level as possible, otherwise the vocoder output level may fluctuate excessively. In many cases, applying heavy compression to the voice feeding the analysis input is sufficient.

Modulated Delay

By modulating the delay time using an LFO the pitch of the delayed signal wavers both sharp and flat at the rate set by the LFO speed. The depth of modulation determines how far sharp or flat the sound goes. The simplest modulation effect is pitch vibrato, where only the delayed sound is used and the sound we hear from the output will be delayed slightly – if the delay time is set to less than 10ms it will be too short to notice. If you set a modulation rate of, say, 4Hz, then turn the depth control up slowly, you should hear the sound being processed take on a wavering effect, not unlike that produced by the mod wheel on a synth.

Phasing

To convert vibrato to phasing, set the mix parameter to give equal amounts of dry and delayed sound and experiment with delay times between 1–10ms. As you adjust the modulation speed and depth, you'll hear the individual harmonics that make up your sound moving in and out of phase with each other, which has the effect of comb filtering the sound in a very dynamic and complex way. As the delay is modulated, the comb frequencies move up and down the audio spectrum producing the classic phaser effect. You can vary which harmonics are affected by changing the basic delay time – the shorter the delay time, the higher the frequencies that are affected and vice versa. Because no feedback is used, the phasing effect is less aggressive than flanging.

While the chapter covering digital delays showed how to set up these modulated effects from scratch using a dedicated DDL, in the context of a multi-effects unit, modulation effects are likely to have their own algorithms, so for a phaser you may only have delay, rate and depth parameters to adjust. Irrelevant parameters may be excluded and the delay time range restricted to that relevant to the particular modulation effect being created. This helps steer the non-experienced user in the right direction, and may allow some other non-standard parameters to be added by the manufacturer.

Flanging

Flanging is similar to phasing but uses a longer maximum delay time and feedback is added to intensify the comb-filtering effect. On more sophisticated units it may be possible to modulate the delay using a source other than the LFO, for example, the input signal's envelope or a rate derived from MIDI clock. Controlling the rate from a varying signal level rather than from a fixed-rate LFO can help make the effect less obviously repetitive, and hence more like tape flanging/phasing.

As with phasing, inverting the phase of the signal fed back to the input allows different harmonics to be accentuated by the filtering process. Try both options and see which you prefer.

Chorus

Chorus is one effect that you can guarantee any multi-effects unit will offer. Technically the effect is similar to vibrato, but with an equal proportion of the dry sound mixed in to give a detuned, ensemble effect.

By setting a longer delay time than for vibrato, say between 30 and 150ms, the effect of the timing differences between instruments is made more pronounced. You can also use very gentle modulation on even longer delays to create a combined chorus and echo effect. The modulation speed is usually set in the range 2Hz to 6Hz and the depth has to be set by ear. The longer the delay time, the less depth will be needed, but the effect of too much depth is immediately obvious as the effect turns from a gentle shimmer into a sickening vibrato.

More sophisticated chorus effects blocks may include multi-tapped algorithms, which produce the effect of multiple chorus devices operating at the same time, helping to disguise the obviously cyclic nature of a single chorus. Where two or more taps are provided, it is normal for these to be panned left and right to create a stereo effect. However, an interesting stereo effect can also be created using a mono chorus by panning the chorus output to one side and the original dry signal to the other side.

Reverberation

Reverberation has been discussed in detail earlier in the book, but the most obvious variable is the time the reverb takes to die away after a percussive sound such as a handclap or drum beat. For contemporary music production, decay times of between one and three seconds are the most useful, though typical multi-effects units have a far wider range to allow for the creation of special effects. In addition to having a choice of environment-type algorithms (usually rooms, plates, halls and chambers and ambience), there will probably be gated and reverse effects available too. Some gated effects are produced simply by generating a burst of early reflections of a nominally equal level, though some still allow you to create it from separate reverb and gate 'blocks'. After decay time, the most important parameters relate to pre-delay time and the brightness of the reverb, the latter often controlled via a high-frequency damping parameter. More sophisticated units may also provide control over the reverb density and diffusion (the rate at which the reverb complexity builds up).

Panners

A basic autopanner is simply a device that automatically pans a mono signal from left to right and back again, usually under the control of an LFO. Some units incorporate options for triggering the pan from MIDI notes or syncing it to tempo via MIDI clock, in which case it's possible to synchronise the panning to the tempo of the music. A more recent advance is the inclusion of 3D panning, an effect that combines left/right panning with psychoacoustic front/back panning and, in some cases, simulated doppler shift. In 3D panning, level changes are combined with EQ changes to make the signal appear as though it is moving in a circle in front of the listener rather than simply following a straight line. As the sound pans, it appears alternately closer to the listener, then further away.

There are now numerous plug-ins that offer the ability to pan signals in elaborate ways, often creating the illusion that the width of pan is greater than the width between the speakers, but as with any dramatic effect you need to decide why you are using it and then apply it in an artistic context.

Rotary Speakers

Rotary speaker cabinets were originally used by organ players to add an interesting chorus/vibrato to the otherwise static electronic organ sound. The most famous of these is the Leslie cabinet, which creates its effect by means of a rotating, slotted baffle spinning around a stationary, vertically facing bass speaker, augmented by a rotating horn running at a different speed (balanced by a dummy horn) to carry the high end. A motor and pulley system provides two operating speeds, and because of mechanical inertia, the system takes a finite time to change between these two speeds.

In a multi-effects unit, the rotary speaker effect is usually created by a combination of modulated delay and filtering, but as far as the user is concerned there may only be fast, slow and off speed options to select from. The inertia effect is simulated by using a special LFO that changes speed over a period of a second or so rather than instantly, and the skill of using a rotating speaker (or emulation) is to operate the speed

change at appropriate points during the performance to provide the right feel. This effect also works well on guitar, synth pads and sometimes even on voice. The quality of the simulation varies from unit to unit with some sounding quite convincing, while others sound much the same as chorus.

So far, the best rotary simulations I've heard have been from software plug-ins such as the Native Instruments B3, where the rotary cabinet may be used as a separate effects plug-in to treat other audio tracks. This plug-in features a high degree of user adjustment, including the individual rotor speeds, the rate of acceleration when the speed is changed and the mic positions from which the effect is perceived.

Ring Modulator

The ring modulator has been extensively used over the years for producing sci-fi voice sounds, and works by combining two audio signals in such a way as to produce an output comprising only the sum and difference frequencies of the two inputs, with the original frequencies completely suppressed. Generally a voice or other audio signal is modulated using a fixed-frequency oscillator, resulting in a metallic, robot-like output. Because the output comprises only sum and difference frequencies, the result is almost invariably musically unmeaningful, but it is still useful as a special effect. Modulation using more complex waveforms, or even modulating one piece of audio with another, generally results in an even more chaotic output signal.

Pitch Shifters

Most effects units have a counterpart in nature – reverb and delay being obvious examples – but pitch shifting is very much a special effect in the strictest meaning of the word. Pitch shifters seem to attempt the impossible: they produce a copy of the input signal that is shifted up or down in pitch by as much as two octaves, but without changing the overall duration of that sound. If you varispeed a tape to create a pitch change, the increased tape speed needed to cause an increase in pitch also causes a reduction in duration.

A typical pitch shifter usually allows a coarse pitch change to be set in semitones (with a maximum range

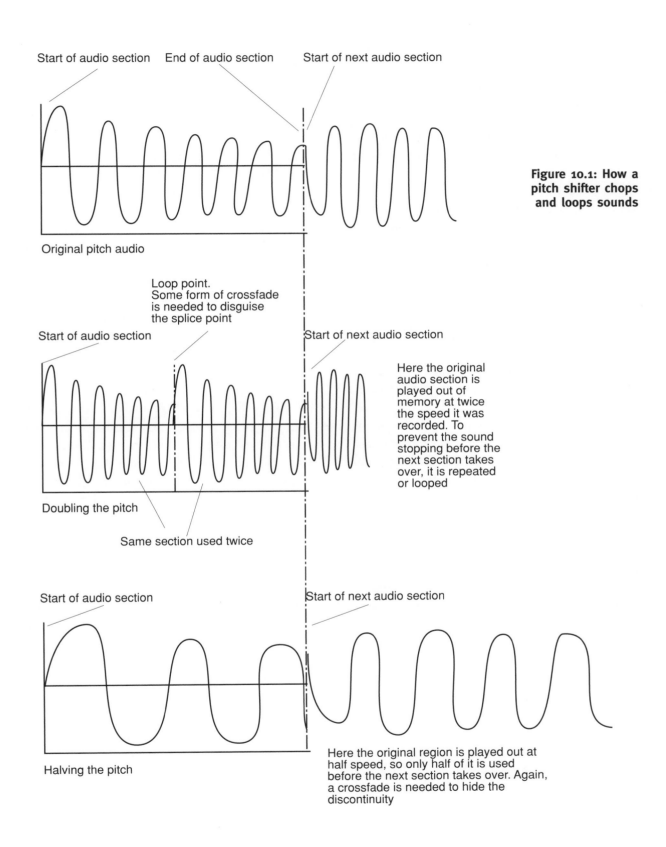

Start of audio section   End of audio section   Start of next audio section

Original pitch audio

Figure 10.1: How a pitch shifter chops and loops sounds

Loop point.
Some form of crossfade is needed to disguise the splice point

Start of audio section

Start of next audio section

Here the original audio section is played out of memory at twice the speed it was recorded. To prevent the sound stopping before the next section takes over, it is repeated or looped

Doubling the pitch

Same section used twice

Start of audio section

Start of next audio section

Halving the pitch

Here the original region is played out at half speed, so only half of it is used before the next section takes over. Again, a crossfade is needed to hide the discontinuity of +/- one or two octaves) with a further fine control providing continually variable tuning over a range of a semitone or so. In purely musical terms however, a straightforward pitch shifter has limited applications as only parallel octaves and fifths tend to be useful in most melodic applications. Pitch shifters also suffer technical limitations, and the best way to understand how these might affect you is to see how a pitch shifter actually works.

As with a DDL or digital reverb unit, the original signal must be converted into a digital form, and the hardware has a lot in common with the simple DDL. With a DDL, a signal is digitised then stored in RAM, where it is clocked out again a set time later, but to achieve pitch change the data must be clocked out at a different rate from that at which it was clocked in. This obviously creates problems, because if the RAM memory is emptied faster than it is being filled, it will eventually run out. Similarly, if the data is clocked out at a reduced rate to create a downward pitch shift, what do you do with the surplus data once the RAM is full?

The answer is that the input signal is chopped into very short sections and each one processed before the next one comes along. There's inevitably some processing delay in pitch shifting and, as a rule, the longer the individual sections being processed, the bigger the delay. Where the sound is being increased in pitch, the short section is repeated until the next chunk of audio is read, so if the pitch is being doubled, each section will be used exactly twice. Where the sound is being reduced in pitch, only part of each section is used before a new one takes its place and in the case of dropping by an octave, exactly half of each section will be used. This might seem very crude – and in may ways it is – but if the sections are made short enough, the nature of the stored waveform is unlikely to have changed by very much over the duration of each section. Figure 10.1 shows how a pitch shifter chops and loops sounds.

The real skill comes in joining up these short sections as smoothly as possible, because even though the waveform might have changed only a little, the phase is unlikely to be exactly right to join seamlessly with the sections on either side. If you try

to do a straight join, you'll hear a click at the end of each section, but if you try to hide this with a crossfade, the phase differences during the overlapped sections will cause a drop in level – the practical outcome of this is that the shifted sound is affected by a very fast vibrato, making it sound out of tune. The larger the amount of pitch shift, the more obvious this vibrato effect becomes.

Different designers have refined their own systems for minimising the glitching between sections but, from my experience, most of the pitch-shifting systems included in low- to mid-price multi-effects units tend to glitch quite noticeably unless the degree of pitch shift is kept very small. As a rule, shorter audio sections retain a higher degree of accuracy for percussive sounds, whereas longer sections produce a smoother overall sound at the expense of timing accuracy. Not only does a long audio section mean a longer overall delay, it may mean that short effects, such as the percussive hit of a drum, are played out twice if you're taking the pitch up.

At the high end of the market, advanced DSP techniques are used to optimise the section splice points, and these give much better results than budget models but at significantly more cost. In the mid-price range, some systems offer a mode optimised for monophonic signals where the splice points are constantly optimised to match the frequency and waveform of the input audio. This type of device is often used to process single-note guitar lines or vocals.

Facilities

Virtually every pitch shifter has both coarse and fine pitch controls, but there are other parameters that may be placed under user control to make the effects more versatile. By detuning the input signal by a few cents (a cent is one-hundredth of a semitone) and then delaying it by 100ms or so, it's possible to create reasonably convincing ADT effects, and with such small pitch-shifting amounts even a budget unit will sound reasonably smooth. As with most other delay-based effects, the pitch shifter will include a dry/wet mix control, though it's still possible to set the control to 'all wet' and use the aux send/returns of a mixer.

At longer delay times, the feedback may be increased to recirculate some of the pitch-shifted sound, and again most units have a feedback parameter or control. If you haven't heard this effect before, it's very unusual because each time the signal recirculates it is shifted further in pitch causing a kind of spiralling effect. For example, if you set up a four-semitone shift range and a delay time of half a second or so, the note being played will run up a diminished musical scale. Shorter delays and higher amounts of feedback give an ethereal pitch-swirling effect that you've probably heard countless times before on low-budget sci-fi films or TV programmes.

Yet another useful facility is to have two or more independent pitch shifts that can be set up at once so that, for example, you can have your original sound plus a fifth up, an octave up and an octave down. Level and pan parameters may be provided for each shifted sound.

MIDI Control

As with most multi-effects parameters, MIDI control is possible – providing the model you have supports this mode of operation. It's quite common, for example, to be able to input MIDI note numbers from a keyboard or sequencer to control the amount of pitch shift. This is often organised so that playing middle C on the keyboard produces no pitch shift, with notes either side of it shifting the signal up or down by a corresponding number of semitones. For example, if you play a B (one semitone down from middle C), whatever pitch is being processed will drop by one semitone relative to its original pitch. Working this way takes some getting used to, but it does mean that you can program a vocal harmony line into a MIDI sequencer to control the pitch of a vocal line played from a multitrack synced to the sequencer. All that you have to remember is that you're programming using intervals to determine how much pitch shift you want and you don't play the actual notes of the harmony.

More advanced machines dispense with the need to indulge in these mental gymnastics by tracking the pitch of the incoming audio. This means that only monophonic lines can be processed (pitch tracking doesn't work on polyphonic music), but at least the notes you play on the keyboard can be the notes you actually want – the software works out the actual amount of shift for you. A good unit of this type can be very useful for fixing vocal tracks where the singer goes out of tune on certain notes, because all you need to do is press the required key just before the note in question and the pitch will be pulled exactly to that note. It's also possible with many pitch shifters to control the pitch in real time from a keyboard pitch-bend wheel. This again is useful for bending badly sung notes precisely into pitch.

More sophisticated hardware pitch shifters and plug-in software may have dedicated vocal correction modes, and though it's invariably better to get the singer to hit the right note in the first place, having the means to correct faulty vocals is very useful if you're working on a track after the singers have gone home.

Auto-Tune

Auto-Tune is a special kind of pitch shifter (available both as hardware and as a software plug-in) that is designed to correct vocal pitching problems. It works rather like the automatic harmony generator described in the previous section, except the pitch shifter only moves the audio to the nearest note in a user-definable scale. For example, if the key were set to C major and the singer was singing the note of D slightly sharp, this would be shifted back down to D to correct the pitching error.

Clearly if the pitch correction worked too fast, all the natural inflections in the voice would be removed (which is exactly how the vocal sound in Cher's 'Believe' single was created) so a control is included that sets the rate at which correction is applied. Set properly, natural scoops and vibrato are unaffected, but sustained notes still settle on the correct pitch. In addition to being able to define user scales, it is also possible to set notes that Auto-Tune should ignore, thus restricting pitch correction to only those notes that are needed. Other facilities include the means to reduce existing vibrato or even to add new vibrato.

Auto-Tune (plug-in only) also includes a graphical pitch correction mode for more surgical corrective work where the user can modify the pitch of individual notes on screen. Using a computer mouse, the pitch

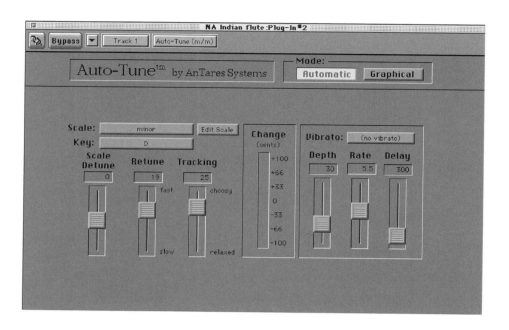

Figure 10.2: AnTares Auto-Tune

graph can be 'dragged' to a new position – for example, to correct a note that drops flat over a period of time. Once the necessary adjustments have been made, the file can be processed to permanently incorporate all the desired changes.

Software Advantages

When it comes to changing pitch without altering length – or changing the length of a piece of music without changing the pitch – non-real-time pitch-shifter software has the advantage over real-time hardware systems because it is possible to analyse the sound file before processing, enabling them to optimise their operating parameters to suit the material being processed. It's also likely that either the computer or the host DSP card, depending on the system, will have a lot more processing power available than a budget hardware unit. Furthermore, the computer doesn't have to work in real time – it can process an audio file off-line allowing it to take more time over doing a good job. Figure 10.2 shows a screen shot taken from the popular Antares Auto-Tune vocal pitch-correction package.

The better software pitch-and-time manipulation packages do a surprisingly good job, enabling a piece of music to be adjusted in tempo or pitch by several per cent without any obvious trace of processing. Similar algorithms are used within samplers to 'time-stretch' or 'time-compress' things like drum loops to make them fit the tempo of the song being worked on.

Other Auto-Tune Applications

The main purpose of Auto-Tune is to tighten up vocal pitching – something it does very well – but it can also be used to produce creative effects and to improve monophonic instrument performances. As explained in the preceding section, forcing incoming notes to the right pitch is only part of the story, because if that was done too efficiently you'd end up with a very robotic-sounding, pitch-quantised performance.

To avoid this problem there's a slider to adjust the rate at which correction takes place, though very interesting effects can be created by applying different rates of pitch correction to monophonic instruments. One very effective demonstration I heard used a theremin as the input source and, as you know, theremins produce a continuously variable pitch and so are very difficult to play with any musical precision. With Auto-Tune's tracking set to its fastest, the theremin sound was forced to produce only discrete, stepped pitches, just like a keyboard. However, setting a longer correction rate enabled the instrument to be played apparently normally, but whenever a sustained note was played, it would glide smoothly into perfect pitch. The same technique can be used with other variable pitched instruments such as cellos, fretless bass guitars and acoustic double bass. I've also used Auto-Tune to tidy up the sound of a North American native Indian flute I have, as not all its notes play exactly at concert pitch.

More Creative Uses

Because Auto-Tune doesn't apply formant correction, any sound pulled far from its original pitch sounds unnatural in the same way any conventionally pitch-shifted signal would. This isn't usually a problem, because the normal amount of pitch correction is less than half a semitone, but the effect can be abused in creative ways by deliberately setting large scale intervals. For example, you could set up a target scale containing only octaves and fifths, then no matter what you sing it will be forced to one of two notes – very effective for world-style music or to create interesting drone parts.

In this example, the voice timbre is transformed in proportion to the pitch difference between the note being sung and the nearest scale note that it is eventually shifted to. To illustrate what I mean, imagine a continuously rising sung note: there would be no pitch change until you got within range of the next note in the target scale but the timbre of the note would change as the pitch shifter worked harder and harder to maintain the pitch. In this example, the pitch shifter might attempt to push the pitch of the note down to compensate for you singing higher, so the timbre will take on a darker, bigger quality. Then, when you get within range of the next note in the scale, the timbre will flip as the pitch shifter pushes the pitch upwards and the timbre will change quite abruptly to take on a speeded-up quality.

I have also discovered some interesting tricks using electric guitar: set to a normal pitch correction rate, Auto-Tune can compensate for incorrectly bent notes in a guitar solo, but by speeding up the correction rate some very interesting things start to happen. Now when notes are bent, they slur rapidly between the notes in the target scale rather than gliding smoothly, lending the whole performance an eastern flavour.

Intelligent Harmony

It's not a huge step from intelligent pitch correction to creating intelligent harmonics, providing – once again – that the input signal is monophonic so that its pitch can be tracked. Depending on the unit, there may be preset harmony scales (major, minor, blues and so on) that the user can choose in conjunction with a musical key, after which the device creates a musically valid harmony of two or more parts in real time. Such technology is commonly used to help live solo vocal performers create their own harmonies and is even installed as part of elaborate karaoke systems, but more sophisticated units are made for studio use where the quality of harmony can be surprisingly realistic. Various proprietary strategies are employed to keep the pitch-shifted vocals sounding natural, with varying degrees of success.

Shifted Formants

A problem with all simple pitch shifters is that a voice quickly becomes 'Mickey Mouse' or 'Darth Vader' sounding as it's shifted up or down, though some dedicated vocal units hide this by using clever vocoding techniques combined with the pitch shifting. However, a better approach is to apply so-called formant correction, and already there are a number of software-based pitch shifters that have this facility.

So, what is formant correction? When a singer sings a new note, certain components of the sound stay the same – the throat and chest cavity resonances, for example. However, with conventional pitch shifting these seem to change along with the pitch, so as the pitch gets higher, the chest and throat of the singer seem to get smaller. It's the same with stringed instruments: the body size seems to reduce as the pitch is pushed up, so a violin dropped by an octave might sound more like a cello or bass. Formant correction preserves the fixed resonance that characterises an instrument or voice while allowing the pitched element of the sound to change, resulting in a much more natural sound. Alternatively, you could deliberately move the formants to make a male voice appear female, or vice versa. Though current formant shifting technology doesn't sound entirely natural, this is going to be a hugely important area in the not-too-distant future, and is set to change the nature of recorded vocals.

Voice Changers

It's also possible to change the character of a vocal without changing the pitch at all and, as these processes become more sophisticated, they'll enable people to change their voices to sound more like they always wanted them to sound – one day they may even be able to emulate other singers. Powerful DSP technology is enabling this area to progress very quickly, so expect some remarkable developments over the next few years. Though you can't yet dial E for Elvis, it is possible to add 'growl' and specialised vibrato to a voice as well as apply formant shifting. Currently a joint venture between TC Electronics and IVL of Canada is leading the way in this field.

Applications

A pitch shifter is connected like any other 'effect' in that it can either use the aux send return system or be patched in via an insert point. If, however, you're using the device to process a single voice, then connecting via an insert point may be more appropriate. If the device has a stereo output, you can always route the second output to the insert return, panned hard left and right.

One of the most popular applications of a pitch shifter is to detune a sound slightly to produce a chorus effect – even a low-cost pitch shifter can do this effectively. As most pitch shifters can produce at least two simultaneously shifted signals, a good way to do this is to create equal and opposite shifts of up to ten cents so that the average pitch is still correct. Panning the shifted sounds to either side and leaving the original sound in the middle gives a nice thickening effect with lots of stereo spread that sounds more natural than conventional chorus. This works well not only on vocals but on also on string, brass and synth pad sounds.

Increasing the delay of the two outputs to between 20 and 100ms produces a nice ADT emulation and, as mentioned earlier, even a budget shifter will sound smooth enough for detuning work.

Whole-tone harmonies are of limited use unless they're octaves or fifths, but of more concern is the glitching effect that occurs with such large shifts. Octaves can be used to give solo guitars a pseudo bass accompaniment (or shifted up to create a 12-string effect), which works well on riffs or arpeggios, but you may have to keep the shifted level very low to hide the glitching. Not only does glitching make the sound seem unnatural, it also makes it sound unacceptably out of tune.

Such large shifts are probably best suited to special effects, and producer Tony Visconti once confided in me that he'd used one of the original Eventide Harmonizers to create the deep snare drum sound on David Bowie's 'Let's Dance' record. This was achieved by adding a pitched-down version of the snare into the mix and choosing the best amount of pitch shift by ear. Kick drums can also be made monstrously deep, but unless the inherent processing delay of the pitch shifter is low, drums might seem out of time or flammy (doubled) after processing. On a hard-disk workstation, delayed tracks can usually be pulled back into time using a negative track delay of a few milliseconds, but the doubling or flamming effects that sometimes affects drums can't be cured.

The spiralling effects that are achieved by combining pitch shift, delay and feedback are generally unmusical, but are useful as spot effects. Even squeaking a plectrum along an electric guitar string results in a wild cacophony of sound that might be useful in a dance song intro.

Within the context of a multi-effects algorithm, pitch shifting may be used as an alternative to chorus (and sometimes it takes less processing power than chorus), not only as an overt effect, but also to process the input to other blocks such as reverb or chorus. Similarly, you can drop the input to a reverb unit by an octave – or push it up an octave – while leaving the original sound dry. The heavier the subsequent processing, the better disguised any glitching will be, so try octave shifts in conjunction with heavy overdrive, swept filters or heavy flanging. Even the least sophisticated pitch shifter can be useful if you use it within its limitations.

Multi-FX Building Blocks

Multi-effects units also tend to contain building blocks based on signal processors such as mixers, equalisers, gates, compressors, exciters, speaker simulators, overdrive effects and swept resonant synth-style filters. Mixer modules are included because within a multi-effects unit the signal can generally be routed in many different ways, through several combinations of effects blocks. Every time two effects block outputs have to be mixed together, or when a dry signal has to be mixed with the output of an effects block, a mixing element is needed. As far as the user is concerned, it's usually only necessary to adjust levels as the effect algorithm includes mixers wherever they are needed, but one or two specialised units give you separate access to mixer elements so that you can, in effect, build your own algorithms.

When the output of one effects block is fed into the input of another there will be no need for a mixer (series connection), but when the outputs from two parallel effects blocks need to be combined, a mixer will be required. Individual effects blocks may also incorporate mixing elements, for example, a delay block requires a mixer to balance the dry and delayed sound and to mix the recirculated sound with the input to create delay feedback effects.

Simpler multi-effects units may be limited to connecting the individual effect blocks in a series chain, and the simplest of these place the blocks in a preset order, leaving the user with choice of which blocks to use and which to turn off. In some cases, different multi-effect algorithms (in effect different multi-effect chains) are available for vocal, guitar, keyboard and so on. More sophisticated systems allow the user to rearrange the individual blocks into a different order, and it's quite common for both series and parallel connection to be permitted. Figure

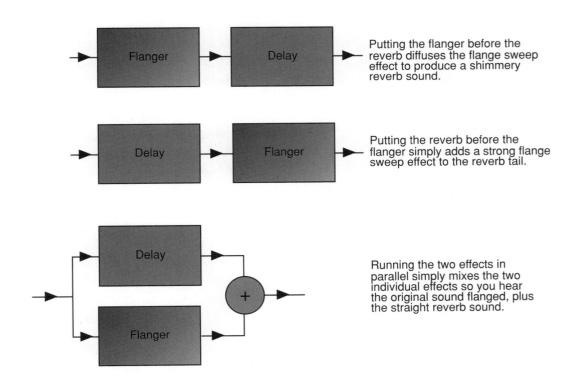

Putting the flanger before the reverb diffuses the flange sweep effect to produce a shimmery reverb sound.

Putting the reverb before the flanger simply adds a strong flange sweep effect to the reverb tail.

Running the two effects in parallel simply mixes the two individual effects so you hear the original sound flanged, plus the straight reverb sound.

Figure 10.3: Series and parallel routing options

10.3 shows an example of both series and parallel routing options.

Equalisation

There's no big mystery about equalisation, but it does come in several guises – specifically shelving, parametric and graphic. The familiar treble and bass controls provide both cut or boost at the extremes of the audio spectrum, and these tend to be based on shelving filters. The various EQ types are covered earlier in the book, so there's no need to cover them in detail again here. In addition, there may be high- and low-cut filters with steep slopes (between 12 and 24dB/octave) with variable cut-off frequencies.

While a shelving equaliser is a 'broad stroke' kind of a tool, parametric equalisers are far more precise devices, which can be tuned to specific areas of the audio spectrum as narrow as a single semitone. A single parametric equaliser has three controls for cut/boost, frequency and bandwidth, where bandwidth determines how wide a band of frequencies is affected. Depending on the power of the multi-effects unit, parametric equalisation may be offered in single-band or multi-band formats.

Graphic equalisers have the advantage of simplicity, though you obviously lose the physical fader control once you get into multi-effects-box territory. Even so, some units provide a graphic-style readout on the display so that you can still see the shape of the curve you have set up.

Sweep Filters

The filter used in a typical analogue synthesiser is closely related to the parametric equaliser – the main difference is that the frequency of the filter can be controlled electronically rather than being left to the user. For example, an LFO could be used to sweep the frequency up and down, or an envelope could be generated to provide a filter sweep. You'll probably also find that the filter can be set to a higher Q and at the highest Q setting the filter may break into self-oscillation. Some of the more sophisticated processors include not only resonant synth-type filters, but also a variety of possible control sources, including envelopes derived from the input signal level, MIDI-triggered envelopes, LFOs, etc.

Gates

An amp/speaker simulator can be as simple as a filter circuit that mimics the amplifier and loudspeaker voicing of a typical guitar amplifier. Many multi-effects units now include amp/speaker simulators as well as overdrive, which enables the user to create a fully produced guitar sound within the one unit. The output may then be recorded without further processing. In addition to creating authentic miked guitar-amp sounds, amp/speaker simulators are also useful for warming up digital synths where a fatter, more 'analogue' sound is desired.

More sophisticated amp simulators can be created digitally by using DSP processing in combination with specially devised algorithms to accurately emulate real-life amplifiers and speaker cabinets. A number of guitar amplifiers and preamps already operate on this principle with physically modelled amp simulation also making an appearance in some multi-effects processors. Software equivalents are also available as DSP plug-ins for hard-disk audio workstations.

Done properly, modelling can convincingly replicate the tonal and overdrive characteristics of classic guitar-amplifier-and-speaker combinations as well as traditional guitar effects like wah-wah and fuzz.

Serious guitarists may still want to use their own analogue distortion pedals before a multi-effects box, and that's fine, but digital overdrive can also be used to great effect on organ and pad sounds if it is used in moderation. Drum sounds and loops may also be 'crunched up' in interesting ways.

Choosing Multi-Effects

Today's, the sheer range of multi-effects units available is bewildering and covers the price range from low budget to pro studio. Before choosing one, you should think about both your budget and about what you really want to do with the unit once you've bought it. If this last point seems obvious, consider that, when it comes to mixing, at least one of your effects is likely to be a room or plate reverb, so if you've got only a single multi-effects unit to play with, you may find most of its features are unused when you're mixing.

Compressors

The most popular use of dedicated compressors is to control vocal, drum or bass levels, though in the context of a multi-effect unit they may also be used to add sustain to guitars, to reshape the decay characteristics of a reverb decay, or to compress the input or output to one of the other effects blocks. In other words, the compressor is more likely to be used in a creative rather than corrective mode in a multi-effects environment. Because compressors increase the level of program noise during quiet passages, they are often used in conjunction with a gate. As a rule, the gate goes before the compressor.

Ducking

Ducking is a technique for controlling the level of one signal according to the level of another signal. For example, the radio DJ's voice that causes the background music to 'duck' in level every time he speaks is a perfect example of ducking.

Some multi-effects boxes now include ducking delay and ducking reverb algorithms, the idea being that when the playing is busy, the effect remains at a low level so as not to get in the way. However, when there's a pause the effect swells up to its full level. The user generally has control over the degree of ducking that takes place. Effect ducking of this type can serve to keep a mix uncluttered while still creating the illusion that heavy effects processing is being used.

Enhancers

There are several types of enhancer on the market today – as explained in the chapter on that subject – but most tend to create a sense of brightness and transparency by manipulating the high-frequency end of the spectrum. Within a multi-effects unit, exciters may be used to brighten individual instruments or, if the routing will permit it, they may be placed after another effects block to brighten only one component of the sound – for example, the output from a reverb or delay. Alternatively, you may want to create a multi-effects patch for stereo mastering, which might include a series connection of compressor, equaliser, limiter and enhancer.

Morphing

Morphing isn't so much an effect as a way of changing one effect into another. Rather than simply crossfading two different effects patches, morphing involves changing the parameter values of the first effect over a period of time so that it actually becomes the second effect. Depending on the effects at either end of the morph, what happens in the middle may be musically useful or unusably chaotic. Only a few effects units include an automatic morphing system (usually triggered by the user), but it is possible to set up your own using an effects unit that permits MIDI parameter control. See the chapter on MIDI control for details on how to set up your own morphs. There are also some effects boxes that allow you to use a pedal to morph between two different sets of effect parameters set by the user.

Amp/Speaker Simulators

While keyboards tend to work best through a hi-fi-type of system with a flat frequency response and minimal distortion, guitar and bass amplifiers are 'voiced', which means their frequency response is shaped to suit the instrument rather than being left flat. Furthermore, the loudspeakers and enclosures used in guitar and bass amplification tend to have a very limited frequency response (and often some interesting cabinet resonances), which enables them to filter out the rougher-sounding components of amplifier distortion. If you were to DI a distorted guitar without EQ, the result would be very thin and raspy compared to what you would hear from an amplifier. To make DI'ing the guitar a more practical proposition, an amp/speaker simulator is required.

In most studio situations, effects are added during mixdown rather than when recording, not only so that you can change things at the last minute, but also because recording with a stereo effect takes up two tracks rather than one (less of an issue if you're recording to a computer sequencer). Sometimes a track shortage or a mid-project bounce will force you to commit to an effect, but most of the time they'll be used for the final mix. This being the case, should you buy a separate, dedicated reverb processor to handle your reverb requirements or go for a multi-

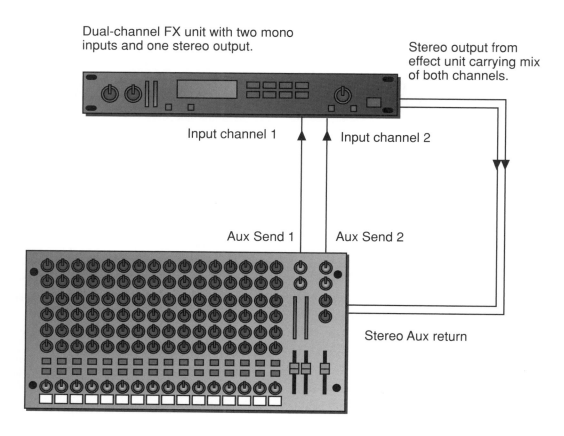

Dual-channel FX unit with two mono inputs and one stereo output.

Stereo output from effect unit carrying mix of both channels.

Input channel 1 Input channel 2

Aux Send 1 Aux Send 2

Stereo Aux return

Figure 10.4: Dual effects unit at mixdown

effects unit? Alternatively, there are units that can be configured as two or more different effects. Most of these enable you to feed one effect via the left input and the other via the right input, which is fine as most stereo effects are created from a mono source. The left and right effect channels are combined at the main outputs to be fed back into the mix via a single stereo return. Most times this doesn't actually lose you any flexibility, and it saves on effects returns. Figure 10.4 shows a two-channel processor set up in this way. Some processors can function as up to four individual effects units with four discrete inputs.

If you choose the multi-channel multi-effects route, it pays to be aware that these devices generally share out their processing power between the different effects in different ways, and you may find that once your dream multi-effect is set up in one channel, you don't have enough power left over to drive a really

good reverb algorithm in the other. While you can get away with a crude reverb as part of a multi-effects patch, for use on vocals or drums, you need the nicest-sounding reverb going. Unless your effects processor has enough power for the job, you'll probably reach the stage where either the reverb or the multi-effects will be compromised.

Another consideration with this type of effect is how you patch it into your system. Reverb is almost always fed direct from a post-fade aux send, but with multi-effects that are being used on just a single track it's sometimes better to patch them into the channel insert point so as to avoid mix buss noise. Clearly, if you have a conventional dual-channel effects box, you can use it only one way or the other, not both. Should you want the ultimate in flexibility, you'll need to make sure that you choose a unit that has multiple stereo outs rather than shared outs so that you're not limited in how you patch things together. Of course it may be that the expense of going this route means it's just as affordable to buy a dedicated reverb box plus a more conservative multi-effects processor (which would be my preferred choice), and in most studios you'll find at least one good dedicated reverb as well as one or more multi-effects devices. Even if you have a digital mixer with in-built multi-effects, you might find you get better-quality reverb from a well-chosen external processor and it's certainly true at the time of writing that a mid-price hardware reverb unit will sound better than a software reverb plug-in.

Effect Combinations

A typical multi-effects unit invariably offers reverb, delay and pitch-based effects. Many also contain building blocks based on some or all of the following signal processors: EQ, equalisers, gates, compressors, exciters, speaker simulators, overdrive effects, resonant synth-style filters, vocoders and digital distortion devices.

Basic multi-effects units may be limited to connecting the various effect blocks in a series chain whereas more sophisticated units either allow the user to rearrange the blocks into a different order or to select from a menu of preset chains designed for different applications. In more sophisticated units, both series and parallel connection may be possible, which makes it possible to create far more complex effects than the simple series chaining shown in Figure 10.3.

Few software plug-ins are presented as multi-effects because of the demands they place on CPU power so it's more usual to combine the plug-ins you need to create your own multi-effects, but I think it is important to point out at this time that most useful effects combinations are fairly simple and generally comprise between two and five individual effects. For example, connecting a low-cut filter, delay and reverb in series is a practical way of setting up a nice delay effect without too much low end.

The majority of audio software that supports plug-ins accepts only series connections, though parallel effects can be set up by using two different aux sends feeding two different effects plug-ins. Additionally,

third party 'shell' programs such as TCWorks' FX Machine or Bias' V-Box allow many plug-in effects to be linked to form complex series/parallel combinations. Such combinations can soon eat up a lot of processing power, especially where high-quality reverb is involved so it pays to keep your sequencer's CPU performance meter visible.

Patch-Change Time

In theory, it's possible to implement a degree of mix automation by switching effects patches via MIDI during a mix. A potential problem here is that patches tend not to switch instantaneously, but instead the effect output is muted for a second or so while the new algorithm is loaded. Indeed, the better effects and reverb units tend to mute the longest as they use more complex algorithms than budget units, and every time a new patch is selected a new algorithm has to be loaded into memory and any audio data in RAM must be flushed out. The solution when switching between algorithms is either to use two different effects units and alternate them, or make sure that the effect is changed over when there's a pause on the track being processed.

MIDI control may also be used to automate the effect level if your multi-effects unit allows you to assign MIDI volume to the input or output level of the effect. In fact, real-time MIDI control can be used to make sophisticated effects changes during a mix providing you don't need to switch to a different algorithm, though be warned that some cheaper units exhibit a phenomenon known as zipper noise. As a rule, most software plug-ins can be adjusted in real time without producing zipper noise, but this is by no means universally true.

Zipper Noise

When a value is changed within a digital effect algorithm, it is done in a series of small discrete steps rather than continuously, as in the case of an analogue control knob. If these steps are big enough, a change in parameters such as level, chorus depth, EQ or delay time may be accompanied by an audible ticking known as zipper noise. Sophisticated units use a system known as linear interpolation to smooth out these steps, resulting in smoother parameter changes. The only way to avoid zipper noise when using effects that suffer from this problem is to make parameter changes during pauses.

Patches

Good effects patches can take a long time to create, and because they're held in battery powered RAM memory, they can occasionally get corrupted by power surges – or fail altogether if the battery dies. These internal batteries last around five years, but when they do fail there's no warning. ROM-based factory patches will, of course, remain.

To avoid this unwanted frustration, back up your patch edits by doing a sysex dump into a sequencer or MIDI data filer. Even if you're one of the minority who doesn't work with sequencers, the chances are that you'll know somebody who has one and who will let you create a back-up copy. Restoring the patches is usually as simple as playing the sequence back into the effects unit and it takes only a few seconds. Storing patches to a sequencer is usually a matter of connecting the MIDI Out of your effects unit to a sequencer, putting a sequencer track into record and executing a sysex dump from within your effects unit's MIDI menu, but check your equipment manuals to make sure there's nothing out of the ordinary about either your sequencer or your effects unit.

Sysex dumps also provide a means for getting third-party patches into your machine, so if you have friends who use the same model effects unit as you, an hour or two spent swapping patches could be quite productive. It's also becoming increasingly common to trawl Internet music sites for effect and synth patches. If you can get the data onto disk in a PC-friendly format, Macs should also be able to read it if they either have recent system software, or a utility such as PC Exchange for those using older operating systems. Of course you can't load patches from a different make or model of unit, even if they appear to use the same basic parameters, because the system-exclusive commands, as the name suggests, are exclusive to that one machine.

If you're interested in getting hold of more patches, your first port of call should be the manufacturer or distributor, where the product specialist should be able to put you in touch with any user groups that may exist. There's also a high probability that the product specialist will have some useful patches he'd be prepared to share with you. More professional effects processors may use a plug-in card system for storing patches, and it's common for specialist effects, or even brand-new algorithms to be available on ROM cards.

Plug-in patches are usually saved in a special 'settings' file that can be backed up in the same way as any other computer data. Effect settings for VST and similar plug-ins are also stored when you save your song so, providing you keep back-ups, you shouldn't risk losing any of your custom effect settings.

While there's no need to feel guilty in using factory patches if they do what you want, the chances are that you'll be able to come up with something more appropriate to your own needs if you're prepared to spend a little time experimenting. If you're the adventurous type, you can jump right in and start creating new effects from scratch, but you'll be surprised how much can be achieved simply by editing the main parameters of some of the existing factory presets, then saving the results into a free user memory. The obvious things to try are changing delay and reverb decay time, and changing the relative levels of the different components of the effect. These edits can be made in just moments, yet by doing them you can transform an okay patch into something that's exactly right for your application.

11 MIDI AND EFFECTS

While MIDI is most often used in the context of sequencers, it can also be a powerful tool in providing real-time parameter control for digital effects. If you've never used MIDI before, the terminology – and indeed the overall concept – can be a little daunting, hence this brief introduction. If you're already familiar with MIDI, then skip to the next part.

Put simply, MIDI (the Musical Instrument Digital Interface), is a standard electronic communication language designed specifically for musical applications that enables two or more MIDI-equipped electronic instruments or devices to be linked together in such a way that useful information can pass from one to the other. You don't have to know anything about digital electronics or computer programming to use MIDI, but you do need to know what type of information it can transmit and how to make use of it.

Physically, MIDI equipment can be identified by the MIDI DIN sockets on the rear panel. On a typical unit, you will see sockets marked MIDI In, MIDI Out and MIDI Thru. These sockets are connected using standard MIDI cables so that MIDI messages may be sent from the transmitting device to the receiving device. A single MIDI connection is a one-way street for data, so MIDI data can go in only one direction.

MIDI instruments are electronic – the keys on an electronic synthesiser are essentially switches that tell the instrument's circuitry what note to play and how loud to play it. When a key is pressed, a note on MIDI message is produced, and when the key is released, there's a corresponding note off message. The pitch of the note played is determined by which key is played, sometimes called the key number or

note number. The harder you hit the key, the louder the sound – a circuit measures how fast the key is pushed down. The faster the key moves, the louder the sound. In MIDI terms, key loudness is known as velocity, because it's related to key speed.

At its simplest, then, a MIDI message comprises a note on message, a note number to tell the instrument what key was pressed, the loudness or velocity of the note and a note off message. That tells us how notes are sent, but MIDI can also transmit data relating to pitch bend, vibrato depth and a host of other useful performance parameters.

All of this data can be sent down a single MIDI cable to control a remote MIDI instrument. The main point to comprehend here is that MIDI isn't a means of transmitting sounds; rather, it's a system for transmitting instructions about what is happening on the master keyboard.

MIDI Channel

The simplest MIDI connection involves plugging the MIDI Out of the keyboard you are actually playing, to the MIDI In socket of a second MIDI keyboard or module. This is shown in Figure 11.1. When you play a note on the master keyboard, the slave instrument will sound the same notes – as long as both instruments are set to the same MIDI channel. So, what's a MIDI channel?

In a more complex MIDI system, you might have a single master device controlling a large number of different instruments or sound modules, and the channel system is the way these modules know which pieces of information to act on and which to ignore. In a typical system, the MIDI Out of the master

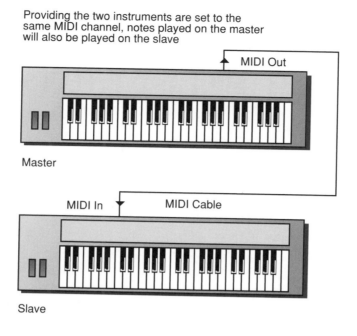

Providing the two instruments are set to the same MIDI channel, notes played on the master will also be played on the slave

MIDI Out

Master

MIDI In   MIDI Cable

Slave

Figure 11.1: MIDI master slave link

instrument (the one sending the MIDI data), goes to the In of the first slave unit, out of the MIDI Thru of the first slave to the MIDI In of the second slave and so on. This is called a MIDI chain and is shown in Figure 11.2 All the modules receive the same MIDI information but, most of the time, we want to be able to select which particular MIDI module responds to the MIDI data.

To keep the data organised, there are 16 MIDI channels, which act like postal addresses for the data being sent. MIDI information can be sent on any one of 16 channels (something you can select on the master device) and the sound modules making up the rest of the system may each be set to receive on different channels. Only when the channels match will the MIDI data be played.

Most modules have a MIDI mode called omni, which allows them to respond to all 16 MIDI channels at once, but this is of little use in normal situations. In normal use, MIDI modules should be set to poly mode (sometimes called omni-off, poly-on), so that they receive data on only one channel.

The need for multiple channels becomes more

apparent when you start using a sequencer. A live performer can generally play only one instrument at a time, but by recording the MIDI data from the master keyboard onto different tracks within a MIDI sequencer it's possible to play this data back on different channels and use it to control several different instruments, each playing a different musical part. Using a sequencer, just one multitimbral sound module or sound card (one that has up to 16 different sound-producing parts, each on a separate MIDI channel) can provide you with a complete backing track, including the drums.

If your recording isn't perfect, you can edit the recorded MIDI data to make changes. Just as a musical score is a series of instructions to the musicians, a MIDI sequence holds a series of instructions, which tell your synths what to play.

Sequencer Setup

Although you might think the musical sequencer is purely a music composing and recording tool, it can also be used to automate certain aspects of your MIDI effects units, so we need to know a little bit

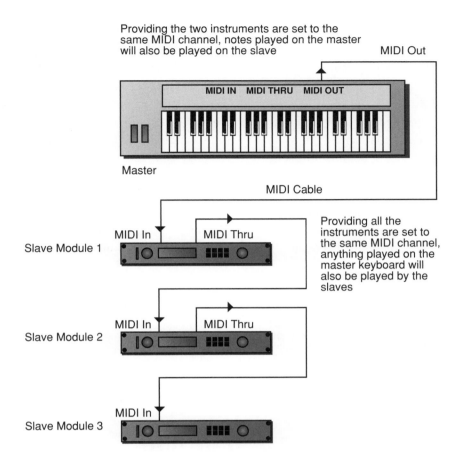

Providing the two instruments are set to the same MIDI channel, notes played on the master will also be played on the slave

MIDI Out

MIDI IN   MIDI THRU   MIDI OUT

Master

MIDI Cable

Slave Module 1   MIDI In   MIDI Thru

Providing all the instruments are set to the same MIDI channel, anything played on the master keyboard will also be played by the slaves

Slave Module 2   MIDI In   MIDI Thru

Slave Module 3   MIDI In

Figure 11.2: MIDI Thru chain

more about the way a typical sequencer is set up. Usually, a MIDI master keyboard is connected to a sequencer via a MIDI cable so that when the sequencer is set to record, any notes played on the keyboard are recorded into separate tracks as MIDI data. Some MIDI instruments have a direct computer connection, but some form of true MIDI interface will still be needed for controlling MIDI effects processors. There can be as many sequencer tracks as you have MIDI channels, but of course you can play back only 16 parts at once if you have sufficient MIDI instruments to do so – for example, a 16-part multitimbral sound module. More advanced systems use multiple MIDI output interfaces to get, in effect, more than 16 MIDI channels, but to look into that now might confuse the issue.

Sequence Editing

A MIDI sequencer is in may ways similar in concept to a word processor – you can delete or replace wrong musical notes, you can use the same phrase more than once by copying it or you can move sections about. In the edit mode, you can change the value, timing and velocity of any notes (or other MIDI data) you've recorded or even build up entire compositions by entering the notes manually.

A sequencer will record any MIDI data you send it (with the exception of MIDI clock or MIDI time code), so unless you deliberately filter out certain types of MIDI data, you can record note on/off, pitch, velocity, aftertouch (a controller that responds to pressure on the keys) and controller information as well as MIDI program changes and even system-exclusive data (which is what you get if you do a patch dump from your instrument). The more flexible MIDI effects units can make use of all this data for real-time parameter control.

Sequenced Data

All the MIDI information recorded in a MIDI sequencer is sent to the receiving device in exactly the same order and with the same timing as you originally played it, though you can change the tempo of the MIDI recording after you've made it. Because the tempo of any recorded controller information also changes with tempo, MIDI effects automation data will always stay in time with the music sequence.

Sequencer Connections

When setting up a sequencer, the master keyboard MIDI Out feeds the MIDI In of the sequencer, the MIDI Out of the sequencer feeds the first MIDI device's MIDI In, and the MIDI Thru from that device feeds the next module's MIDI In socket. This setup is shown below in Figure 11.3. Sadly, it's impractical to daisy-chain instruments together indefinitely because the MIDI signal gets slightly distorted every time it passes through another unit, and eventually there comes a point where the system becomes unreliable. For this reason, larger systems normally include a MIDI Thru box.

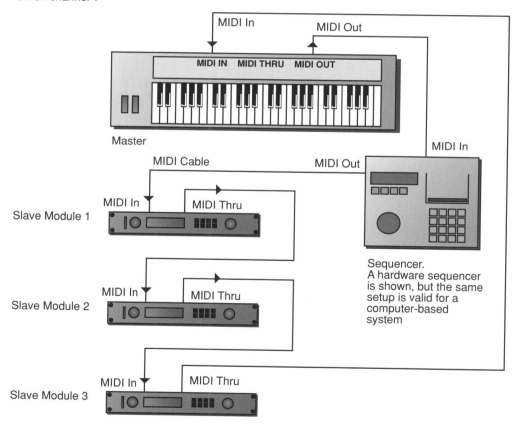

Master keyboard should be set to Local Off mode to prevent creating a MIDI feedback loop. If no Local On/Off facility is provided, set master keyboard to transmit on MIDI channel 1 and set sequencer Thru to Off on channel 1

MIDI In   MIDI Out

MIDI IN   MIDI THRU   MIDI OUT

Master

MIDI In

MIDI Cable   MIDI Out

MIDI In   MIDI Thru

Slave Module 1

Sequencer.
A hardware sequencer is shown, but the same setup is valid for a computer-based system

MIDI In   MIDI Thru

Slave Module 2

MIDI In   MIDI Thru

Slave Module 3

Figure 11.3: Hardware MIDI sequencer setup

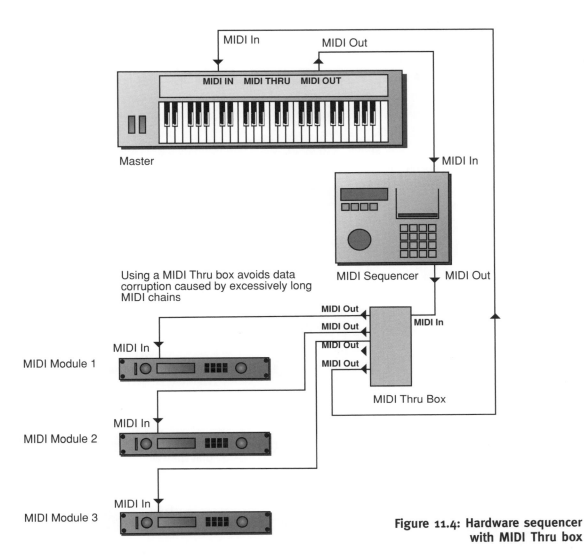

MIDI In

MIDI Out

MIDI IN   MIDI THRU   MIDI OUT

Master

MIDI In

MIDI Sequencer   MIDI Out

Using a MIDI Thru box avoids data corruption caused by excessively long MIDI chains

MIDI Out
MIDI Out
MIDI Out
MIDI Out

MIDI In

MIDI In

MIDI Module 1

MIDI In

MIDI Module 2

MIDI Thru Box

MIDI In

MIDI Module 3

Figure 11.4: Hardware sequencer with MIDI Thru box

MIDI Thru Box

A MIDI Thru Box takes one MIDI input and splits it into several identical MIDI outputs and is connected as shown in Figure 11.4. In a sequencer setup, the thru box would be fed from the MIDI Out of the sequencer – the multiple MIDI Outs can each be used to feed a separate MIDI device or indeed a chain of MIDI devices.

So far, the only MIDI Out that's been used belongs to the master synth and the sequencer; the MIDI Outs of the slave units have been left unconnected. The reason modules have MIDI Outs is so patch data (usually system-exclusive data), can be sent to a computer or MIDI data filter for storage or for editing.

MIDI Program Change

Most MIDI synthesisers and effects boxes are programmable, and individual programs can be recalled almost instantly using MIDI. In a synth, a program would be a number of parameters making up a specific sound, whereas in an effects unit, a patch would correspond to a particular effects patch you'd created, or to one of the factory preset effects.

MIDI provides direct access for up to 128 patches via MIDI messages called program changes. When you change the patch on your master keyboard, a program change command is transmitted from the MIDI Out (unless this function has deliberately been disabled via a menu option) and can be recorded onto a sequencer along with other MIDI data. When this data is sent to a receiving device, it switches to the appropriate patch. Where modules or effects have more than 128 different patch locations, these are stored in separate banks, where each bank contains a maximum of 128 different patches or programs. MIDI bank change commands may then be sent to switch from one bank to another, though at the moment, there are several non-standard bank change message types. Consult your equipment manual to find which one you need. Note that some manufacturers number their patches 1–128 while others number theirs 0–127. This can cause some confusion.

Real-Time Control

It's the performance controls on a synth or master keyboard that are most often used to control effect parameters, though you can enter the data directly into the edit page of your sequencer if you want to work that way. Whenever a pitch-bend or mod wheel is moved, a stream of MIDI data is generated, and part of the programming system of your effects unit will let you select which effects parameter is controlled by which MIDI controller message. For example, you may want to use the keyboard's mod wheel to lengthen the decay time of the reverb or the amount of feedback in a DDL effect. As we'll see later, this control data may be used to control some aspect of a MIDI effects device.

MIDI Volume

On a master instrument that sends master volume information, turning up the master volume slider will send the appropriate control information over MIDI and the receiving instrument will respond to it. Some older instruments do not respond to MIDI volume control, but most modern instruments do. You may also find that your effects unit can make use of MIDI volume in some way.

MIDI Controllers

MIDI controllers have been mentioned a lot, but what exactly are they and how many are there? If you look in the manual for your synthesiser or module, you'll find that a number of additional performance controls are supported by MIDI including sustain pedals, joysticks, sostenuto, pan and many more. These so-

called MIDI controllers are divided into two main types: those that are either on or off, and those that can be varied in fine increments. The latter are known as continuous controllers and, like most MIDI messages, generally comprise up to 128 discrete steps. A sustain pedal has a simple on/off function whereas pan or volume are continuous controllers. Controllers tend to be known by number (I've already mentioned that controller 7 is MIDI master volume), and a full listing is shown in Figure 11.5.

MIDI Modes

The majority of MIDI instruments can be set to work on any of the 16 MIDI channels, though there's also an omni mode that forces the receiving unit to respond to incoming data on all channels. It is also possible to tell an instrument whether to play polyphonically or monophonically, and while polyphonic operation is the most common, mono operation has certain applications when playing bass lines or analogue-style lead lines. The four common MIDI modes are:

- **Mode 1 (Omni On/Poly)** – enables the instrument to play polyphonically but it will respond to all incoming data, regardless of channel

- **Mode 2 (Omni On/Mono)** – nobody really knows what mode 2 is for as most instruments don't support it!

- **Mode 3 (Omni Off/Poly)** – this is the most common mode, which allows instruments to respond to individual MIDI channels and to play polyphonically

- **Mode 4 (Omni Off/Mono)** – reconfigures the receiving synth as several monophonic synths, each on its own MIDI channel. Used mainly when playing melody or bass lines, or for use with guitar synths

MIDI And Tempo

MIDI sequencers and drum machines both send and receive MIDI clock. This is the MIDI equivalent of metronome pulses, but instead of getting four to the bar, you get 96 per quarter note or 384 pulses per

Figure 11.5: MIDI controller table

0	Bank Select		73	Attack Time/Equaliser
1	Modulation Wheel		74	Brightness/Expander-Gate
2	Breath Controller		75	Undefined/Reverb
3	Undefined		76	Undefined/Delay
4	Foot Controller		77	Undefined/Pitch Transpose
5	Portamento Time		78	Undefined/Flange-Chorus
6	Data Entry		79	Undefined/Special Effect
7	Main Volume		80–83	General Purpose 5–8
8	Balance		84	Portamento Control
9	Undefined		85–90	Undefined
10	Pan		91	Effects Depth (Effect 1)
11	Expression		92	Tremolo Depth (Effect 2)
12	Effect Control 1		93	Chorus Depth (Effect 3)
13	Effect Control 2		94	Celeste Depth (Effect 4)
14	Undefined		95	Phaser Depth (Effect 5)
15	Undefined		96	Data Increment
16–19	General Purpose 1 to 4		97	Data Decrement
20–31	Undefined		98	Non-Registered Parameter Number LSB
32–63	LSB for Control Changes 0–31 (where greater resolution is required)		99	Non-Registered Parameter Number MSB
			100	Registered Parameter Number LSB
			101	Registered Parameter Number MSB
64	Damper/Sustain Pedal		102–119	Undefined
65	Portamento		120	All Sound Off
66	Sostenuto		121	Reset All Controllers
67	Soft Pedal		122	Local Control
68	Legato Footswitch		123	All Notes Off
69	Hold 2		124	Omni Mode Off
70	Sound Variation/Exciter		125	Omni Mode On
71	Harmonic Content/Compressor		126	Mono Mode On
72	Release Time/Distortion		127	Poly Mode On

Not all controllers deal with performance control. In addition to the use of the last four controller numbers to change MIDI modes, there are also bank change messages, an all-notes-off message (to cut off notes that may still be playing), local on/off and a reset-all-controllers message, so that all controller values can be reset. Where the initials MSB and LSB are shown, these stand for 'most significant bit' and 'least significant bit' – roughly speaking, coarse and fine adjustments. Both MSBs and LSBs have a possible numerical range of 0–127. Variable controllers have values of between 0 and 127, while switched controllers are usually set at 0 for off and 127 for on. Most instruments will also accept any value of 64 and above as on and any below 64 as off. Pitch bend can provide control in two directions, so its default position is midway between the two extremes – 64.

4/4 bar. MIDI clock makes it possible to sync two or more MIDI devices together where the master device (usually a sequencer) sets the tempo and the slaves followed it precisely. Using MIDI clock you can slave a sequencer to a drum machine or vice versa, or even use a sync box to lock a sequencer to tape.

Even when the master machine is not playing it is still sending out MIDI clock at the current tempo, which means that any connected device knows exactly what tempo to start at when it receives a start command. The MIDI commands for starting and stopping drum machines and sequencers are known as MIDI real-time messages. However, MIDI clock can be used with some effects units to synchronise such parameters as LFOs (low-frequency oscillators) and so on. This is particularly useful if you have a delay effect that is set to lock in with the tempo of a song that includes tempo changes. Using MIDI clock to synchronise your delays you'll find that as the song speeds up, the delay time will shorten proportionally, keeping everything musically tight.

When using MIDI clock with sequencers or drum machines, a MIDI stop command will cause both the master and slave machines to stop running. A MIDI continue restarts the machines playing from the point at which they were stopped while an 'S start' message always forces the master and slave to start from the beginning of the song.

For a MIDI sync setup to work, the master device is switched to internal clock mode while the slave machine is set to external MIDI clock sync. Figure 11.6 shows how a simple MIDI master/slave system works.

MIDI Sync

Both sequencers and drum machines can be synchronised to tape recorders, and the normal way to do this is to have the tape recorder working as a master and the drum machine or sequencer as a slave. Because tape machines don't output MIDI directly, an interface box or sync unit is needed so that MIDI timing data can be recorded onto tape (usually to the highest-numbered track). There are various different types of MIDI sync box, but the simplest uses a system known as Smart FSK, which works with another piece of hidden MIDI information known as MIDI song position pointers (or SPPs). Most modern equipment generates and recognises these. If your sync box uses Smart FSK, you can start the tape anywhere in the song and the sequencer will lock up within a couple of seconds. All you need do is compose your sequence, including tempo changes if there are any, run the sequencer's MIDI Out via the sync box and record the timing code to a spare tape track. When switched to playback and the sequencer is set to external MIDI sync, the sequencer will always follow

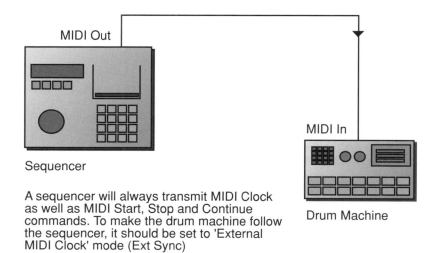

MIDI Out

Sequencer

A sequencer will always transmit MIDI Clock as well as MIDI Start, Stop and Continue commands. To make the drum machine follow the sequencer, it should be set to 'External MIDI Clock' mode (Ext Sync)

MIDI In

Drum Machine

Figure 11.6: Syncing a drum machine

the code on tape, even if you press Play in the middle of a song.

MIDI And Effects

Any MIDI-equipped effects unit will at the very least allow you to change patches using MIDI program change messages. These may be sent from a sequencer or from a keyboard and follow exactly the same format as the program change messages used with keyboards and modules. Where more than 128 patches are available, there may be a MIDI bank change facility to access these. If not, you may have to change the banks manually using front-panel controls.

In the studio, patch changes may be used within songs to add a rudimentary degree of effect automation but, as mentioned earlier in this book, many effects units change their patches too slowly for this to be useful. An alternative is to use a multi-effects unit where there are two effects blocks in parallel – for example a reverb and a chorus – but then use MIDI controller information mapped to the respective levels of the two effects to change their balance during the mix. This way you can instantly switch from reverb to chorus or vice versa, or even use a mix of the two.

To do this, you first need to study the manual that came with your effects unit to see which parameters can be controlled via MIDI. Some offer only a small selection, while other permit MIDI control of absolutely any variable parameter. You then have to assign a controller type to the parameter you want to change and again your effect manual will tell you how to do this. Finally, you have to arrange to send the appropriate controller at the desired time and, though you can do this directly from the physical controls of a keyboard, it may be easier to put the information straight into your sequencer, especially if you have one with a graphical MIDI editor. With a graphical editor, you can simply draw envelopes that correspond to the desired controller values, allowing you to make progressive changes between effects rather than hard changes.

Figure 11.7 shows a pair of parallel effects being controlled in this way via two MIDI continuous controllers. Hard changes within effect algorithms,

for example, turning parts on or off, can be handled using simple switched controllers.

Effect Morphing

An interesting experiment is to set up effects that morph into each other, and to do this you need to choose two effects that use the same parameters, but with radically different values. For example, delay and flanging both use delays with feedback, so to change a flange into a delay, you need to lengthen the delay time while reducing the modulation depth to zero and perhaps changing the feedback value. You can change all these parameters over a period of time using MIDI, and as the values change you'll hear the effect turning from a flange into a delay. Using a graphical editor is the best way to do this as you have only to join the start and end values with straight lines, though it can be interesting to make some values reach their destinations before others. The morph can be as long or as short as you like, and sometimes you'll find that what you get mid-morph is pleasantly unexpected!

Advanced FX Control

I'll be the first to admit that most of the time I'll plug in an effect and change nothing more than its level throughout a mix. However, if you don't have an automated mixer you can assign the effect level (input level is best) to a MIDI controller and automate the whole procedure from your sequencer. However, there's a lot more you can do, so I'm going to finish off this chapter by outlining a few control strategies that you might find useful.

- Use the MIDI note numbers from one of your sequencer's music tracks to control things like reverb decay time of the frequency of a resonant filter. This way you can have a filter that tracks what you play or a reverb that's longer on high notes than it is on low ones.

- I've already mentioned syncing delays to MIDI clock, but you can also sync LFOs. This can be particularly when you're working with dance music, where you might want a cyclic effect to

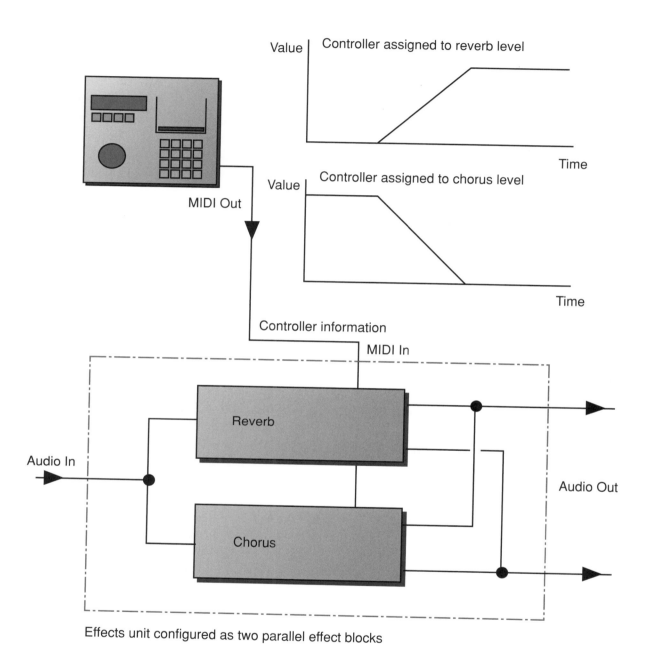

Value | Controller assigned to reverb level

Time

MIDI Out

Value | Controller assigned to chorus level

Time

Controller information

MIDI In

Reverb

Audio In

Chorus

Audio Out

Effects unit configured as two parallel effect blocks

Figure 11.6: MIDI-controlled effects crossfades

lock solidly with the tempo of the track. As with delays, these will follow any tempo changes in your sequenced song.

- Use the pad synth track to feed a resonant chord effect and feed a drum pattern into the audio input of the effects unit. The result will be a chordal ringing that turns a simple drum part into a very complex and atmospheric backdrop.

- Control the depth of a modulation effect via note velocity, so that the harder the instrument plays, the stronger the effect.

- Try some of the techniques from the gate chopping section to do the same with effects. For example, switch the output level of an effect abruptly from zero to one and then back again on each beat and suddenly the effect is a rhythmic element.

12 SOFTWARE PLUG-INS

Over the past few years, many of the traditional recording and signal-processing tasks (once the sole domain of specialised hardware) are now available via software, either using the native processing power of desktop PCs or running on DSP (digital signal processing) cards optimised for audio applications. When the major sequencer manufacturers added both audio recording, mixing and signal-processing capabilities to their systems using only the native processing power of the host computer, the desktop studio finally became a reality. This opened up the world of recording to those musicians who previously might have been able to budget for only a basic MIDI-sequencing system.

For the more sophisticated user who may need to run a number of powerful processing and mixing applications at the same time, even powerful desktop computers can run out of processing power when there's a need to do several processing jobs at the same time, but as computers get faster and more powerful this becomes less of a restriction. An alternative that places less reliance on the host's CPU power is to use a computer audio system that has assistance from DSP cards plugged directly into the PCI expansion slots of a PC or Macintosh computer. These cards can't run the same plug-in software as the host computer as the DSP chips use a different computational system to computer CPUs, but most come with a suite of specially written plug-in software, often including high-quality reverb. One of the main limitations of host-based systems is that insufficient power may be available to run high-end reverb algorithms as these require a lot of power, so moving reverb over to a DSP card makes a lot of sense.

Third-Party Plug-ins

Additional plug-in effects and processing software are available from a number of third-party suppliers, which means that the functionality of the host software (for example, an audio plus MIDI sequencer), may be extended in various ways. However, different versions may be required depending on whether the host system runs on a Mac or PC, and on whether the effects are to run on the native processor or on a DSP system. DSP chips are not generally compatible with those of a different design, and new generations of DSP are appearing all the time so it's important to ensure you buy the correct version of plug-in for your system. Furthermore, different sequencing software may support different plug-in formats and, while the VST standard is supported by a number of major software developers, it is by no means universal. Nevertheless, plug-ins of one kind or another are available for all the major audio recording and sequencing software packages, and for the purpose of this book it is sufficient to treat them in general terms rather than taking a detailed look at each plug-in format.

Native Plug-ins

Native plug-ins rely entirely on the host computer's processor and memory, so the more plug-ins you want to run at the same time the more powerful a processor you will need. Some plug-ins require more processing power than others, reverbs being particularly power-hungry. Sophisticated de-noising and de-clicking software is also processor-intensive but this tends to be used when editing stereo tracks rather than when working in a multitrack environment, so having sufficient CPU power may not be a major concern.

Logic Fat EQ

One way around the need for a powerful processor is to use a non-real-time plug-in. These generally enable you to audition a short loop of audio held in RAM while you adjust the various parameters, then the whole audio file or section of file is processed off-line. The slower the computer, the longer this will take. Unlike a real-time process that doesn't actually change the source audio file, off-line processes are destructive in that either the original file is changed or a new file reflecting the processing changes is created. Today, most plug-ins can be run in real time, though in situations where CPU power is being pushed to the limit it is still possible to process one or more tracks and in effect bounce them to a new track that includes the processing. This frees up CPU power for further real-time processing.

Depending on the type of software package, real-time plug-ins will be deployed in different ways. For example, a MIDI-plus-audio sequencer that includes a virtual mixer and real-time effects may be patched in via virtual insert points or aux sends and returns, while processors would be connected via insert points in the usual way.

In both multitrack and stereo editing packages, plug-ins can sometimes be used to make destructive edits of selected sections of the file as well as the whole file, but it is also possible to use the automation capabilities of plug-ins to process different sections of a piece of audio in different ways in real time. For example, you could program an EQ to change only for choruses or vary the threshold of a compressor at different points within a song.

Using Multiple Plug-ins
One of the advantages of using plug-in effects and processors is that there's no wiring to worry about, they don't take up space in your studio and you don't need a patchbay to connect them. You don't have to worry about whether they have balanced or unbalanced connections and you never suffer from dirty patchbay

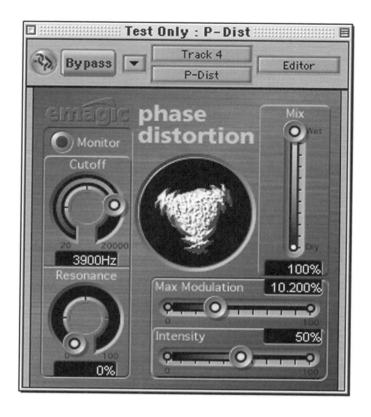

Phase distortion

contacts. Furthermore, all your settings are saved along with your song data, so you don't have to try to remember which effects you used or how much was added to each channel. Seen in this light, the advantages over hardware look overwhelming, but a hardware reverb box will never tell you it hasn't got enough power to do what you want because you're running too many compressors!

Most systems allow a single plug-in to provide multiple occurrences of the same processor, with each appearance having different settings. For example, you may be able to load in a compressor plug-in, then use six of those compressors in different channels of your virtual mixer, all optimised for different program material. The practical limit on how many occurrences of a plug-in may be used at the same time is the amount of processing power and RAM available. More sophisticated systems based on DSP cards, such as ProTools, allow additional DSP

cards to be installed when more processing capability is needed.

Plug-in Types

Virtually any effect or processor that can exist in hardware can be implemented in software – indeed, there are direct software equivalents of famous-name compressors, equalisers, gates, reverbs and so on as well as any number of general purpose EQs, delays and chorus effects. Though digital emulations of specific analogue processors are not always entirely accurate, there are several digital processes that can be done more effectively in software, not least because of the more sophisticated display and interfacing possibilities afforded by a computer screen.

In addition to the more obvious processes, plug-ins can also handle vocal pitch correction, de-noising, de-clicking and other high-level tasks such as azimuth correction of analogue tape masters made on improperly aligned machines. There are physical modelling guitar amp simulators, elaborate dithering systems for optimising bit reduction (used when converting 24-bit recordings to 16-bit CD masters), vocoders and even plug-ins to add deliberate noise and crackle to simulate vinyl recordings. These latter devices are fashionable for making new recordings sound like vintage vinyl samples, and include such parameters as record speed, recording age, amount of surface damage and so on. Other plug-ins for adding digital distortion, reducing bit depth or down-sampling to deliberately introduce quantisation distortion are popular with dance music composers. Surround sound mixing is also supported by many modern sequencers and surround encoding is available through the use of plug-ins, enabling a multi-channel audio workstation to handle TV and film sound mixing as well as producing surround audio mixes.

The plug-in environment allows a few more off-the-wall ideas to flourish, such as multi-band fuzz boxes, unusual dynamic equalisers with user-adjustable compression curves and frequency points, and various interesting metering systems for viewing stereo image, phase, frequency content and so on. There are numerous pitch manipulation packages, stereo width enhancers, 3D-sound positioning algorithms, many types of spectral enhancer and even systems that enable you to analyse the spectral content of commercial recordings then automatically EQ your own recordings to have the same spectrum.

Perhaps one of the most fascinating areas is the ability to emulate real recording environments using a process known as 'convolution' by analysing a recording of a special test signal made in a concert hall or cathedral. Producers have often dreamt of being able to take a magic box into a great sounding room and then somehow capture its effect electronically. By recording the room's influence on a test signal comprising swept tones, tone bursts or clicks, it's possible to build up a model of how that room behaves acoustically, then configure an algorithm to emulate it. Plug-in packages are already available to do this, though I've no doubt they'll become much more sophisticated in the near future.

What interests me even more is the possibility of a system able to analyse the performance of high-quality analogue processors, such as equalisers and

Sony Oxford EQ

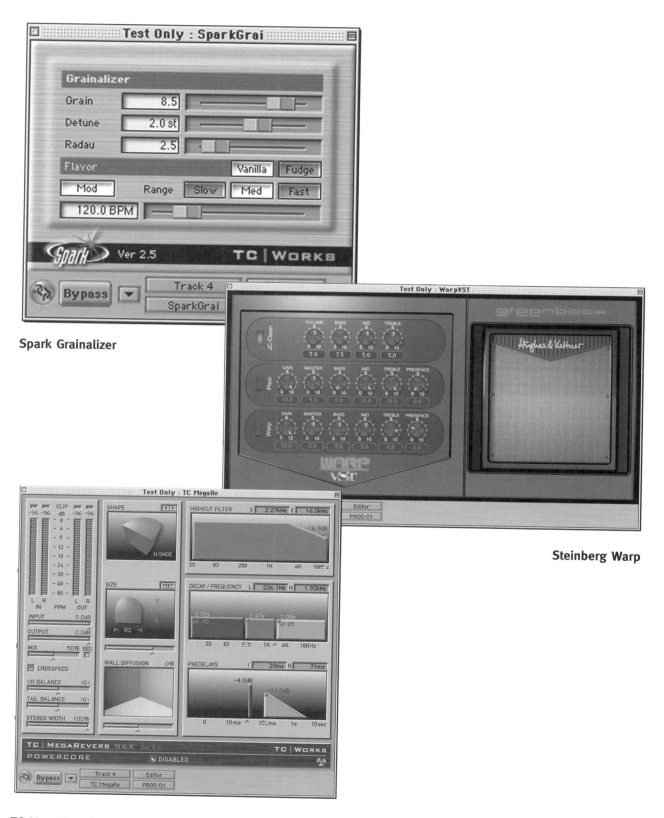

Spark Grainalizer

Steinberg Warp

TC MegaReverb

compressors, then model them in the form of digital plug-ins. Again this is already starting to happen but I foresee it as being a major line of software development in the near future.

At the time of writing, the majority of plug-ins are designed to be used within software recording and editing environments, but already manufacturers of some digital mixers are adding plug-in DSP-processing capabilities to their products so that effects or processing algorithms from third-party designers can be used within the mixer. This can only be a good thing as it gives the end user more choice and may be one way of offsetting the shortage of analogue insert points on a typical low-cost digital mixing console.

The Computer Interface

One obvious advantage of software is that computers are able to provide an excellent graphical interface, so as well as controls and meters, plug-ins often provide dynamic graphs of things like compressor slopes or EQ curves. Another very positive factor is that computers don't have to do everything exactly in real time. For example, if there's a process that could be done more effectively if the computer could analyse the signal a little before processing it (such as lookahead compression), no problem – there's the option of delaying the process for a fraction of a second so that the algorithm gets to look ahead at the material coming along. Where necessary, the whole sound file can be scanned prior to processing as is necessary for procedures such as normalisation, where the gain of the whole file is adjusted so that the very loudest peak coincides with odB FS.

The graphical interface provided by computers opens up some very interesting possibilities – one piece of software I looked at recently enables graphical images to be drawn on screen or scanned in, after which they can be further manipulated using a graphic editing program before being converted into sound. You could even scan in photographs and convert them into sound, though the results aren't always very musical! On this particular package (okay, it was Metasynth!), each pixel of the scanned image functions as a separate oscillator, with pitch being proportional to the height above the bottom of the picture and pan

position depending on the colour of the pixel. To 'play' the image, a cursor moves from left to right at a speed set by the user and, as it passes across the image, a moving vertical line of pixels plays. Various quantising effects can be set up to make the results more musical, and it is even possible to process real audio recordings using the image data to obtain weird filtering effects not obtainable with a regular vocoder. This may seem a little off-the-wall, but at least it's the only package I know of where you can use your album sleeve design to help create the music on the album!

Plug-in Automation

Elsewhere in this book I've described how MIDI effects units may have some of their parameters automated using MIDI controller information. Most plug-ins for the popular sequencers or for Digidesign's TDM ProTools systems may be automated to the extent that any on-screen user control movements may be recorded for automatic replay in sync with the song. While some processes don't lend themselves to automation in any obvious way, effect such as delay, reverb or even guitar-amp simulation can be automated to produce very creative mixes. Now that native-powered effects are very common, anyone who uses a computer can easily experiment with effect automation in the knowledge that all the necessary automation data is stored along with the song.

Software Protection

Software piracy is a major problem in some sectors of the industry so music software tends to be protected, which can be inconvenient for the legitimate user. However, it prevents unlawful copying of the software, which in the long term should mean better product support and lower prices for the end user.

Protection comes in several forms, though the older floppy disk system is being phased out as many modern computers don't come with a floppy disk drive. Perhaps the most common systems in use are the challenge-and-response code, the uncopyable master CD-ROM or the dongle (hardware key).

Dongles typically plug into computer ports, such as the keyboard buss on older Macs, the mouse port on a PC or the USB ports of a newer Mac or PC.

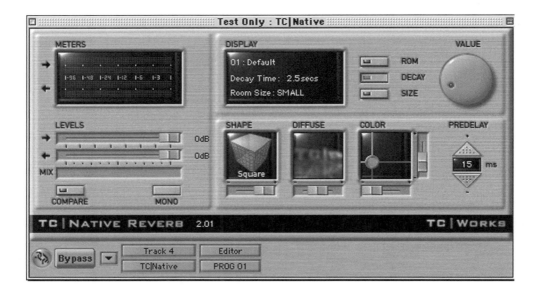

TC Native Reverb

Without them the software won't run so copies are useless to anyone except the legitimate owner as the copies will run only on a machine that has the correct dongle plugged in. Generally this is a good system, though things can get messy when you have multiple dongles hanging from the back of your computer.

Some plug-in manufacturers use a single dongle to authorise whichever of their plug-ins that you have bought, and this usually works via some kind of password system – when you've paid for the plug-in you get a password that effectively upgrades your dongle to run the new as well as existing plug-ins.

A number of companies are making extensive use of the Internet, not only to sell software but also for providing passwords to registered users and for providing software updates. Where a dongle is needed to run the software, the latest versions of all the company's products can be made freely available to all registered users with no risk of piracy.

Limited disk-install copy protection relies on an uncopyable master floppy disk from which the software is installed. If you need to change computers or reformat your hard drive, you first have to de-install all your copy protected software (otherwise the key disk will no longer work), and if you have a lot of software this can be a long job.

A less intrusive system of copy protection involves the use of an uncopyable CD-ROM as the master disk. The software is installed from this CD-ROM in the normal way, but on random occasions, usually when starting the program up, you're asked to insert the master CD-ROM before you can continue working.

Finally, there's the challenge-and-response system. After installing the software from CD-ROM, a challenge code is generated that is unique to your computer hardware. This must be e-mailed or otherwise sent to the software vendor, who will then supply a unique response code that will authorise the software to run only on that specific computer. If you change computers, your software will generate a new challenge code and you'll need to ask for a new response code.

Computing Power

Having effects that can run in real time on a host computer with no additional hardware other than a simple sound card is very attractive and, though there is a limit as to how many plug-ins even the fastest and most powerful computer will run, a modern computer can handle more than enough plug-ins for a typical pop mix, even if some virtual instruments are being used at the same time. The benefits are

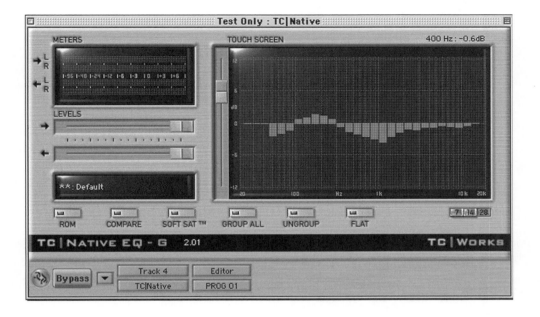

TC Native EQ

convenience, recall of all settings with a song, full parameter automation and cost (many sequencers come with a generous suite of plug-ins built in), but the downside is that really good-quality reverb places a heavy drain on processing resources and so is best either run on a dedicated DSP card or provided by an external hardware reverb unit. The latter option requires at least one spare output on the sound card or audio interface to be used as an aux send to feed the reverb unit.

Other than the fact that the control panels are all on screen as opposed to physical – and that there may be more limitations as to the way effects can be interconnected than with hardware – there's very little difference between using real and virtual effects/processors. When I first started out in recording, my outboard equipment comprised a spring reverb, a compressor, a tape loop echo unit and a few guitar effects pedals. Today, even the first-time buyer gets much more than that with a basic sequencing system.

13 PRODUCTION AND EFFECTS

The term 'record producer' is somewhat flexible and different producers are quite likely to define their jobs in different ways. A simplistic definition might be that a producer is responsible for the commercial success of a recording and also for overseeing the recording process. In other words, he is part artistic director, part musical arranger, part accountant and part personnel manager. There's a lot of psychology involved in being a good producer!

This book is concerned mainly with the creative aspects of the role, although even that can be hard to define precisely, so if you want to know more about production, read *Recording And Production Techniques*, also from Sanctuary Publishing. Some producers might simply take a back seat, tossing in the odd suggestion here and there while others may rearrange the whole song, change the instrumentation, bring in session players, or even replace most of the musical performances with samples. The typical producer, if there is such a creature, lies somewhere between these two extremes, but whatever the approach, a good producer must be able to view the work objectively and to make decisions on that basis. Some producers will stay away from the recording session for long periods to retain their objectivity, while others sit next to the engineer all the way through the project, so there's no rigid job description. Successful producers have obviously hit upon an approach that suits both them and their clients, and in truth each project has to be approached differently depending on the experience and skill of the artists being produced.

It's essential that a producer has a good 'bedside manner' when working with the same musicians in the same studio for what often amounts to weeks at a time. Recording can be very stressful, so the producer's ability to defuse confrontational situations and get everybody delivering their best is perhaps one of the most important facets of the job. Ask any studio manager what makes a good engineer or producer and the chances are that he'll place the ability to work with other people above technical ability.

Project-Studio Production

If you're reading this book, the chances are that you have your own recording system, which you use mainly for your own projects. In the project studio the engineer, producer and the performer are often the same person, which is a mixed blessing. One advantage of combined roles is that there's no risk of communication problems – you'll always know precisely what you want but, on the other side of the coin, it can be very difficult to remain objective when you're so deeply involved in all aspects of a project. It's also quite difficult to work in isolation, and experience has shown that the best musical ideas happen when you have somebody else to bounce your ideas off.

Things are very different in a commercial environment, so if you're working with other musicians in your studio, what is the best way to approach a recording job? Probably the most important thing to do at the outset is to listen to what your clients actually want to achieve. Do they actually want any production input or do they simply want you to engineer? In professional studios a good engineer often ends up having as much creative input as the producer – but rarely gets the credit for it! Find out what instruments the band uses, what sounds they like and dislike; if they're aiming for a commercial sound you need to be familiar with the market they're aiming for. Check out who else is in that market and see if you can borrow some records to see what they sound like – it's all good background material. Also – and this is very important – try to get the band to make a demo tape for you to listen to. It doesn't have to be anything special – a cassette of a rehearsal should be fine. This will give you an idea of the song type and structure as well as any obvious strengths and weaknesses the band has. Whether you're called in to produce or not, if you want the band to come back and use your studio again, or if you want them to recommend it to others, you'll need to emphasise their strengths, help steer them around their weaknesses and generally be supportive at all times.

Musical Arrangements

There is no hard-and-fast rule on how to arrange a good pop song, otherwise everybody would be doing it, but whether the material is pop, dance or folk, most musicians can spot the major flaws in other people's demos very quickly. Other than obvious problems such as out-of-tune singing, out-of-time-playing or the lack of an emotionally involving performance, most of the problems stem from poor song structure or arrangement, specifically sections in the wrong order, or bridge sections and solos too long or too repetitive. Even dance music, which seems at first listening to be extremely repetitive, has a lot of changes thrown in to keep the listener's interest. Too many otherwise decent songs have been ruined by poor structure – we live in a society where the sound-bite is king and short attention spans are the norm, so a successful song needs to get to the point pretty quickly. With inexperienced bands there's also the danger of the five-minute guitar solo or the predictable four-chord sequence that repeats eight times between each verse! It's very easy to fall into this trap, especially if the band's main experience is playing live, because on record there's no visual stimulus to keep the interest going. Part of the producer's job is to recognise these problems and suggest fixes without upsetting any egos!

Instrumentation

Assuming the verses and choruses are the right length and in the right place, does the song develop from start to finish, and is there too much (or too little) going on? A mix can easily get cluttered if there are two or more instruments occupying the same part of the audio spectrum, especially if they conflict with the vocalist in any way. Instruments become difficult to distinguish, the vocals get buried and you end up with a muddled, closed-in sound. I like to think that in a good mix the listener can hear the space around each individual instrument and voice rather than being confronted by an impenetrable wall of sound. It's an established scientific fact that if the listener has to strain to differentiate between sounds in a mix, the effort will make the mix fatiguing to listen to.

Consider the example where you have two rhythm guitars, and both players want to use a distorted sound, perhaps because that's what they've heard on records or that's what they use live. Distortion can certainly give a guitar an exciting edge, but use too much and you'll thicken the sound, destroy the dynamics and generally take up space that might be better used some other way. Distortion not only levels out the dynamics of the guitar, it also adds a huge number of artificially generated high-frequency harmonics, which cause the guitar's spectrum to spread. If the two guitars sound quite similar you might find that by the time you've added the bass and drums the mix is already too full. Very often you can reduce the amount of distortion when recording, especially on chordal parts, perhaps adding some compression to keep the sound even and solid-sounding. Changing the rhythm guitar style slightly to damp or space out individual chords can also produce a better-defined rhythm part than letting the chords blur into one another.

Similar problems occur with synthesised sounds, not least because so many players rely on factory patches, and factory patches are often designed to sound big and impressive when played on their own in the music shop! Put those same sounds in to a mix with other instruments and, once again, all the space may be gone. Either reprograming suitable sounds or using high- and low-pass filters to reduce the slice of the audio spectrum occupied by the instrument may be all that's necessary.

Spectral Mixing

To address the problems just outlined requires effort from both the players and the engineer. As suggested, the players may be able to reduce the amount of guitar distortion, choose different synth patches or change their performance styles, and these should be the first things you check before moving onto the use of effects and EQ to try to solve the problem. Listening to albums in a similar style should get you into the right ball park here as the sounds you (or the players) imagine you need may be quite different when you come to analyse them. Here's a simple example: if you decide you want some tinkly bell or synth percussion at the top of the mix, it's probably not a good idea to have the drummer playing four or eight to the bar on a ride cymbal for all he's worth as the sounds occupy the same part of the audio spectrum. Instead, try a closed hi-hat pattern, or at the very least a less ringy or less busy ride cymbal part.

One important engineering solution to cluttered mixes (after all the arrangement issues have been addressed) is to employ a technique sometimes called spectral mixing, where the problematic instruments are filtered to narrow the area of spectrum they occupy. Very often you can use a steep high-pass filter to trim off the bottom octave from a guitar or synth part, and rather than make the sound of the overall mix appear thin, it actually strengthens it, because now the bass and drums can be heard more clearly. Similarly, a low-pass filter can be used to trim away some of the unwanted high end from a distorted guitar part or over-bright synth so that it takes up less space. If there are two guitars, each can be EQ'd differently, and if this isn't enough try using different amp sounds or pick-up settings on one of the guitars to make it sound different at source. I tend to call the process of trimming the top and bottom of a sound using a shelving equaliser 'bracketing' as it makes it easier to visualise what you are actually doing.

Often the EQ that you get in a mid-price mixing console isn't tight enough for spectral mixing so a good external parametric can be a big help. However,

the variable frequency 12dB/octave side chain filters that many gates have can be wonderful for bracketing when you're doing spectral mixing in a hardware-based studio. Just set the gate to key listen mode so you hear the filters, not the gate, then use the high- and low-frequency controls to 'bracket' your sound. In a software-based recording system, plug-ins are ideal for this purpose as high- and low-cut filters take relatively little processing power. To cite another example, I was recently asked to comment on a mix that included both a bass guitar and an arpeggiated bass synth. Both bass parts sounded fine individually but were a mess when played together. The solution was to use EQ and heavy compression to beef up the bass guitar part and then use a low-cut filter to remove all the low end from the arpeggio to redefine it as a rhythmic element rather than as a supportive bass part.

The Devil In The Detail

Most music relies on a backbone of bass and drums, so make sure these are properly arranged and tightly played before you proceed. Also pay special attention to bass guitar sounds, because although some sound big in isolation they can virtually melt into the background when the other instruments are added. As a rule, a bass sound with a lot of middle will stand out better than one with a lot of deep bass and a thin wiry twang at the top. Heavy compression (using a high ratio of 8:1 or more) plus EQ boosting between 250 and 500Hz can add a lot of definition to a bass guitar part.

This book is mainly about using effects, but when it comes to mixing, knowing when to leave an effect out can be more important than choosing what effect to put in. There's often a temptation to add too much reverb but, as explained earlier, if you use too much the spaces in the music will get filled up, making the music sound congested and lacking in space. If you use a budget reverb or plug-in, this will be a more serious problem than if you are using a fairly serious studio reverb. Often you'll need only the slightest hint of reverb or ambience to take the dry edge off a close-miked sound – you don't need to place everything in a virtual cavern.

Bass guitars are normally kept pretty dry unless the instrument is fretless, in which case a little slow chorus and ambience reverb might help it breath, providing the song leaves it sufficient space. Slow or moody songs can sound great with an appropriately treated fretless bass. If the reverb clouds the low end, simply use two mixer channels instead of aux returns so you can use the channel EQ to roll some low end off the reverb output. This trick also works when adding reverb to drums, though if your reverb unit or plug-in includes low cut filtering, you can apply it there rather than using up mixer channels.

The Bass End

Bass guitar, bass drums and other low-frequency sound sources should generally be panned to the centre of the mix so that the heavy load of the bass frequencies can be shared equally by the two speakers in a stereo system. In a surround mix, it may be wise to feed them to all three front speakers. As a rule, low-frequency sounds don't provide strong auditory clues to direction anyway, so keeping deep bass sounds panned centre isn't too much of a restriction. Bass sounds with a lot of top do sound more directional, but again, unless you really need to push them to one side for specific artistic reasons it's best to leave them in the centre. If you want to add stereo movement to something like a fretless bass, adding a stereo chorus (or a mono chorus panned to one side and the dry sound to the other) will usually do the trick while still spreading the load between the two speakers reasonably evenly. Always do a mono check with stereo effects as some effects become much less pronounced when heard in mono and the outputs of some older designs of stereo chorus actually cancel out altogether when summed to mono. Though most new sound systems are stereo (or even surround), mono compatibility is still an important issue for music destined to be heard over mono TVs or transistor radios.

Staying with bass sounds a while longer, bass guitars often need compressing to keep their level under control, and even if you've compressed a little during recording, there's no reason not to compress even more when you mix. Just keep in mind that the more dBs of compression you add, the more you bring up any background noise, so you may want to gate the bass before compressing it further. The attack of the bass sound can be modified to some extent after recording by adjusting the attack time of the compressor or by using a transient enhancer. As a rule, ensure that the release time is as fast as you can set it without the level pumping unacceptably.

To change the tonality of a bass guitar, you need an equaliser, but you're likely to get better results with a multi-band parametric or even a good graphic equaliser than you are with the EQ on your desk. However, don't waste too much time trying to get a great bass sound in isolation as it will almost certainly sound quite different when the rest of the mix is added. In fact there's a good argument for not EQing anything too extensively until you have a reasonable balance setup that you're happy with. If you find the bass lacks punch, a little boost at 80 to 100Hz should help, but keep in mind that punch and audibility are not the same thing. The part of a bass guitar that you actually hear rather than feel tends to be between 200 and 400Hz.

If the bass sound comes from a synth or sampler, then compression is unlikely to be necessary, though you can EQ the sound in just the same way as you would the real instrument. The same applies to effects but, as ever, use effects sparingly on bass sounds.

Drums In The Mix

Drum sounds are very much a matter of personal taste and are influenced by current musical fashion, but it's probably fair to say that few contemporary music styles require a recorded drum kit to sound exactly like its acoustic counterpart. Exceptions to this rule include jazz and indie music, where more recognisable drum sounds are appropriate.

If the drums have been close miked and are recorded on separate tracks, then gating can be used to make the sound tighter and more separate. A compressor with a medium attack time, or a transient enhancer can be used to add more snap to the individual drum sounds, and of course EQ can be employed to add punch or remove boxiness. Boost between 80 and 120Hz adds weight, while a little

6kHz boost will sharpen up the attack. Boxy toms can be tamed by pulling back at 150 to 250Hz and air can be added to the whole kit by boosting the overhead mics by a dB or two at around 15kHz using a low Q setting. A harmonic enhancer can also help brighten up a dull drum sound. However, make sure that the drum sound you end up with complements the song you're working on. Too many engineers have a stock drum sound that they always recreate, regardless of whether it suits the song or not.

Snare drums can be interesting because no two are quite the same. The type of drum will define its sound, so it's no good expecting a deep metal sound from a metal piccolo snare or, for that matter, a metallic ring from a deep wood shell model. You can cheat by adding depth to snare drums or kick drums using a pitch shifter, but as a rule the drum sound is largely defined at source.

If you're working on a project where the snare or kick drum sound turns out to be inappropriate and you can't persuade the drummer to do it again, consider gating it and using the gated signal to trigger a sampler or drum machine. The new sound may then be used instead of the original sound or layered with it, but remember that the contribution of the original sound in the overhead mics will remain. If you have a drum machine that accepts audio triggers, you can feed the gated drum sound directly into the drum machine, but if not you'll need a MIDI gate or a pad-to-MIDI converter brain from an electronic drum system. If there's a lot of spill on the snare (or kick) track, a gate with side chain filters will help reduce the risk of false triggering.

Percussion Effects

General reverb treatment is a matter of taste but, for use with drums, settings with a decay of less than 1.5 seconds are often most appropriate. The impression of loudness isn't just a matter of having something loud in the mix, it's also about what's going on between the beats – the quieter the spaces between the beats, the greater the sense of contrast and the louder the sound seems. If you fill these spaces by choosing a reverb setting that's too long, the sense of power will be diminished. It's for this

reason that gated reverb sounds so powerful – there's lots of contrast, but because the gated sound is so tied in with fashion, it's down to you to decide if you can get away with using it. For a more conventional sound, try an ambience or small room algorithm.

Toms may be treated with a similar setting to snares, but as I said earlier in the book, toms generally have plenty of sustain of their own, so you don't usually need a very long reverb. Heavy reverb can sound impressive in an exposed drum fill in a rock track, but in a busy pop mix it's just more mess to deal with!

More Obvious Effects

Fortunately, although there are ground rules that caution us to moderation, there are many cases where the bold use of effects can transform a mix in a positive way, not least in the case of dance music. Interesting rhythmic patterns can be set up using tempo-synchronised delays with drums to create straight or triplet repeats.

Being more subtle, you could use a synchronised delay, then use the delay to feed a reverb unit set so that you get to hear only the wet sound repeated. Alternatively, feed a kick drum into a short delay with lots of feedback for a metallic drone. You can use the delay time to tune this to the pitch of the rest of the track, perhaps gate the result in time with the music to create a chopped effect and use it instead of a bass line! There's also the pitch shifter, which can be used to shift the input to the drum reverb, so the reverb appears to come from a differently tuned kit. You must allow yourself time to play about with effects like this just for the fun of it, because only then will you know what kind of effect you can create 'on the spot' when a suitable project comes along or when a client suddenly asks you to suggest something a little different. When you're actually in the middle of a project involving other musicians, there's often little or no time for experimentation.

Rhythm Section

Some engineers like to work on one sound at a time while others bring up all the faders and take it from there. If you're still gaining experience, it can be helpful to try to sort out the rhythm section first, but again, don't spend too much time perfecting the EQ and effects as these will probably change as the rest of the mix is added. Also resist the temptation to make every sound a killer sound that will stand proud at the front of the mix, because there simply isn't room for everybody at the front. Instead, organise your mix like a group wedding photo with the important elements front centre and the odd relatives further back or off to the sides. Take particular care picking your kick drum sound as this is the bedrock that supports the rest of a pop mix. If you work with samples and find you need a lot of EQ and processing to get what you need, it may be better to search for another sound that works with less processing.

Vocals In The Mix

There are very few vocalists who can control their singing dynamics to the degree that no further compression is needed. Even if some compression has been applied during recording, it's common to need more during the mix, but as with any use of compression, you have to keep an ear open for noise or over-emphasised breath noises when heavy compression is needed. Often it's best to gate the vocal before compression to prevent noise build-up during pauses. Take care when setting up the gate so as not to lose any word endings or even the important breaths that start phrases. Rather than gating the breaths out completely, use the gate's range control to reduce them to an artistically acceptable level. Sometimes you can't find a perfect setting and the gate will occasionally trigger from headphone spill or other noises, but these occurrences may be completely hidden in the mix. If in doubt, check using headphones as they're often far more revealing of detail than loudspeakers. As a rule, a little unwanted spill is better than bits of wanted audio being chopped off short, so if the gate action is too obvious, change the range setting to a smaller value.

It's because a wrongly set gate can ruin a recording that I recommend the majority of gating is left until the mixing stage – that way you can always have another go if the gate setting was wrong. Furthermore, gating as you mix also removes any noise that you may have picked up on recording your vocal to multitrack, especially if you're still using an analogue tape machine.

Not only does compression ensure that vocals remain audible at all times during the song, helping them sit more naturally in the mix, it also makes the vocal sound more up front, intimate and confident. If you have several tracks of backing vocals all needing compression, these can be routed via a stereo subgroup and a two-channel compressor inserted into the group insert points. As a rule, the compressor's stereo link mode should be switched on. This doesn't provide as much control as compressing the individual backing vocal tracks, but it does provide a reasonable level of control without tying up too many compressors. You can also try the trick with a linked multi-channel gate to make sure all the backing vocalists finish their words at the same time. This is described in the section covering gates and their applications.

Because vocals tend to be recorded in a fairly dry studio environment, some reverb is nearly always necessary to create a sense of the music existing in a real space. However, unless you have an artistic reason for choosing a longer reverb time, try a shorter room or ambience setting first as this will create a more intimate, uncluttered sound. Where a longer reverb is called for, try using a longish pre-delay to provide a little separation between the vocals and the reverb that follows. It's also a psychoacoustic fact that brighter-sounding reverbs help keep a sound up front when you need a stronger reverb effect, but keep an ear open for over-emphasised sibilance. De-ess the reverb feed if necessary.

Lead vocals are traditionally positioned near the centre of the mix – though there is nothing to say you can't experiment – while backing vocals are often split left and right to enhance the stereo width of the mix. Weak vocals can be double-tracked by getting the singer to repeat the performance on a spare track, then play both back together. Done properly, this sounds better than ADT or other artificial methods, and if the singer has trouble ending the words the same time both takes, get them to miss off hard consonants and 's' sounds from the ends of words when they do their second take.

If the singer can't do a good natural double track, try setting up an ADT using a 30 to 60ms delay time and adding a little gentle modulation or pitch detuning. This technique can also be useful in thickening backing vocals. If the dry and affected sounds are panned to opposite sides, a wide stereo image can be created, though you don't always have to go for the widest stereo image if you don't want to. A further refinement of ADT is to add reverb only to the delayed sound, not to the original.

If the vocals are still having a hard time being heard over a busy backing track, try putting the guitars and any keyboards through a stereo subgroup and then patch in a compressor (or gate with ducking facility), configured as a ducker and triggered by the vocals. Adjust this so that the subgroup ducks in level by around 2 to 3dB when the vocals are present, and set the attack and release times by ear for the most natural result. However, don't compress the bass and drums as these rhythm-section elements are expected to sound consistent. Not only will this make the vocal more audible, but the slight level pumping that results can also make the song seem more powerful and exciting.

At the recording stage, try to assess whether the singer has sibilance problems on 's' and 't' sounds that will show up in the final mix. If this is the case, you can use a de-esser, but before going for a corrective measure, try to fix the problem at source by trying a different mic and changing the mic position. Often a good dynamic mic used instead of a capacitor mic will do the trick.

A pop shield should always be used while recording, and if you don't have one you can make one by stretching a piece of fine stocking material over a wire frame and placing it midway between the singer and the mix. Without a pop shield you're almost certain to hear some popping caused by explosive 'b' and 'p' sounds. Don't let the foam wind shields supplied with the mics lull you into a false sense of security – these often dull the sound and do little to reduce popping.

Finally, if you need the vocals to sound more 'present' but don't want to risk adding harshness or exaggerating any sibilance, use an air EQ setting by boosting at around 15kHz with a Q of around two.

You should need only one dB or two of boost to make the vocal sound more airy and transparent, and because the boost is applied mainly to very high frequencies the amount of sibilance shouldn't be increased significantly.

The Vital Mid Range

Most of the meaningful information in an audio mix resides in the mid range, which is why monitors with a limited bass response often appear to be more revealing of detail. Vocals occupy a position in the lower mid range, though the harmonics that lend clarity to speech extend well beyond 3kHz. It's seldom practical to leave a gap in the audio spectrum between 200Hz and 3kHz so as to allow the vocals to exist without competition, so instead you have to examine the musical arrangement and check that what does exist within that range doesn't obscure the vocals to any serious degree. It's for this reason that acoustic guitars and those with single-coil pick-ups work well in busy mixes – they have a bright, well-defined sound, yet they don't fill up the lower mid range excessively. Guitars with humbucking pick-ups produce a thicker sound and work well in a rock band context where the line-up is fairly small and the sound needs filling out.

Keyboard pads, particularly very textural ones, should be kept reasonably low in the mix, and in some cases, their effect may almost be subliminal. If they're too obvious, they're probably acting as musical filler, destroying your contrast. A great many mistakes can be made at the song arrangement stage, so I can't stress too highly that the arrangement should be thoroughly examined before recording starts. It can help to record MIDI parts to a sequencer, even if the player is capable of performing well enough to record the instrument directly. This allows inappropriate sounds to be changed at the mixing stage without the need to re-record. Anything that makes mixing easier has to be good news, and sometimes something as simple as changing a chord inversion or altering a strummed guitar style to make it more staccato can make a significant improvement to a song. By paying more attention to planning (and this is where the rough demo comes in very handy), you can be more creative when it comes to mixing rather than constantly having to be finding ways around problems.

The Salvage Scenario

If you're presented with a finished multitrack recording to mix, you can only really vary the levels, the EQ settings and the use of effects. Congested sounds can be thinned out by 'bracketing' with EQ as described earlier, sounds can be ducked in level to reduce conflicts and, more drastically, unsuitable musical parts can be omitted altogether. Depending on how the drums are recorded, it may be possible to replace some or all of them by triggering sampled sounds or suitable alternatives from a drum machine or module, but another useful and simple technique is to balance the close-miked sounds against the overhead mics differently.

If the recording is well made, the overhead mics will produce a fairly natural kit sound, so you may need to add only a small amount of the close-miked tracks to give the right overall balance. On the other hand, if you want a close-miked, tight drum sound, use less of the overheads (perhaps even rolling off some bottom end) and try gating the close mics if spill is a problem. Add a tight ambience reverb and you can end up with a much cleaner sound. Overall compression of the drum mix can also work in some cases, using the compressor attack time to vary the attack sound of the drums.

If you find yourself faced with lifeless sounds on tape – as may happen when the guitar parts and bass parts have been DI'd in an unimaginative way – try feeding the tracks back out through a good guitar combo and re-record them onto spare tracks using microphones. If you have no spare tracks, you can do this live as you mix as long as the amplifier and mic are in another room. I've even heard of one producer who salvaged a poor snare drum sound by playing the snare track back through a guitar combo with a real snare drum up against the speaker. Every amplified hit caused the real snare to sound, and this was miked up and added back into the mix. Often these low-tech experiments produce the most useful and individual results!

Stereo Positioning

So far I've suggested that the vocals, the bass drum, the snare drum and the bass guitar or synth should be panned to the centre of the mix, but I'm not advocating that you mix everything in mono. Far from it: there's plenty of scope to add width, depth and interest to a mix using panning and effects. For example, synths – other than those used to provide bass lines – can be panned to any position in the mix, as can real or sampled brass, guitars and additional percussion. Effects too can be panned to different positions in the mix.

It's worth repeating at this point that panning isn't the same thing as true stereo, but it's so universally used in contemporary music production that, with the addition of a good stereo reverb to provide the illusion of space, most instruments can safely be recorded in mono. Pianos and live ensembles tend to be recorded in true stereo, but this requires a stereo pair of mics and two recorded tracks panned left and right in the mix. It's always good to try stereo miking once in a while, just so you can see how the results differ from panned mono, but don't worry if you don't have enough tracks or if you don't want to record in stereo – panned mono is fine for most pop music applications.

Stereo synths are sometimes best sequenced during the mix where the sequencer is synced to the multitrack recorder. This saves recorded tracks (two would be needed to keep the sound in stereo) and gives you the opportunity to substitute alternative sounds or edit the existing ones if they don't work well in the mix. However, on a MIDI/audio sequencer that can play back more tracks than you normally need, it can be helpful to record external synths to audio tracks so that you can make use of plug-in effects and mix automation. This also makes sense when you are using a software recorder with surround mixing facilities to create a surround mix.

To create the widest possible stereo image, you either pan the two channels hard left and right, or use a stereo enhancement device to make them seem even wider, but in many situations it's better to restrict the stereo image of an instrument to a narrower range. For example, a piano or drum kit panned hard left and right will sound as though it fills the entire width of the imaginary stage that exists between the speakers, but you don't often get 20 foot wide pianos or drum kits! By narrowing the range a little, you can give the instruments a more natural stereo perspective and gain the opportunity to move it off centre. For example, you could pan between hard left and centre. Think of your stereo soundstage as a real stage and try to position the instruments on it as realistically as possible. Of course this only applies to traditional pop mixes – experimental music or dance music can be handled any way you feel is artistically suitable, as can surround mixes.

To push a sound back in the mix, try some of the tricks described in the reverb section – for example, making the sounds a little less bright and/or using a higher level of reverb mixed with the dry sound. By making the sound quieter than you might normally mix it, it will appear to fade into the distance.

Digital reverb has the wonderful property of being able to create an apparently stereo sound from a mono source. In real life, many sounds emanate from a single point in space, and it's only the sound reflections from nearby surfaces that give a stereo context. Digital reverb does this by simulating the reflections that occur within a real building, and where you don't want to add an obvious reverb treatment to the sound, a good ambience or small room setting will create the desired impression. Such short treatments are particularly useful when you're dealing with dry synth sounds, drum machines or close-miked real instruments, as the human hearing system seems to demand the auditory clues that give a sound spatial context.

Textural pads or string sounds can be enhanced by adding a little chorus and reverb or delay, though most modern instruments will have these effects built in, so there should be no need to tie up an external processor. In fact having different effects in each synth module provides an enormous amount of scope for effects creation, even if you have only one or two dedicated effects processors. You do, however, have to know how the internal effects within a multitimbral keyboard are deployed, and this differs from one model to another. Some are configured like a mixer with one or two discrete effects blocks, but there are often restrictions associated with effects such as distortion or EQ, which process the entire signal. Take the time to read your equipment manuals and see how these restrictions might affect you. If you're using external effects, try pitch detuning as an alternative to chorus.

The Final Mix

When first setting up a mix, set the mixer to 'neutral' with all the aux sends set to zero and set all the EQ controls to their central positions. Pull all the faders down and check that all the routing buttons are up. This helps avoid problems later on as it's easy to overlook a signal that's routed somewhere you don't want it to go. The PFL metering system should be used for each input in turn to optimise the gain setting for minimum noise and distortion; the PFL meter should just go into the red on signal peaks.

Where possible, organise logical groups of sounds into subgroups – that way you'll be able to control the mix using fewer faders. Drums, for example, are often recorded on four or more tracks, so route these to a stereo subgroup. Backing vocals or keyboards can also be grouped effectively.

I like to set up an initial balance in mono without effects and with the EQ flat. Effects, EQ and compression can be introduced next. On channels where EQ will not be needed at all, bypass it, and mute all unused monitor inputs. Gates or expanders can be used to clean up tape tracks (or noisy synths) though care must be taken to match the release time of the gate to the sound being gated. Unused mixer channels (this applies specifically to analogue mixers) should not only be muted but also unrouted (all the routing buttons in their up position) to prevent unnecessary noise being added to the mix.

Some mixes can simply be set up with most of the faders left in the same position throughout the mix, but most times some tracks will need adjustment as the mix progresses. For example, guitars might have to come up slightly during solos; vocal levels may need a little extra 'riding' to keep them under control. When you think you have a good balance, and you've marked the faders where any changes need to be made (or set up the automation if you have an automated mixer or software audio system with automation), don't just run the mix and move on – take a short rest, have a cup of coffee, and perhaps listen to a few CD tracks in the same style to help restore your sense of perspective. This will also help your ears recover if you've been monitoring a little too loudly, though I always advocate doing most of the mixing at the kind of levels you think the record buyer might be using at home. Heavy rock, for example, may sound great at 120dB on a pair of wardrobe-sized studio monitors, but the real skill is to make it sound big on a pair of small hi-fi speakers playing at 85dB.

When you go back to your mix, check it on speakers, with headphones (these show up little distortions and noises that speakers might miss), and again on speakers but listening from outside the studio door. Listening from outside seems to show up balance errors that can be overlooked when you're right in front of the speakers. If you have mix automation, also listen with your eyes closed as the visual feedback from things like sequencer displays can be very misleading.

Remember that when mastering to digital media, such as DAT, there's no headroom above 0VU FS, which means excessively loud signals will sound distorted. Try to keep your peak level around 3dB below 0dB FS so as to allow a little headroom for unexpected signal peaks.

When you're happy, do the mix and then make a good cassette copy without noise reduction – or better still burn a CD-R – and check it on as many different stereo systems as you can, including the one in your car. I tend to be wary of mixes transferred to cassette as these can sound different on other systems due to reasons of alignment or tape and may not necessarily give a clear idea of how your mix really sounds. If your mix sounds reasonably good on all of the different systems you play it on, then you've probably got it about right. If it sounds wrong on all of them, for example, always bass heavy or bass light, then your monitoring system may have problems.

In reality, no monitoring system is perfect, but if you choose speakers that are honest rather than flattering, and get to know how your system sounds with commercial CDs, you can make good mixes even with modest speakers in a less than ideal room. It's all about getting to know your equipment.

14 SURROUND-SOUND CONCEPTS

Surround audio was first mooted in the form of quadraphonic vinyl records, but for various technical and social reasons that particular format did not enjoy lasting success. However, surround audio is the established format for cinema sound, and now that many home users are buying DVD players and surround speaker systems, the opportunity has once again arisen for record companies to produce music recordings in a surround format.

The main point to note about surround sound is that it relates to audio reproduction using more than the two speakers required for conventional stereo reproduction. Though there are some systems based on psychoacoustic processing that claim to provide a surround experience from only two speakers, true surround require four or more loudspeakers positioned around the listening position at specifically defined locations, and in the case of cinema-format surround sound, five separate speakers plus an optional sub-bass speaker are needed.

Current Surround Formats

The first successful domestic surround format was Dolby Pro Logic used for reproducing the analogue soundtracks of films recorded on VHS and also transmitted along with some TV programs. Modern films and DVD, however, employ a more advanced type of digital surround reproduction that provides five discrete channels of audio plus a sub-bass channel (this is the 5.1 format) for low-frequency sound effects, such as earthquakes and explosions. The '5' in 5.1 refers to the three front speakers and two rear speakers (left, centre, front, left-surround and right-surround) while the '.1' refers to the audio

channel feeding the LFE (low-frequency effects) sub-bass speaker.

It is perfectly possible to use just the audio capabilities of DVD video to provide music in a surround format, but now that the final specifications for DVD audio-only discs (DVD-A) have been agreed, and suitable players are being built, we also have the opportunity to enjoy a higher-quality, audio-only format. DVD-Audio is a quite different format to that used for DVD-V and is based upon 5.1 format, 24-bit, 96kHz uncompressed audio. It also includes options for 192 and even 384kHz sample rates, which is technically superior to CD and offers similar sound quality to the Sony/Philips SACD high-definition audio format. The benefits of 96kHz are questionable as far as the typical consumer is concerned so I can't see many music producers going to the expense of upgrading their systems to record and mix at 192kHz (or even twice that). What's more, I anticipate that a lot of DVD releases will be remastered from original multitrack recordings originally made for stereo release, or even 'folded out' from existing stereo masters, so the ultra-high sample rate argument is largely academic.

The problem with new standards is that they are so good, everybody wants one, so along with DVD-V and DVD-A we see competing (and mutually incompatible) systems such as Digital Theatre Systems' DTS and Sony's Super Audio CD (SACD). Furthermore, 5.1 film soundtracks may be included in the Dolby Digital or DTS format. Many commercial DVD players are designed to play DTS format recordings as well as DVD-V, (though most require a separate decoder for DTS surround playback) but we are a little way off having one player that can accommodate all the competing formats. At the time of writing, very few DVD players can handle SACD discs or provide full DVD-A compatibility, though it is expected that universal players capable of replaying all formats will soon become available. Once a significant number of consumers are geared up to replay music mixed in surround rather than simply stereo, there will be pressure upon music producers to mix songs in surround, probably in addition to stereo. Indeed, this is already happening, even where the surround version of the record isn't planned to be released until some unspecified time in the future.

Surround For Music

For the music producer, surround provides both technical and artistic challenges, but it opens up creative possibilities that could never be fully explored in stereo. On the technical side, it means employing a multi-speaker surround monitoring system and having access to mixing facilities that can handle surround and not just stereo. Then there's the question of what recording format to use for the multi-channel surround master, followed by the technical issues involved in producing a playable surround DVD. As you might imagine, the authoring issues surrounding DVD production are rather more complex than those presently faced in stereo mastering and CD master production, but providing the master recording is made as six discrete audio tracks in a format that the mastering house can read, the musician/engineer need not be too concerned about the technicalities of DVD production.

Why Consider Surround?

Conventional CD players are already being superseded by DVD players, the majority of which can play back 5.1 audio as well as your old CDs at the very least. Then there's the Sony/Philips Super Audio CD (SACD) format, which though only supported by some DVD players at this time, also has standalone audio players. All new Sony DVD players are able to replay SACD discs and of course DVD-A is a format that any DVD player with surround outputs should be able to play back. Because of these factors, record companies,

film producers, television producers, computer games developers and so on are increasingly expected to provide surround audio tracks as a matter of course, even though they may not be needed for release in that format initially.

The 5.1 Format

The 5.1 loudspeaker arrangement used in home theatre systems and cinemas comprises three speakers in front of the listener and two behind, all capable of handling full-range audio. These are augmented by a sub-woofer fed from the low-frequency effects (or LFE) channel. All 5.1 means therefore is that the system comprises five full-range speakers (ideally 20Hz and 20kHz) plus an LFE channel. A 7.1 system would comprise seven full-range speakers plus an LFE channel.

For accurate playback, the speakers in a 5.1 system must be placed in precise locations around the listener in order to reproduce the intended listening experience (though we all know that most home theatre system owners put the speakers wherever they'll fit!).

The LFE channel isn't strictly necessary for musical use as music rarely contains very low-frequency special effects, and different surround music mix engineers disagree as to whether it should be employed or not. My own view is that most home cinemas are set up with the LFE channel way too loud so as to make explosions more impressive, so if this was used for important musical information the mix could end up sounding ridiculously bass heavy.

Data Compression

In all probability, commercial surround material will be mastered by a specialist mastering facility, but it is inevitable that surround authoring software will become more readily available to the home studio owner. When this happens, potentially confusing issues will arise, not least being the use of data compression to make all that audio fit onto a DVD and still leave room for the picture. Dolby Digital is a familiar term associated with 5.1 surround film releases where Dolby is responsible for the AC3 data-reduction system being used. In fact both Dolby Digital and DTS are different types of multi-channel audio

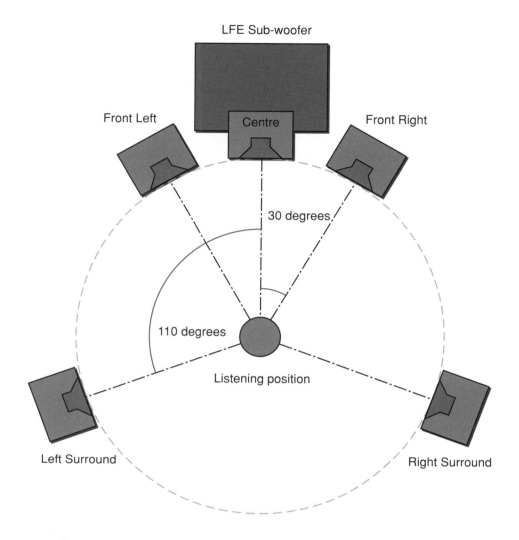

Figure 14.1: 5.1 speaker system

data-reduction systems commonly used in both film work and DVD, but the important point here is that the quality of data reduction is very high and shouldn't be compared with more lossy data compression systems such as MP3.

While consumer Dolby Digital is associated only with DVDs, I'm particularly excited about DTS as a music format for the project studio as it can be recorded onto a regular CD-R yet can still be played back by the majority of DVD players. Note that although some DVD players can decode DTS directly, most simply provide a data feed via their digital outputs for use with an external DTS encoder.

Microsoft has also created its own surround encoding process, which is being supported by a small number of consumer DVD players and Apple is expected to announce something similar.

DVD-A

DVD-A (DVD-Audio) was devised as a means of using the entire storage capacity of DVD to provide high-quality, multi-channel audio playback at 24-bit, 96kHz (or higher) resolution. Unlike sound for picture, DVD-A doesn't have to employ the same lossy data compression techniques as used for video because there is no picture data to accommodate, but nevertheless, a specialised, loss-less data packing system (MLP or Meridian loss-less packing) is used to increase the available playing time. A space saving of roughly 2:1 can be achieved using this system, yet the reconstructed data on playback is exactly the same as the original.

The 5.1 Speaker layout

The physical positioning of the loudspeakers in a 5.1 system (as defined by the International Telecommunications Union, or ITU) states that the front three speakers should be arranged with the angle between the left/right and centre speakers set at 30 degrees as shown in Figure 14.1. Fortuitously, this leaves the front left and right speakers correctly placed for playing regular stereo mixes, so the same monitoring system can be used for stereo and 5.1 surround.

All three front speakers should be positioned on an arc centred at the listening position so that all are equidistant from the listener. The rear speakers are also positioned at points on this imaginary circle, again shown in Figure 14.1. These are set up at an angle of 110 degrees from the centre front speaker, plus or minus 10 degrees. The rear speakers are known as surrounds and are generally abbreviated to Ls and Rs.

Positioning of the LFE speaker is less critical because of the low frequencies involved, but some experimentation may be required to find a position that gives a nominally even level of bass. Unfortunate positioning that coincides with room mode dimensions or their multiples can result in some notes being too loud and others too quiet. Starting with the LFE beneath the centre speaker is probably a good starting point, but always follow the speaker manufacturer's guidelines in this respect.

To achieve accurate monitoring for film mixing, standard playback levels are used, though in music mixing these are less likely to be observed. The main criteria is that all five full-range speakers are calibrated to produce exactly the same level at the monitoring position for the same magnitude of input signal. Commercial surround amplifiers usually have some in-built calibration system for achieving this, usually

by sequencing bursts of pink noise around the speakers in a special setup test mode.

Practical Systems

Although full-range speakers are specified for the five main speakers in a 5.1 playback system, this is clearly impractical in a domestic situation, and the number of systems available with tiny speakers indicates that there must be an alternative. The practical solution is to use smaller speakers with a limited low-frequency range and then to feed the missing low end to the sub-woofer along with the genuine LFE information. This is known as 'bass management'. Taken to extremes, this will compromise spatial accuracy at mid and low frequencies, but it is an acceptable compromise for consumer systems and, implemented carefully, a practical solution for the smaller studio too. In a typical studio system, it is unlikely that frequencies above 80Hz would be diverted from the main speakers into the sub-woofer.

The cut-off frequency of the LFE channel is defined as 120Hz for film mixing, though some engineers have been known to set a lower value (say 80Hz) for music-only applications so as to minimise overlap between the LFE channel and the full-range speakers.

Calibrating the replay level of the sub-woofer is more difficult than with the five main speakers – you can't use the same noise burst because of the restricted bandwidth of the LFE channel. Where bass management is being used, it may be acceptable to play known material through the system and then adjust the LFE level by ear until you get what seems like the correct balance of bass to the rest of the mix.

Though not very scientific, a good pair of ears can be more useful than measuring equipment, especially in smaller rooms. If you buy the speakers and surround amplifier as a matched package, there may also be a calibrated setting to provide the optimum main/LFE balance.

Choosing A 5.1 System

The simplest way to set up surround monitoring in the smaller studio is to use a powerful, commercial surround amplifier combined with passive speakers. While I am on the whole a big fan of active speakers,

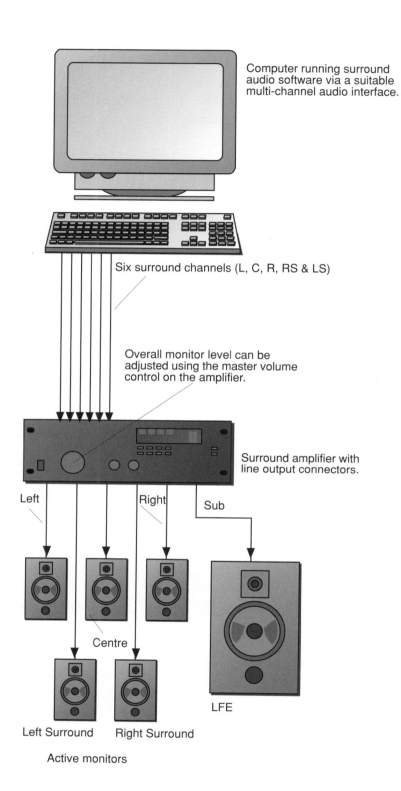

Computer running surround audio software via a suitable multi-channel audio interface.

Six surround channels (L, C, R, RS & LS)

Overall monitor level can be adjusted using the master volume control on the amplifier.

Surround amplifier with line output connectors.

Left

Right

Sub

Centre

LFE

Left Surround   Right Surround

Active monitors

Figure 14.2: Active monitoring via surround amp with line outs

it is rather more difficult to control the level of an active surround system than a passive one as very few project studio mixers have dedicated surround monitoring capabilities, even though they may cater for surround mixing.

It is vital that all five main loudspeakers are matched in terms of their main characteristics and the best solution is to use five identical speakers. Where this is not possible, some manufacturers provide smaller speakers from the same family and with the same general characteristics, other than bass extension, that can be used as surrounds. Additionally, the company may also produce a centre speaker that can be used horizontally rather than vertically, which can be useful when trying to maintain a line of sight through a control room window.

Where active speakers are employed, these must be used either with a mixer that provides surround monitoring control or be used with a separate surround monitoring controller. Currently these tend to be expensive, so a cheaper option may be to buy a commercial surround amplifier that provides line-level outputs as well as amplified feeds for passive speakers. The signal output from your mixer must then be split to feed both the multitrack recorder used to record the six discrete channels of the surround mix and to feed the controller/surround amplifier as shown in Figure 14.2.

Given that most MIDI-plus-audio sequencers now include the ability to handle surround mixing (often with automatable parameters), it is relatively easy to experiment with surround mixing once a suitable monitoring system has been set up. As you may have gathered from the brief explanations of the different surround formats in common usage, authoring any form of surround material to create a production master involves a lot of specialist knowledge and mistakes can be very expensive as some faults may not show up until you've had a batch of discs manufactured. I'm sure that more software will appear to make this task easier, but at the time of writing, it's probably best to mix your surround material onto six tracks of an ADAT or DA88, or save them as discrete audio files on CD-ROM, then use a competent mastering house to create the master for you. The

possible exception is DTS where software for systems such as ProTools and Digital Performer is already available. DTS has the attraction that it can be recorded onto regular CD-R, but the downside is that many DVD players will only play back DTS discs in stereo unless a dedicated DTS decoder is connected.

Practical Surround

When we experience live music in ambient surroundings, the majority of what we hear is in fact reflected sound coming from all the surfaces of the venue, not just from the musicians in front of us. When working in stereo, we use digital reverberation to try to create a sense of spaciousness, but it is always played back from speakers in front of the listener and so fails to create a convincing sense of envelopment. The attraction of surround sound is that it helps us escape the boundaries of stereo and to create music that really does surround the listener.

As you already know from working in stereo, the individual musical elements of a mix may be mono or stereo, and in the case of mono, panning plus the application of effects is used to create a sense of stereo width or placement. Surround productions can incorporate mono, stereo and full surround elements, the latter usually furnished by surround microphone systems such as the Soundfield (coincident point source) or an array of numerous discrete microphones roughly analogous to the surround version of a stereo-spaced pair. However, you don't have to buy a Soundfield microphone or multiple extra discrete mics to work in surround any more than you have to employ stereo miking techniques to create stereo records. It's more likely, in pop music production at any rate, that working with mono and stereo sources most of the time will suffice.

Surround Mixing

Mixing in surround means having access to the surround equivalent of a pan pot that can move signals from front to back as well as from left to right. A further width control is also useful when working with stereo sources and control over how much signal is fed to the centre speaker is also required. Many of the better sequencers now include surround mixing as standard by providing multiple mix busses, virtual joystick surround positioning control and separate sends for each mixer channel to feed the surround LFE channel.

The main mixer control requirements for surround panning is the ability to pan front/back as well as left/right and to adjust the width of stereo source material. If your sequencer offers surround mixing, then that's a great help, but if you're working with more traditional hardware that offers no surround support you may need to improvise a little. Even the affordable hardware digital mixers offering surround support tend to be less flexible than software (and seldom offer surround monitoring facilities), so the alternative is to find ways of getting the job done using equipment originally designed for stereo. A surround mixer, or a stereo mixer being used for surround mixing, must have at least six busses that can be used to carry the six elements of the surround mix, and at the channel level some way must be found of panning the signal left and right and between the front and rear busses. Many stereo mixers designed for multitrack recording have enough busses, but obviously they're not fitted with surround pan controls. One possible solution is to use two channels fed from the same source and to route one to the front left/right busses and the other to the rear (surround) left/right busses. Conventional panning can then be used to move the signals left or right in the mix while adjusting the relative levels of the signal sent to the front and rear busses provides a means of front/back positioning. This doesn't address the issue of the centre speaker or the LFE channel, but this is easily catered for by using two sends, one to feed signal to the LFE channel and one to feed some of the signal to the centre speaker as shown in Figure 14.3.

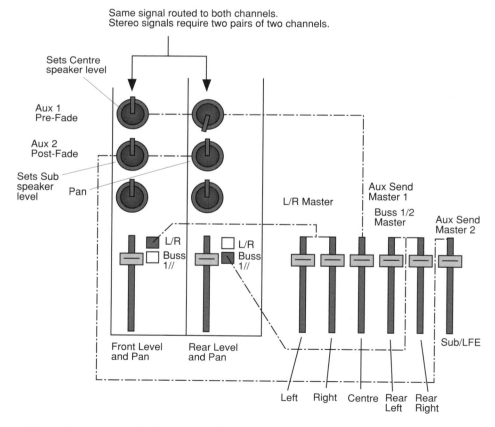

Figure 14.3: Using mixer channels for surround

Positioning a sound within the surround mix in this way is cumbersome, but it can be done. Things get more difficult, however, when you want to move a sound around in real time as you end up having to adjust several controls at once. That being the case, unless you're planning to keep most elements static in the surround mix, you're better off buying a mixer with some basic surround mixing capability. For example, Yamaha's 03D and 02R digital consoles include a surround mode in which automatic panning is possible based on preset patterns, such as arcs and circles, and adjustable pan rates. Although these are useful for some effects, they're not nearly as flexible as having a joystick that can position sounds anywhere within the surround mix using a single movement. When positioning a sound manually on a console without surround panning, you generally need to operate at least two separate controls, and that's without considering what happens to the centre channel, so it's important to understand that while you can make a perfectly acceptable surround mix using a multi-buss stereo mixer with enough input channels, you will face a number of practical limitations that will render some mixing techniques extremely difficult or even impossible. At least if you have mix automation, you can fine tune some of the more impossible multi-control moves until they sound right. In this respect, sequencers offering surround mixing are far more flexible than most hardware.

Surround Effects

Exotic surround processors are already available, such as the TC System 6000 that can handle dynamics and surround reverb (amongst other things), but a number of professional engineers use processors designed for stereo for their surround mixing without finding too many limitations. For example, if you want to create surround reverb, you can either use a single stereo reverb and use surround panning to position it midway between the front and rear speakers, or you can use two different stereo reverbs, one feeding the front left and right speakers and the other the left/right surrounds. Adding a little delay to the rear reverb or using a reverb algorithm with a slower reflection build-up can create a very convincing sense of spatial envelopment.

Software And Surround

The typical project studio combines an audio-plus-MIDI sequencer with external MIDI hardware, and while some of the lateral thinking described earlier must be used to create surround panning effects from external stereo sound modules, it's much easier to deal with sounds generated within the sequencer (audio tracks and virtual instruments) as these can be treated using the surround capabilities of the internal virtual mixer before being fed into the external mixer to be merged with the hardware-generated sounds. On a conventional mixer, six mono channels would be needed to route the six surround feeds from the computer sound card or interface to the six mixer busses being used to handle the surround mix, as shown in Figure 14.4.

Using automation for level and surround panning changes is straightforward using software, and though most processing plug-ins are still designed for stereo use, there are some surround plug-ins appearing that offer interesting creative possibilities. To work as described, you need an audio output card or interface with at least six outputs, and if you're working with a digital mixer that can accept an ADAT or other standard digital multi-channel audio interface card, then choosing a computer audio interface with a compatible multi-channel digital output simplifies things.

If you want to use external MIDI synths as well as virtual ones, one option is to add a hardware mixer with plenty of inputs and at least four output busses plus a couple of pre-fade send busses to feed the six surround streams to your mastering recorder. However, a perfectly practical alternative if you want to do everything within the computer is to record the external synth parts into the computer as audio tracks, so that they can be processed via the sequencer software's virtual surround mixer. This approach has the advantage that your surround mix can be recorded into the computer and saved on the hard drive, avoiding the need for an external multitrack mastering recorder. Where possible, audio files should be saved as 24-bit, 96kHz, though lower resolution formats can still be converted by the mastering house where necessary.

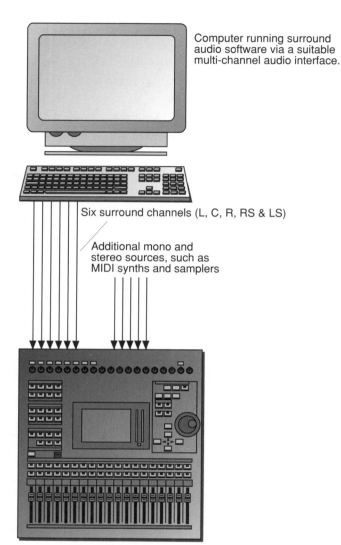

Computer running surround audio software via a suitable multi-channel audio interface.

Six surround channels (L, C, R, RS & LS)

Additional mono and stereo sources, such as MIDI synths and samplers

Figure 14.4: Computer surround through hardware mixer

Mixer able to handle surround mixing

Monitoring Practicalities

Finding space for surround monitoring in a small studio can be a problem, but if you don't have room for five full-range speakers, you can use smaller speakers with a restricted low-frequency range and use the sub-bass speaker to reproduce the missing bottom end as well as the LFE. This requires a surround amplifier with a bass management system so that the low-frequency energy from the main speakers can be redirected to the sub-bass speaker. In active systems, the bass management electronics is often housed in the LFE speaker so all the other speakers connect to that.

If you decide to use passive monitors, the solution is simple and straightforward: buy a reasonably powerful domestic surround amplifier/ decoder with separate analogue inputs for all six surround components. You can connect your master surround output busses to these inputs, using split cables if necessary to allow you to feed a multitrack recorder at the same time. The amplifier's volume control is used to control your surround mix level and monitor switching means you can play back your stereo mixes or CDs through the same system without repatching.

Active Monitoring

Things are less simple if you use active speakers, though there are commercial surround decoder/amplifiers that have individual line-level ins and outs that you can use in much the same way as described for passive speakers. Specialist surround monitoring controllers are available but most cost far more than a suitable surround amplifier.

One compromise solution is to use the multiple buss outs from your surround mixer or audio interface directly into the mastering recorder (for example, an ADAT or DA88), then feed your active monitors from the output of the recorder. The limitation is that when the optimum recording level is being fed into the recorder, the monitors will play back at a fixed level determined by how you set the gain pots on their back panels. It's easy enough to set this up for a sensible monitoring level, but there are always occasions on which you need to check the mix at a different level or turn down the monitors to answer the phone.

When you're at the tracking stage, you can turn down the mixer buss outs (physical or virtual) to reduce the feed to the multitrack recorder, but when you're actually mixing, your monitoring level is effectively fixed, determined by the optimum record level. Figure 14.5 over the page shows this arrangement.

Surround Mastering

The surround mix recorder can be any high-quality recorder capable of recording six tracks simultaneously, ideally at 20-bit resolution or higher. Six spare sequencer tracks in a software-based setup, or a standalone ADAT/DA88 or a hard disk multitrack machine will do the job well enough (stick to a standard track identification system so you know which part of the surround mix is on what number tape track), but you can replay your surround mix only from this master until you've had a disc made. Unfortunately, surround is not yet like stereo when you can simply burn a CD and play it back on your friend's hi-fi system.

To create a disc that can be played back on a home theatre system, you need to decide what surround format you want to release your work in, then transfer your work onto DVD (or DTS encoded CD-R). This part of the process requires specialist hardware and/or authoring software to create the necessary AC3 files (for Dolby Surround) or DTS files and to add the metadata – all the additional 'invisible' data that DVDs require that we didn't have to deal with when working with stereo CDs. Once the files have been created, you then have to burn that information onto a DVD using compatible 'burning' software.

Currently, the most painless way (other than financially, of course!) of getting a DVD master is to have a commercial mastering house do the job for you, and if you're a professional producer this is probably the route you'd take anyway. However, it can be frustrating not to be able to create listening copies straight after mixing, so the situation won't be an entirely happy one until cheaper and simpler means of surround DVD mastering are available to the project studio owner.

Artistic Considerations

I've spoken to a number of engineers already involved in surround mixing, and I have been surprised by the number of differing views on what is and what is not artistically acceptable. The whole and only point of surround audio is to present the listener with a more interesting or more involving listening experience, so in one sense there are no rules, but even so, there are 'considerations'. Surround music is still a relatively new art form, and at least one element of the debate centres around whether or not we want guitar solos coming out from behind the sofa, or is it better to leave all the instruments at the front and use the surrounds to add ambience and depth? Another concern is more practical and involves the use of the centre speaker.

The centre speaker in a film theatre generally carries the dialogue and other sounds that need to be keyed to the centre of the visual image (the screen) while the left and right speakers carry the stereo elements of the soundtrack. Because of our exposure to conventional stereo systems, we're used to hearing stereo with no centre speaker (in other words relying

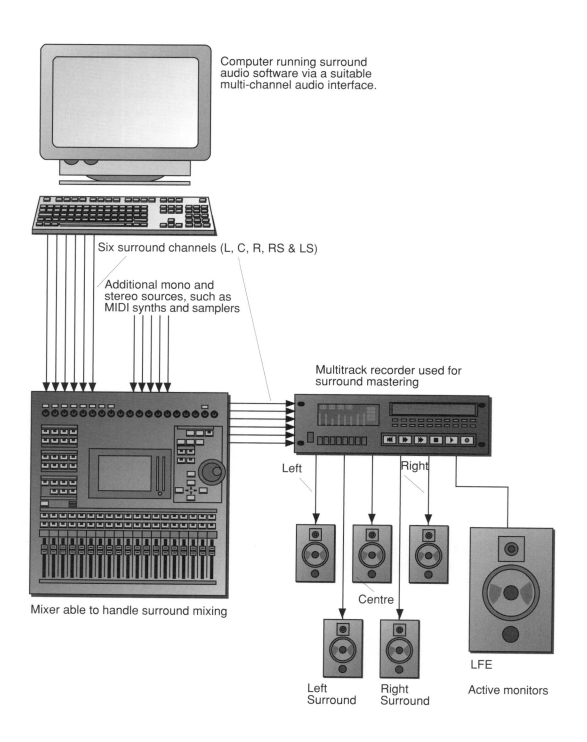

Computer running surround audio software via a suitable multi-channel audio interface.

Six surround channels (L, C, R, RS & LS)

Additional mono and stereo sources, such as MIDI synths and samplers

Multitrack recorder used for surround mastering

Mixer able to handle surround mixing

Left

Right

Centre

Left Surround

Right Surround

LFE

Active monitors

Figure 14.5: Active monitoring via multitrack recorder

on a phantom centre image), so mixing with all the mono components coming from a centre speaker sounds different from what we're used to, and because of the axial response of the human ear, it also makes the signal sound tonally different.

Some producers and engineers think it's best to put the voice and solo instruments in the centre channel while others may prefer not to use the centre channel in this way and instead stick with the phantom centre image we're all used to from listening to two-speaker stereo. Putting centred sounds in the centre speaker has the benefit that their position is less ambiguous if the listener isn't exactly in the sweet spot between the speakers, but in my experience it also makes the stereo soundstage appear narrower in some way than the usual two-speaker approach, possibly because all that comes from the front left and front right speakers are the stereo components of the sound and not the mono components normally needed to build a phantom centre image.

I have spoken to at least one producer who likes to exploit the difference between the centre speaker and the conventional phantom centre image by using both in a mix. For example, a double-tracked vocal might appear once in the centre speaker with the second version panned to the centre of the left and right speakers. The version in the centre speaker usually seems to sit slightly in front of the phantom image, an effect that can be exploited when you want to push lead vocals to the front and backing vocals to the rear. Simply put the lead vocal in the centre speaker only and the backing vocals in the left/right speakers only.

My main concern over using the centre speaker is that domestic playback systems are often very badly set up, and while the stereo left/right balance may be okay, there's a good chance that the centre speaker level will be a dB or two too loud or too quiet, and that the LFE channel will be much too loud.

If, on playback, the centre channel is a few dB adrift of its correct level balance, a carefully crafted mix could end up with the vocals, bass guitar, kick drum and any other centre-panned sounds noticeably too high or low in the mix, and of course the consumer will assume he's listening to a badly mixed record, not a badly set up sound system.

The low-frequency effects channel (the '.1' part) is not mandatory in all surround formats and not all home systems will have a proper LFE speaker, so you can never be certain that something you place in the LFE channel will be heard by the listener. Normal bass will be reproduced, however, even when small satellite speakers are being used as a bass speaker and bass management system is always provided as part of a serious domestic system. For mixing in surround, it's probably safest to ensure that your mix sounds right heard on just the full-range speakers and never put anything into the LFE channel that you can't afford to lose.

Dynamics In Surround

When compressing a stereo mix, it is usual to employ a stereo compressor that has the ability to link its side chains so that both channels always undergo exactly the same degree of gain reduction, regardless of the relative balance of the two channels at any one time. The reason for doing this is that by applying the same gain reduction to both channels, there will be no unwanted image shifts that might otherwise occur if a peak in one channel were to result in significantly more gain reduction on that channel than on the other.

Strictly speaking, a surround mix should be treated the same way, using five channels of compression with linked side chains, and this is one facility provided (digitally) by the TC System 6000 processor. Nevertheless, I've spoken to engineers who have tried both linked side chains and independent stereo compressors for the front and rear left/right signals plus a regular mono compressor for the centre channel. Clearly, using an independent compressor for the centre channel isn't going to cause any left/right image shifting, and similarly, using linked stereo compressors for the front left/right and surround left/right channels will also avoid left/right image shifts. However, because the front and rear compressors are working independently of each other, it is conceivable that front/rear image shifts could occur, though in typical mix situations, this problem appears not to arise to any significant extent.

The Surround Element

The discussion so far has really related to the reproduction of stereo via three front speakers rather than the usual two, but what should you feed into the surrounds? This is mainly a matter of art rather than science, but again, there are 'considerations'. For acoustic recordings, the room acoustics (or simulated room acoustics) can be used to provide the listener with a 'best seat in the house' listening experience where the music still comes mainly from the front and the reverberant field comes from both the front and the surround speakers. The next step up from this is to push some elements of the mix slightly towards the surrounds to increase the apparent width of the mix, but still keep the sound coming predominantly from the front.

Anything more dramatic can be distracting, especially if the music is accompanying a video where all the action is on a screen in front of you, but there's no reason at all not to conceive music where different sounds do come from different directions, effectively placing the listener in the middle of the performance rather than in the audience. The more conservative producer may decide to play safe, just moving some of the effects or incidental instrument parts out to the sides or even to the rear while others may place a different instrument in each corner of the room. As with the introduction of stereo, I expect there to be some horrendous excesses before a general consensus of good taste is arrived at, so don't go spinning sound sources around in 360 degrees all the time as you'll only make your listeners feel ill. Having said that, there will always be room for the odd dramatic effect used in context, and for more subtle surround effects such as panning delays that move around the speakers.

Processing Back Catalogue

When CD was launched, a lot of marketing energy was put into remastering back-catalogue material for the new format and DVD surround audio seems to be going the same way. Where possible, engineers will go back to the original multitrack tapes and remix these for surround in as artistically sympathetic a way as possible, but sometimes the master multitrack tapes are no longer available or there is no budget for extensive remixing. In these cases, a lot can be done simply by processing an existing stereo master, though there is a limit to what can be achieved compared with doing a full surround remix.

Mastering engineers routinely split a stereo signal into its mid and side (using a mixer or special hardware to derive sum and difference signals) components so that they can process the mono (centre-panned) components of a mix differently from the left/right (difference) information. For example, they may wish to EQ or compress the vocals and other centre panned elements of the mix without changing the way the rest of the mix sounds, or conversely they may want to add extra reverb to the stereo elements of a mix without affecting the lead vocal.

Once the middle and/or side elements have been processed, they can be recombined – once again by deriving sum and difference signals to provide a stereo mix with the desired modifications in place. This technique of splitting a stereo mix into its middle and side components is obviously very useful when processing stereo mixes for surround as various techniques can be used to wrap the 'side' components around the room while leaving the centre sounds intact.

Also, because the centre sounds can be extracted, they can be sent to the centre channel if required. One simple technique used to 'unwrap' the sound is to feed some of the side signals into surround channels and also to add artificially generated 'rear of room' reflections that create a more convincing sense of space. This is something that could easily be achieved using software mastering plug-ins, but in my view the real adventure begins when we conceive new projects for surround listening and approach both the composition and arrangement with that in mind.

Summary

Surround sound as an audio format is still in its infancy and it is too early to tell yet whether it will take over from CD as the standard audio format within the foreseeable future. My impression is that although surround provides us with a lot of opportunities for being creative with mixing and production, the conventional stereo CD will remain the consumer standard for many years to come.

GLOSSARY

AC
Alternating current.

Active
Describes a circuit containing transistors, ICs, tubes and other devices, that requires power to operate and is capable of amplification.

Active Sensing
System used to verify that a MIDI connection is working, which involves the sending device sending frequent short messages to the receiving device to reassure it that all is well. If these active sensing messages stop for any reason, the receiving device will recognise a fault condition and switch off all notes. Not all MIDI devices support active sensing.

A/D Converter
Circuit for converting analogue waveforms into a series of values represented by binary numbers. The more 'bits' a converter has, the greater the resolution of the sampling process. Current effects units are generally 16 bits or more with the better models being either 20- or 24-bit.

ADSR
Envelope generator with attack, sustain, decay and release parameters. This is a simple type of envelope generator and was first used on early analogue synthesisers, though similar envelopes may be found in some effects units to control filter sweeps and suchlike.

AFL
After fade listen; a system used within mixing consoles to allow specific signals to be monitored at the level set by their fader or level control knob. Aux sends are generally monitored AFL rather than PFL (see *PFL*) so that the actual signal being fed to an effects unit can be monitored.

Aftertouch
Means of generating a control signal based on how much pressure is applied to the keys of a MIDI keyboard. Most instruments that support this do not have independent pressure sensing for all keys, but rather detect the overall pressure by means of a sensing strip running beneath the keys. Aftertouch may be used to control musical functions such as vibrato depth, filter brightness, loudness and so on, though it may also be used to control some parameters of a MIDI effects unit, such as delay feedback or effect level.

Alpha
Release version of software which may still contain some bugs (see *Beta*).

Algorithm
Computer program designed to perform a specific task. In the context of effects units, algorithms usually describe software building blocks designed to create specific effects or combination of effects. All digital effects are based on algorithms.

Aliasing
When an analogue signal is sampled for conversion into a digital data stream, the sampling frequency must be at least twice that of the highest frequency component of the input signal. If this rule is disobeyed, the sampling process becomes ambiguous as there are insufficient

points to define each cycle of the waveform, resulting in enharmonic sum and difference frequencies being added to the audible signal. (See *Nyquist Theorem*.)

Ambience

Result of sound reflections in a confined space being added to the original sound. Ambience may also be created electronically by some digital reverb units. The main difference between ambience and reverberation is that ambience doesn't have the characteristic long delay time of reverberation – the reflections mainly give the sound a sense of space.

Amp

Unit of electrical current. (Also abbreviation for 'amplifier'.)

Amplifier

Device that increases the level of an electrical signal.

Amplitude

Another word for level. Can refer to sound levels or electrical signal levels.

Analogue

Circuitry that uses a continually changing voltage or current to represent a signal. The origin of the term is that the electrical signal can be thought of as being 'analogous' to the original signal.

Anti-Aliasing Filter

Filter used to limit the frequency range of an analogue signal prior to A/D conversion so that the maximum frequency does not exceed half the sampling rate.

Application

Alternative term for computer program.

ASCII

American Standard Code for Information Interchange. A standard code for representing computer keyboard characters by binary data.

Attack

Time it takes for a sound to achieve maximum amplitude. Drums have a fast attack, whereas bowed strings have a slow attack. In compressors and gates, the attack time equates to how quickly the processor can change its gain.

Audio Frequency

Signals in the human hearing range, nominally 20Hz–20kHz.

Aux

Control on a mixing console designed to route a proportion of the channel signal to the effects or cue mix outputs (aux send).

Balance

This word has a dual meaning in recording. It may refer to the relative levels of the left and right channels of a stereo recording, or it may be used to describe the relative levels of the various instruments and voices within a mix.

Balanced Wiring

Wiring system which uses two out-of-phase conductors and a common screen to reduce the effect of interference. For balancing to be effective, both the sending and receiving device must have balanced output and input stages respectively.

Bandpass Filter

Filter that removes or attenuates frequencies above and below the frequency at which it is set. Bandpass filters are often used in synthesisers as tone-shaping elements.

Bandwidth

Means of specifying the range of frequencies passed by an electronic circuit such as an amplifier, mixer or filter. The frequency range is usually measured at the points where the level drops by 3dB relative to the maximum.

Binary

Counting system based on only two states – one and zero, representing on and off.

Bios

Part of a computer operating system held on ROM

rather than on disk. This handles basic routines such as accessing the disk drive.

Bit
Binary digit, which may either be 1 or 0.

Boost/Cut Control
Single control that allows the range of frequencies passing through a filter to be either amplified or attenuated. The centre position is usually the 'flat' or 'no effect' position.

Bouncing
Process of mixing two or more recorded tracks together and re-recording these onto another track.

BPM
Beats per minute.

Breath Controller
Device that converts breath pressure into MIDI controller data.

Buffer
Circuit designed to isolate the output of a source device from loading effects due to the input impedance of the destination device.

Buffer Memory
Temporary RAM memory used in some computer operations, generally to prevent a break in the data stream when the computer is interrupted to perform another task.

Bug
Software fault or equipment design problem.

Buss
Common electrical signal path along which signals may travel. In a mixer, there are several busses carrying the stereo mix, the groups, the PFL signal, the aux sends and so on. Power supplies are also fed along busses.

Byte
Piece of digital data comprising eight bits.

Cardioid
Meaning 'heart-shaped', describes the polar response of a unidirectional microphone.

Channel
In the context of MIDI, 'channel' refers to one of 16 possible data channels over which MIDI data may be sent. The organisation of data by channels means that up to 16 different MIDI instruments or parts may be addressed using a single cable.

Chase
Term describing the process whereby a slave device attempts to synchronise itself with a master device. In the context of a MIDI sequence, chase may also involve chasing events – looking back earlier in the song to see if there are any program changes or other events to be acted upon.

Chord
Three or more different musical notes played at the same time.

Chorus
Effect created by doubling a signal and adding delay and pitch modulation.

Chromatic
Scale of pitches rising in semitone steps.

Click Track
Metronome pulse that helps musicians keep time.

Clipping
Severe form of distortion that occurs when a signal attempts to exceed the maximum level that a piece of equipment can handle.

Clone
Exact duplicate. Often refers to digital copies of digital tapes or discs.

Common-Mode Rejection
Measure of how well a balanced circuit rejects a signal that is common to both inputs.

Compander

Encode/decode device that compresses a signal while encoding it, then expands it when decoding it.

Compressor

Device designed to reduce the dynamic range of audio signals by reducing the level of high signals or by increasing the level of low signals.

Computer

Device for the storing and processing of digital data.

Conductor

Material that provides a low resistance path for electrical current.

Console

Alternative term for mixer.

Contact Enhancer

Compound designed to increase the electrical conductivity of electrical contacts such as plugs, sockets and edge connectors.

Continuous Controller

Type of MIDI message used to translate continuous change, such as from a pedal, wheel or breath control device.

Crash

Term relating to malfunction of computer program that necessitates restarting the program.

Cut-And-Paste Editing

The ability to copy or move sections of a recording to new locations.

Cutoff Frequency

The frequency above or below which attenuation begins in a filter circuit.

CV

'Control voltage' used to control the pitch of an oscillator or filter frequency in an analogue synthesiser. Most analogue synthesisers follow a one-volt-per- octave convention, though there are exceptions. To use a pre-MIDI analogue synthesiser under MIDI control, a MIDI to CV converter is required.

Cycle

One complete vibration of a sound source or its electrical equivalent. One cycle per second is expressed as 1Hz (Hertz).

Daisy Chain

Term used to describe serial electrical connection between devices or modules.

Damping

In the context of reverberation, damping refers to the rate at which the reverberant energy is absorbed by the various surfaces in the environment.

DAT

Digital audio tape. The commonly used DAT machines are more correctly known as R-DAT because they use a rotating head similar to a video recorder.

Data

Information stored and used by a computer.

Data Compression

A system for reducing the amount of data stored by a digital system. Most audio data compression systems are so-called lossy systems as some of the original signal is discarded based on psychoacoustic principles designed to ensure that only components that cannot be heard are lost.

dB

Decibel. Unit used to express the relative levels of two electrical voltages, powers or sounds.

dBm

Variation on dB referenced to 0dB = 1mW into 600 ohms.

dB Per Octave

Means of measuring the slope of a filter. The more dBs per octave, the sharper the filter slope.

dBv (dBu)

Variation on dB referenced to 0dB = 0.775 volts.

dBV

Variation on dB referenced to 0dB = 1 volt.

dbx

Commercial encode/decode tape noise reduction system that compresses the signal during recording and expands it by an identical amount on playback.

DC

Direct current.

DCC

Stationary head digital recorder format developed by Philips. Uses a data compression system to reduce the amount of data that needs to be stored.

DCO

Digitally controlled oscillator.

DDL

Digital delay line.

Decay

Progressive reduction in amplitude of a sound or signal over time. In the context of an ADSR envelope shaper, the decay phase starts as soon as the attack phase has reached its maximum level. During decay, the signal level drops until it reaches the sustain level set by the user. The signal then remains at this level until the key is released, at which point the release phase is entered.

De-esser

Device for reducing the effect of sibilance in vocal signals.

Defragmentation

The process of rearranging the files on a hard disk so that all the files are as contiguous as possible, and that the remaining free space is also contiguous.

detent

Physical click stop in the centre of a control such as a pan or EQ cut/boost knob.

DI

Short for 'direct inject', where a signal is plugged directly into an audio chain without the aid of a microphone.

DI Box

Device for matching the signal level and impedance of a source to a tape machine or mixer input.

Digital

Electronic system that represents data and signals in the form of codes comprising 1s and 0s.

Digital Delay

Digital processor for generating delay and echo effects (see *DDL*).

Digital Reverb

Digital processor for simulating reverberation.

DIN Connector

Consumer multipin signal connection format, also used for MIDI cabling. Various pin configurations are available.

Direct Coupling

Means of connecting two electrical circuits so that both AC and DC signals may be passed between them.

Disc

Used to describe vinyl discs, CDs, MiniDiscs and DVDs.

Disk

Abbreviation of 'diskette', but the term is now used to describe computer floppy, hard and removable disks.

Dither

System of adding low level noise to a digitised audio signal in such a way as to extend the low level resolution at the expense of a slight deterioration in noise performance.

DMA

Direct memory access. Part of a computer operating system that allows peripheral devices to communicate directly with the computer memory without going via the central processor or CPU.

Dolby

An encode/decode tape noise reduction system that amplifies low-level, high-frequency signals during recording, then reverses this process during playback. There are several different Dolby systems in use: types B, C and S for domestic and semi-professional machines, and types A and SR for professional machines. Recordings made using one of these systems must also be replayed via the same system.

DOS

Disk operating system. Part of the operating system of PC and PC-compatible computers.

Driver

Piece of software that handles communications between the main program and a hardware peripheral, such as a soundcard, printer or scanner.

Drum Pad

Synthetic playing surface that produces electronic trigger signals in response to being hit with drum sticks.

Dry

Describes a signal that has had no effects added.

DSP

Digital signal processor. A powerful microchip used to process digital signals.

Dubbing

Adding further material to an existing recording. Also known as overdubbing.

Ducking

System for controlling the level of one audio signal with another.

Dump

To transfer digital data from one device to another. A Sysex dump is a means of transmitting information about a particular instrument or module over MIDI, and may be used to store sound patches, parameter settings and so on.

DVD

Digital versatile disc. High-capacity disc format capable of storing multi-format data.

Dynamic Microphone

Type of microphone that works on the electric generator principle, where a diaphragm moves a coil of wire within a magnetic field.

Dynamic Range

Range in decibels between the highest signal that can be handled by a piece of equipment and the level at which small signals disappear into the noise floor.

Early Reflections

The first sound reflections from walls, floors and ceilings following a sound created in an acoustically reflective environment.

Effect

Device for treating an audio signal in order to change it in some creative way. Effects often involve the use of sophisticated delay circuits, and include such treatments as reverb and echo.

Effects Loop

Connection system that allows an external signal processor to be connected into the audio chain.

Effects Return

Additional mixer input designed to accommodate the output from an effects unit.

Encode/Decode

A system that requires a signal to be processed prior to recording, then that process reversed during playback.

Enhancer

Device designed to brighten audio material using techniques such as dynamic equalisation, phase shifting and harmonic generation.

Envelope

The way in which the level of a sound or signal varies over time.

Envelope Generator

Circuit capable of generating a control signal, which represents the envelope of the sound you want to recreate. This may then be used to control the level of an oscillator or other sound source, though envelopes may also be used to control filter or modulation settings.

Equaliser

Device for selectively cutting or boosting selected parts of the audio spectrum.

Event

In MIDI terms, an event is a single unit of MIDI data, such as a note being turned on or off, a piece of controller information, a program change, and so on.

Exciter

An enhancer that works by synthesising new high-frequency harmonics.

Expander

Device designed to decrease the level of low level signals and increase the level of high level signals, thus increasing the dynamic range of the signal.

Expander Module

Synthesiser with no keyboard, often rack-mountable or in some other compact format.

Fader

Sliding potentiometer control used in mixers and other processors.

FET

Field-effect transistor.

Figure Of Eight

Describes the polar response of a microphone that is equally sensitive both front and rear, yet rejects sounds coming from the sides.

File

Meaningful list of data stored in digital form. A 'standard MIDI file' is a specific type of file designed to allow sequence information to be interchanged between different types of sequencer.

Filter

Electronic circuit designed to emphasise or attenuate a specific range of frequencies.

Flanging

Modulated delay effect using feedback to create a dramatic, sweeping sound.

Floppy Disk

Computer disk that uses a flexible magnetic medium encased in a protective plastic sleeve. The maximum capacity of a standard High Density disk is 1.44Mbytes.

Flutter Echo

Resonant echo that occurs when sound reflects between two parallel, reflective surfaces.

Foldback

System for feeding one or more separate mixes to the performers for use while recording and overdubbing. Also known as a 'cue' mix.

Formant

Frequency component or resonance of an instrument or voice sound that doesn't change with the pitch of the note being played or sung.

Format

Procedure required to ready a computer disk for use. Formatting organises the disk's surface into a series of electronic pigeon holes into which data can be stored. Different computers often use different formatting systems.

Fragmentation

The process by which the available space on a disk drive gets split up into small sections due to the storing and erasing of files. See *Defragmentation*.

Frequency

Indication of how many cycles of a repetitive waveform occur in one second. A waveform that has a repetition cycle of once per second has a frequency of 1Hz (Hertz).

Frequency Response

Measurement of the frequency range that can be handled by a specific piece of electrical equipment or loudspeaker.

FSK

Frequency shift keying. A method of recording a sync clock signal onto tape by representing it as two alternating tones.

Fundamental

All sounds comprise a fundamental or basic frequency plus harmonics and partials at a higher frequency.

FX

Short for effects.

Gain

Amount by which a circuit amplifies a signal.

Gate

Electrical signal generated when a key is depressed on an electronic keyboard. This is used to trigger envelope generators and other events that need to be synchronised to key action.

Gate

Electronic device designed to mute low level signals so as to improve noise performance during pauses in the wanted material.

General MIDI

Addition to the basic MIDI spec to assure a minimum level of compatibility when playing back GM format song files. The specification covers type and program number of sounds, minimum levels of polyphony and multitimbrality, response to controller information and so on.

Glitch

Describes an unwanted short-term corruption of a signal, or the unexplained, short-term malfunction of a piece of equipment. For example, an inexplicable click on a DAT tape would be termed a glitch.

GM Reset

Universal Sysex command, which activates the General MIDI mode on a GM instrument. The same command also sets all controllers to their default values and switches off any notes still playing by means of an all-notes-off message.

Graphic Equaliser

An equaliser whereby several narrow segments of the audio spectrum are controlled by individual cut/boost faders. The name comes about because the fader positions provide a graphic representation of the EQ curve.

Ground

Electrical earth or 0 volts. In mains wiring, the ground cable is physically connected to the ground via a long conductive metal spike.

Ground Loop

Condition that is likely to lead to the circulation of currents in the ground wiring of an audio system. When these currents are induced by the alternating-current mains supply, hum results.

Group

Collection of signals within a mixer that are mixed, then routed through a separate fader to provide overall control. In a multitrack mixer, several groups are provided to feed the various recorder track inputs.

GS

Roland's own proprietary extension to the General MIDI protocol.

Hard Disk

High capacity computer storage device based on a rotating rigid disk with a magnetic coating onto which data may be recorded.

Harmonic

High-frequency component of a complex waveform.

Harmonic Distortion

Addition of harmonics that were not present in the original signal.

Headroom

The safety margin in dBs between the highest peak signal being passed by a piece of equipment and the absolute maximum level the equipment can handle.

High-Pass Filter

Filter that attenuates frequencies below its cut-off frequency.

Hiss

Noise caused by random electrical fluctuations.

Hum

Signal contamination caused by the addition of low frequencies, usually related to the mains power frequency.

Hz

Short for Hertz, the unit of frequency.

Impedance

Can be visualised as the 'AC resistance' of a circuit, which contains both resistive and reactive components.

Inductor

Reactive component that presents an increasing impedance with frequency.

Initialise

To automatically restore a piece of equipment to its factory default settings.

Insert Point

Connector that allows an external processor to be patched into a signal path so that the signal now flows through the external processor.

Insulator

Material that does not conduct electricity.

Interface

Device that acts as an intermediary to two or more other pieces of equipment. For example, a MIDI interface enables a computer to communicate with MIDI instruments and keyboards.

Intermodulation Distortion

Form of distortion that introduces frequencies not present in the original signal.

I/O

Part of a system that handles inputs and outputs, both digital and analogue.

IPS

Inches per second. Used to describe tape speed.

IRQ

Interrupt request, part of the operating system of a computer that allows a connected device to request attention from the processor in order to transfer data to it or from it.

Jargon

Specialised words associated with a specialist subject.

k

Abbreviation for 1,000 (kilo). Used as a prefix to other values to indicate magnitude.

kHz

1,000Hz.

LCD

Liquid crystal display.

LED

Light-emitting diode, a type of solid-state lamp.

Limiter

Device that controls the gain of a signal so as to prevent it from ever exceeding a preset, user-defined level. A limiter is essentially a fast-acting compressor with an infinite compression ratio.

Line Level

Nominal signal level, about -10dBV for semi-pro equipment and +4dBu for professional equipment.

Linear

Describes a device where the output is a direct multiple of the input.

Load

Electrical circuit that draws power from another circuit or power supply.

Local On/Off

Function to allow the keyboard and sound-generating section of a keyboard synthesiser to be used independently of each other.

Logic

Type of electronic circuitry used for processing binary signals comprising two voltage levels.

Loop

Circuit where the output is connected back to the input.

Low-Frequency Oscillator (LFO)

Oscillator used as a modulation source, usually below 20Hz. The most common LFO waveshape is the sine wave, though there is often a choice of sine, square, triangular and sawtooth waveforms.

Low-Pass Filter (LPF)

Filter that attenuates frequencies above its cut-off frequency.

LSB

Least significant byte. If a piece of data has to be conveyed as two bytes, one byte represents high value numbers and the other low value numbers, much in the same way as tens and units function in the decimal system. The high value, or most significant part of the message is called the MSB (Most Significant Byte).

mA

Milliamp, or one thousandth of an amp.

MDM

Modular digital multitrack; a digital recorder that can be used in multiples to provide a greater number of synchronised tracks than a single machine.

Memory

Computer's RAM used to store programs and data. This data is lost when the computer is switched off and so must be stored to disk or other suitable media.

Mic Level

Low-level signal generated by a microphone.

Microprocessor

Specialised microchip at the heart of a computer.

MIDI

Musical instrument digital interface.

MIDI Analyser

Device that gives a visual readout of MIDI activity when connected between two pieces of MIDI equipment.

MIDI Bank Change

Type of controller message used to select alternate banks of MIDI programs where access to more than 128 programs is required.

MIDI Control Change

Also known as MIDI controllers or controller data, these messages convey positional information relating to performance controls such as wheels, pedals, switches and other devices. This information can be used to control functions such as vibrato depth, brightness, portamento, effects levels, and many other parameters.

MIDI Controller

Term used to describe the physical interface by means of which the musician plays the MIDI synthesiser or other sound generator. Examples of controllers are keyboards, drum pads, wind synths and so on.

(Standard) MIDI File

Standard file format for storing song data recorded

on a MIDI sequencer in such a way as to allow it to be read by other makes or model of MIDI sequencer.

MIDI Implementation Chart

A chart, usually found in MIDI product manuals, providing information as to which MIDI features are supported. Supported features are marked with an o while unsupported features are marked with an X. Extra information may be provided, such as the exact form of the bank change message.

MIDI In

Socket used to receive information from a master controller or from the MIDI Thru socket of a slave unit.

MIDI Merge

Device or sequencer function that enables two or more streams of MIDI data to be combined.

MIDI Mode

MIDI information can be interpreted by the receiving MIDI instrument in a number of ways, the most common being polyphonically on a single MIDI channel (poly-omni off mode). Omni mode enables a MIDI instrument to play all incoming data regardless of channel.

MIDI Module

Sound generating device with no integral keyboard.

MIDI Note Number

Every key on a MIDI keyboard has its own note number ranging from 0–127, where 60 represents middle C. Some systems use C3 as middle C while others use C4.

MIDI Note Off

Message sent when key is released.

MIDI Note On

MIDI message sent when note is played (key pressed).

MIDI Out

MIDI connector used to send data from a master device to the MIDI In of a slave device.

MIDI Port

MIDI connections of a MIDI-compatible device. A multiport, in the context of a MIDI interface, is a device with multiple MIDI output sockets, each capable of carrying data relating to a different set of 16 MIDI channels. Multiports are the only means of exceeding the limitations imposed by 16 MIDI channels.

MIDI Program Change

Type of MIDI message used to change sound patches on a remote module or the effects patch on a MIDI effects unit.

MIDI Splitter

Alternative term for MIDI Thru Box.

MIDI Sync

Description of the synchronisation systems available to MIDI users – MIDI clock and MIDI time code.

MIDI Thru

Socket on a slave unit used to feed the MIDI In socket of the next unit in line.

MIDI Thru Box

Device that splits the MIDI Out signal of a master instrument or sequencer to avoid daisy chaining. Powered circuitry is used to 'buffer' the outputs so as to prevent problems when many pieces of equipment are driven from a single MIDI output.

mixer

Device for combining two or more audio signals.

Monitor

Reference loudspeaker used for mixing. Or...

Monitor

Action of listening to a mix or a specific audio signal. Or...

Monitor

VDU display for a computer.

Motherboard

The main circuit board within a computer into which all the other components plug or connect.

MTC

MIDI time code; a MIDI sync implementation based on SMPTE time code.

Multisampling

Creation of several samples, each covering a limited musical range, the idea being to produce a more natural range of sounds across the range of the instrument being sampled. For example, a piano may need to be sampled every two or three semitones to sound convincing.

Multitimbral Module

MIDI sound source capable of producing several different sounds at the same time and controlled on different MIDI channels.

Noise Shaping

System for creating digital dither so that any added noise is shifted into those parts of the audio spectrum where the human ear is least sensitive.

Non-Registered Parameter Number

Addition to the MIDI spec that allows Controllers 98 and 99 to be used to control non-standard parameters relating to particular models of synthesiser. This is an alternative to using System Exclusive data to achieve the same ends.

Non-Linear Recording

Describes digital recording systems that allow any parts of the recording to be played back in any order with no gaps.

Nyquist Theorem

The rule that states that a digital sampling system must have a sample rate at least twice as high as that of the highest frequency being sampled in order to avoid aliasing. Because anti-aliasing filters aren't perfect, the sampling frequency has usually to be made more than twice that of the maximum input frequency.

Ohm

Unit of electrical resistance.

Omni

Meaning all, refers to a microphone that is equally sensitive in all directions, or to the MIDI mode where data on all channels is recognised.

Open Reel

Tape machine where the tape is wound on spools rather than sealed in a cassette.

Oscillator

Circuit that generates a periodic electrical waveform.

Overdub

To add another part to a multitrack recording or to replace one of the existing parts.

Pad

Resistive circuit for reducing signal level.

Parallel

Means of connecting two or more circuits together so that their inputs are connected together, and their outputs are all connected together.

Parametric EQ

Equaliser with separate controls for frequency, bandwidth and cut/boost.

Patch

Alternative term for 'program', referring to a programmed sound within a synthesiser that can be called up using program change commands. MIDI effects units and samplers also have patches.

PFL

Pre-fade listen; a system used within a mixing console to enable the operator to listen to a selected signal regardless of the position of the fader controlling it.

Phantom Power

48v DC supply for capacitor mics, transmitted along the signal cores of a balanced mic cable.

Phase

The timing difference between two electrical waveforms expressed in degrees where 360 degrees corresponds to a delay of exactly one cycle.

Phaser

Effect that combines a signal with a phase-shifted version of itself to produce creative filtering effects. Most phasers are controlled by means of an LFO.

Pick-up

Part of a guitar that converts the string vibrations to electrical signals.

Pitch Bend

Special control message specifically designed to produce a change in pitch in response to the movement of a pitch bend wheel or lever.

Pitch Shifter

Device for changing the pitch of an audio signal without changing its duration.

Poly Mode

Most common MIDI mode, allowing an instrument to respond to multiple simultaneous notes transmitted on a single MIDI channel.

Polyphony

Ability of an instrument to play two or more notes simultaneously. An instrument that can only play one note at a time is described as monophonic.

Post-Fade

Aux signal taken from after the channel fader so that the aux send level follows any channel fader changes. Normally used for feeding effects devices.

PPM

Peak programme meter; a meter designed to register signal peaks rather than the average level.

PPQN

Pulses per quarter note. Used in the context of MIDI clock derived sync signals.

PQ Coding

Process for adding pause, cue and other subcode information to a digital master tape in preparation for CD manufacture.

Pre-emphasis

System for applying high-frequency boost to a sound before processing so as to reduce the effect of noise. A corresponding de-emphasis process is required on playback so as to restore the original signal, and to attenuate any high-frequency noise contributed by the recording process.

Pre-Fade

Aux signal taken from before the channel fader so that the channel fader has no effect on the aux send level. Normally used for creating foldback or cue mixes.

Print-through

The undesirable process that causes some magnetic information from a recorded analogue tape to become imprinted onto an adjacent layer. This can produce low level pre or post echoes.

Program Change

MIDI message designed to change instrument or effects unit patches.

Pulse Wave

Similar to a square wave but non-symmetrical. Pulse waves sound brighter and thinner than square waves, making them useful in the synthesis of reed instruments. The timbre changes according to the mark/space ratio of the waveform.

Pulse-Width Modulation

Means of modulating the duty cycle (mark/space ratio) of a pulse wave. This changes the timbre of the tone; LFO modulation of pulse width can be used to produce pseudo-chorus effects.

Punching In

Action of placing an already recorded track into Record at the correct time during playback, so that the existing material may be extended or replaced.

Punching Out

Action of switching a tape machine out of Record after executing a punch in.

PZM

Pressure zone microphone. A type of boundary mic.

Q

Measure of the resonant properties of a filter. The higher the Q, the more resonant the filter and the narrower the range of frequencies that are allowed to pass.

Quantising

Means of moving notes recorded in a MIDI sequencer so that they line up with user-defined subdivisions of a musical bar, for example, 16s.

RAM

Abbreviation of Random Access Memory. This is a type of memory used by computers for the temporary storage of programs and data, and all data is lost when the power is turned off. For that reason, work needs to be saved to disk if it is not to be lost.

R-DAT

Digital tape machine using a rotating head system.

Real Time

Describes an audio process that can be carried out as the signal is being recorded or played back. The opposite is off-line, where the signal is processed in non-real time.

Release

The time taken for a level or gain to return to normal.

Resistance

Opposition to the flow of electrical current. Measured in ohms.

Resonance

Same as Q.

Reverb

Acoustic ambience created by multiple reflections in a confined space.

RF Interference

Interference far above the range of human hearing.

Ring Modulator

A device that accepts and processes two input signals in a particular way. The output signal does not contain any of the original input signal but instead comprises new frequencies based on the sum and difference of the input signals' frequency components. The best known application of ring modulation is the creation of 'Dalek' robot voices but it may also be used to create dramatic instrumental textures. Depending on the relationships between the input signals, the results may either be musical or extremely dissonant – for example, ring modulation can be used to create bell-like tones. (The term 'ring' is used because the original circuit that produced the effect used a ring of diodes.)

Roll-off

The rate at which a filter attenuates a signal once it has passed the filter cut-off point.

ROM

Abbreviation for Read-Only Memory.

Sample

Digitised sound used as a musical sound source in a sampler or additive synthesiser.

Sampling

Process carried out by an A/D converter where the instantaneous amplitude of a signal is measured many times per second (44.1kHz in the case of CD).

Sample And Hold

Usually refers to a feature whereby random values are generated at regular intervals and used to control another function such as pitch or filter frequency. Sample and hold circuits were also used in analogue synthesisers to 'remember' the note being played after a key had been released.

Sample Rate

Number of times an A/D converter samples the incoming waveform each second.

Sawtooth Wave

So called because it resembles the teeth of a saw, this waveform contains only even harmonics.

SCSI

Abbreviation of Small Computer System Interface (and pronounced 'skuzzi').

Sequencer

Device for recording and replaying MIDI data, usually in a multitrack format, allowing complex compositions to be built up a part at a time.

Sibilance

High-frequency whistling or lisping sound that affects vocal recordings, due either to poor mic technique, excessive equalisation or exaggerated vocal characteristics.

Side Chain

Part of the circuit that splits off a proportion of the main signal to be processed in some way. Compressors use the side chain signal to derive their control signals.

Signal

Electrical representation of input such as sound.

Signal Chain

Route taken by a signal from the input of a system to the output.

Signal-To-Noise Ratio

The ratio of maximum signal level to the residual noise, expressed in decibels.

Sine Wave

The waveform of a pure tone with no harmonics.

Single-Ended Noise Reduction

Removal or attenuation of the noise component of a signal that doesn't require previous coding, as in the case of Dolby or dbx.

Slave

Device under the control of a master device.

SMPTE

Time code developed for the film industry but now extensively used in music and recording. SMPTE is a real-time code and is related to hours, minutes, seconds and film or video frames rather than to musical tempo.

SPL

Sound pressure level, measured in decibels.

SPP

Song position pointer (MIDI).

Square Wave

Symmetrical rectangular waveform. Square waves contain a series of odd harmonics.

Standard MIDI File

Standard file format that allows MIDI files to be transferred between different sequencers and MIDI file players.

Step Time

System for programming a sequencer in non-real time.

Stereo

Two-channel system feeding left and right loudspeakers.

Stripe

To record time code onto one track of a multitrack tape machine.

Sub-bass

Frequencies below the range of typical monitor loudspeakers. Some define sub-bass as frequencies that can be felt rather than heard.

Subcode

Hidden data within the CD and DAT format that includes such information as the absolute time location, number of tracks, total running time and so on.

Sweet Spot

Optimum position for a microphone, or for a listener relative to monitor loudspeakers.

Sync

System for making two or more pieces of equipment run in synchronism with each other.

Tape Head

Part of a tape machine that transfers magnetic energy to the tape during recording, or reads it during playback.

Test Tone

Steady, fixed level tone recorded onto a multitrack or stereo recording to act as a reference.

THD

Total harmonic distortion.

Thru

MIDI connector that passes on the signal received at the MIDI In socket.

Tracking

System whereby one device follows another. Tracking is often discussed in the context of MIDI guitar synthesisers where the MIDI output attempts to track the pitch of the strings.

Transducer

Device for converting one form of energy to another.

Triangle Wave

Symmetrical triangular-shaped wave containing odd harmonics only, but with a lower harmonic content than the square wave.

TRS Jack

Stereo-type jack with tip, ring and sleeve connections.

Unbalanced

Describes a two-wire electrical signal connection where the inner or hot or +ve conductor is usually surrounded by the cold or -ve conductor, which forms a screen against interference.

Velocity

The rate at which a key is depressed. This may be used to control loudness (to simulate the response of instruments such as pianos) or other parameters on later synthesisers.

Vocoder

Signal processor that imposes a changing spectral filter on a sound based on the frequency characteristics of a second sound. By taking the spectral content of a human voice and imposing it on a musical instrument, talking instrument effects can be created.

Warmth

Subjective term used to describe sound where the bass and low mid frequencies have depth and where the high frequencies are smooth-sounding rather than being aggressive or fatiguing.

Waveform

Graphic representation of the way in which a sound wave or electrical wave varies with time.

White Noise

Random signal with an energy distribution that produces the same amount of noise power per Hz.

XG

Yamaha's alternative to Roland's GS system for enhancing the General MIDI protocol.

XLR

Type of connector commonly used to carry balanced audio signals including the feeds from microphones.

Zero-Crossing Point

Point at which a signal waveform crosses from being positive to negative or vice versa.

Zipper Noise

Audible steps that occur when a parameter is being varied in a digital audio processor.